Introducing the

OLD TESTAMENT

INTRODUCING THE
OLD TESTAMENT

by
FREDERICK L. MORIARTY
S.J.

LONDON
BURNS & OATES

BURNS & OATES LIMITED
25 Ashley Place, London S.W.1

First published 1960
This edition   1966

IMPRIMI POTEST:
> JAMES E. COLERAN, S.J.
> *Provincial*

NIHIL OBSTAT:
> ROBERT A. DYSON, S.J.
> *Diocesan Censor Deputatus*

IMPRIMATUR:
> ✠ RICHARD CARDINAL CUSHING
> *Archbishop of Boston*
> February 2, 1959

PRINTED IN GREAT BRITAIN
BY LOWE AND BRYDONE (PRINTERS) LTD., LONDON

To *TOM*

PREFACE

IT IS very encouraging to realize that we can today speak of the Catholic biblical revival as a fact and not simply as a hope for the future. Indeed, one would find it hard to recall a period in the history of the Church when there was such a swelling stream of books, pamphlets, and articles dealing with the Bible. And no small part of this literature is devoted to the Old Testament. That much still remains to be done should only encourage the many scholars who are capable of making some positive contribution to a better understanding of Sacred Scripture. Misunderstandings have not been entirely removed and many difficulties are as yet unsolved, as Pius XII reminded us over fifteen years ago in his great Encyclical *Divino Afflante Spiritu*. But to this reminder he immediately added: "We should not lose courage on this account; nor should we forget that in the human sciences the same happens as in the natural world; that is to say, new beginnings grow little by little and fruits are gathered only after many labors."

The present work is a modest attempt to present some of these fruits to the general reader. The author cannot claim that these are the harvest of his own toil; he gladly acknowledges an immense debt to the patient and rewarding efforts of many scholars, Catholic and non-Catholic. To enumerate all of his creditors would be a hopeless task.

A fair number of accurate and interesting introductions to the Bible by Catholic writers are now on the market and we may expect more to follow. This book also claims to be an introduction to the Old Testament, but after a different fashion. As far as the author can ascertain no Catholic writer has tried to build his presentation of the Old Testament around its leading characters. History is never so interesting as when it takes the form of historical biography, and the author believes that, with the proper adjustments, the same literary genre can serve the cause of sacred history. The fifteen individuals chosen span the two thousand years of Israel's unique historical experience. These men differ markedly in temperament, natural gifts, power of expression, intensity of feeling; only one thing unites them, the pervasive presence of God, blessing, warning, approving, chastising, and, in all, preparing men for the hour when He would become man and fulfill the promises of the Old Testament.

The author has frequently let the sacred writers speak for themselves in the belief that use of the Old Testament is the best way to acquire that savor for its enduring message, and to realize what the ancient Hebrew meant when he called the God of the Bible "a living God." The author will be abundantly rewarded if this effort leads some readers to the living water of God's word to man.

CONTENTS

TABLE OF DATES

Introducing the

OLD TESTAMENT

ABRAHAM OUR FATHER

Then Joshua said to all the people, "Thus says Yahweh, the God of Israel: 'In former times your fathers lived beyond the River, among them Terah, the father of Abraham and Nahor; and they served other gods. Then I brought your father Abraham from beyond the River and led him through all the land of Canaan and I multiplied his offspring and gave him Isaac' . . ." (Josh. 24:2–3).

JOSHUA spoke these words at a solemn covenant ceremony held at the ancient shrine of Shechem. They are a terse admission of the fact that the ancestors of Abraham were polytheists, serving strange gods in the land of Mesopotamia; they are also a reminder of the divine initiative in making a fresh start with Abraham. Here and elsewhere in the Hebrew tradition it is a fundamental article of belief that the vocation of Abraham marks a clean and sharp break with the past. It was a journey of faith. In the New Testament as well, the author of the Epistle to the Hebrews proudly points to Abraham and his coheirs Isaac and Jacob as models of faith. Abraham is the father of all who believe because he turned his back on a world he knew and, with nothing more than a promise, set out "not knowing where he was going . . . for he was looking for the city that has the foundations, of which city the architect and the builder is God" (Hebr. 11:10).

Until recent times the period known as the Patriarchal Age was treated with a generous dose of skepticism. Some doubted the very existence of the Patriarchs as individuals, preferring to think of them as personifications of Hebrew tribes living in a dim and legendary past. Others might be willing to concede that they once existed and played some role in Hebrew history, but resignedly confessed that they and their times were lost

1

beyond recall. A more sophisticated view saw in the patriarchal narratives retrojections of ideas and customs which prevailed in the period of the monarchy (1000–587 B.C.). These last critics were confident that the stories about the Patriarchs in Genesis could tell us a good deal about life and belief in the time of the kings of Israel and Judah, but precious little about the period of the Patriarchs (2000–1700 B.C.).

If the situation has changed drastically today — and no one who understands the facts can doubt it — the credit goes first and foremost to the archaeologist and linguist whose combined efforts have set the Patriarchal Age in an entirely new light. In the past twenty-five years a bewildering amount of new material has been turned up and it has revolutionized our knowledge of that part of the world which very deservedly is called "The Cradle of Our Civilization." Within one generation we have seen whole cultures saved from the oblivion of millennia, new and unsuspected scripts and languages brought to light, entire civilizations reconstructed. Who in 1920 had ever heard of Ugarit and its great epic literature? How much did we know of the Hurrians and the Hittites, both of whom, as we shall see later, had an influence on the culture of the Patriarchs which goes a long way toward explaining some of the puzzling customs and incidents in the Genesis story? But before beginning to exploit some of this new material it will be worthwhile to describe the sources of the Genesis narratives and to suggest, at least tentatively, how they came to assume their present form. There cannot be the slightest doubt that our present biblical text of Genesis is the result of a long process, beginning with orally transmitted material and ending with the finished literary product we now read in our bibles.

THE SOURCES

We who depend so much for communication upon the written word are all too prone to underestimate the importance of oral tradition in the ancient world. Both the ancient Near

East and the classical world depended greatly upon memorization for the transmission of vital material to posterity. This is as true of religious belief as it is of folklore; both depended upon oral recitation for their dynamic retention in communities where few could read or write. Where writing was known and practiced, it was usually as an aid to memory or a check upon it, but not a substitute for the oral recital. In the early religious life of Israel oral recitation was the normal way of retaining and reliving the great deeds which Yahweh had once performed for His people. The call of Abraham and the liberation from Egypt are two of the best examples of the *magnalia Dei*. These saving acts of God challenged the Israelite here and now to respond in love and obedience as the past came to living reality in the present. The importance of oral transmission must not, however, be exaggerated, and any approach toward reconstructing the history of our biblical text must take into consideration both methods of transmission, the oral and the written. The reaction against an excessively literary and bookish handling of the ancient material was most salutary, but the pendulum should not swing too far in the other direction.

What does all this have to do with the composition of Genesis and the other early historical books? If one reads with any care the first five books of the Old Testament (the Pentateuch) he soon becomes aware that we do not have here a simple, straightforward, and scientific account of historical events in the manner of a modern historical work. The past is not retold for its own sake, but for the very practical purpose of instructing, edifying, and inviting men to see God's hand in their history. When a modern reader hears a story his first question is usually, "Did this really happen?" When the ancient Israelite head a story he would ask, "What does it mean?" The first concern of the Israelite historian was the significance of the event narrated. This does not mean that he was indifferent to historical truth or that he falsified the facts at his disposal. But he was aiming at the theological significance of his narrative and did not seem to be particularly disturbed about inconsistency in details. We may not find this kind of historiography to our taste, but there is no other course except to take the Semitic historian as we find him.

In the Pentateuch there are great differences in content, style, and literary form. Incidents are repeated, usually with different details; and, as we have said, the author does not seem to have bothered harmonizing diverging accounts of the same event. To give some kind of a satisfactory explanation of these peculiarities of Hebrew historical writing, modern scholars have come to see the early books of the Old Testament as the product of a welding together of four strata or layers of traditions which represented centuries of slow growth through both oral and written transmission. Sometime after the Exile of the sixth century B.C., a critical period in Israelite history, these four sources or traditions were put together in the form we now find in the text of the Old Testament. W. F. Albright has succinctly summarized this formative process:

> The Hebrews brought with them from their original Mesopotamian home the hallowed cosmogonic stories which they had learned there. To these ancient stories, handed down for uncounted centuries by word of mouth, were added the poetic narratives of the Patriarchs, which were subsequently adapted to the form of prose saga in which they have survived in the Hebrew Bible. Then came the soul-shaking events of the Exodus and the Wanderings, which were handed down in poetry and prose, together with the teachings and institutions of Moses. Gathered together in various compilations, the documents of the Mosaic Age were gradually formed into a single collection, which was completed in approximately its present form before the Restoration at the end of the sixth century B.C. The contents of our Pentateuch are, in general, very much older than the date at which they were finally edited; new discoveries continue to confirm the historical accuracy or the literary antiquity of detail after detail in it. Even when it is necessary to assume later additions to the original nucleus of Mosaic tradition, these additions reflect the normal growth of ancient institutions and practices, or the effort made by later scribes to save as much as possible of extant traditions about Moses. It is, accordingly, sheer hypercri-

ticism to deny the substantially Mosaic character of the Penta-
teuchal tradition.[1]

Since these traditions or compilations, which amount to four
versions of Israel's sacred history, assume such great importance
in studying that history as it was remembered and faithfully
set down by her sacred writers, it will not be out of place to
describe the characteristics of each of them. It should be noted
that this process of compilation in no way destroys the essential inner unity of the Old Testament as the revelation of the
living God Who covenants with His people Israel. Nor should
we forget that all four traditions go back ultimately to that
period in which Israel was formed as a nation, and that epoch
is dominated by one outstanding personality — Moses. We have
every reason, then, to speak of the Mosaic authorship of the
Pentateuch.

1. *The Yahwist Tradition* (J)

The name is derived from the frequency with which God is
called by the sacred name "Yahweh." To this tradition we owe
many of the most colorful and lively passages in the historical
records of Israel. It is primitive and archaic in character, but
extremely subtle in its handling of human psychology. For
delineation of life and character the Yahwist is unexcelled. The
style is concrete and vivid and, while the tradition shows a
special interest in the problem of sin (Gen. 3), there is also a
joyous confidence in the promises made by God to the Fathers.
To this tradition belong the older of the two creation accounts
(Gen. 2:4–25), the narrative of the Fall, the story of Sodom
and Gomorrha, much of the patriarchal history and some of
the most vivid incidents in the life of Moses. This tradition
pictures the relation between God and man as one of special
intimacy, sometimes naïvely anthropomorphic, and its greatest
preoccupation is with the stirring history of salvation. The call
of Abraham, the promises of Yahweh and His miracles, are the

---

[1] W. F. Albright, *The Archaeology of Palestine* (Baltimore: Penguin Books,
1956), pp. 224–225.

dominating ideas in the Yahwist's history. It is usually associated with the Kingdom of Judah, and its definitive literary fixation, in all probability, should not be placed after the tenth century B.C. The work of the Yahwist was the first great national and religious epic, and a most plausible time for its composition would be the end of David's rule or the beginning of the brilliant reign of Solomon.

2. *The Elohist Tradition (E)*

This takes its name from its preference for "Elohim" as the name of God. Less dramatic and vivacious than the earlier tradition, it is more consciously artistic than the Yahwist without, however, attaining the sonorous rhetoric of the Deuteronomic prose. Avoiding the anthropomorphisms of the Yahwist, the Elohist stresses the transcendence of God, the stern and demanding sovereign. The differences between the two narrative styles should not, however, obscure the likelihood that J and E are simply two versions or recensions of an original epic whose nucleus goes back to the thirteenth century B.C. When the Philistines smashed the unity of the tribal confederacy in the eleventh century B.C., it is quite probable that the two traditions were transmitted separately, J in the south and E in the north, until their definitive fixation and eventual combination in the eighth century B.C. The Elohist tradition breathes the spirit of the vigorous prophetic movement which developed in North Israel after the victories of Elijah and Elisha over the gods of Canaan.

3. *The Sacerdotal Tradition (P)*

In viewpoint and style P differs greatly from J and E. The book of Leviticus is the best example of this tradition, which is concerned especially with liturgical, chronological, and genealogical matters, though moral or inner motivation is not absent. It seems that the scribal representatives of this tradition gave the Pentateuch its final framework. This source is an excellent illustration of the important difference between the final setting down of the material which is, in this case, relatively late, and the antiquity of some of its contents. Here as elsewhere in the Bible it is extremely important to distinguish carefully between the age of the material incorporated and the date of the ultimate redaction of this material. As countless examples teach us, centuries can elapse between the one and the other. The sacerdotal tradition is usually identified by its great concern with the cult; it is fond of classifying and schematizing; it has lucidity, precision, and completeness but is almost wholly lacking in the freshness and dramatic vividness of the Yahwist tradition.

4. *The Deuteronomic Tradition (D)*

This includes not only the book of that name but a whole history of Israel including the books of Joshua, Judges, Samuel, and Kings. This Deuteronomic history has a nostalgic quality expressed in a homogeneous style easily identified by characteristic words and phrases. D also has a unified theology built around the idea that Israel is God's chosen people and that she owes to God a total, all-absorbing loyalty. God has revealed in the Law a way of life for Israel and in loving obedience to that Law Israel would find her security and prosperity:

> And now, Israel, what does Yahweh, your God, ask of you but to fear Yahweh, your God, to walk in all His ways, to love and serve Yahweh, your God, with all your heart and with all your soul, to keep the commandments and statutes of Yahweh which I command you this day for your own good? Behold, the heavens, even the highest heavens, belong to Yahweh, your God, as well as the earth and everything on it. Yet Yahweh loved your fathers exceedingly and chose their seed after them, you above all peoples, as on this very day (Deut. 10:12–15).

The above is a sample of the style and spirit of the Deuteronomic tradition, which starts with the idea of election and then summons the nation to obedience.

These four sources are not merely historical accounts of Israel; all disclose a definite theological perspective from which they view the events of Israel's life as a nation. The Yahwist

unfolds with patriotic fervor the glorious destiny of Israel and
sees it as the fulfillment of the promises made to the Fathers
of the young nation. Under God's providence great odds have
been overcome, a Promised Land has been entered. The part
played by the divine initiative is very prominent in this tradition. The Elohist tradition shares with its older counterpart the
pride in Israel's attainment of her goal through God's grace;
there is also the same confidence in the future of the nation
because of the special protection of God. The sacerdotal tradition has been compared to St. Augustine's *City of God* in that
both describe a spiritual commonwealth erected on the ruins
of an old order. Israel is God's holy congregation and her vocation consists in the observance of the Law in all its details. The
Deuteronomic tradition not only lays down the grave duty of
obedience to God's statutes in reciprocation for God's love and
choice of this people, but explains the disasters which overtook
Israel as divine punishment for her infidelities.

I WILL MAKE A GREAT NATION OF YOU

To what class of people did Abraham and his people belong?
How do they fit into the complex ethnic and cultural picture
of the ancient Near East? To answer these questions we must
take a look at what was happening when the Patriarchal Age
opens, shortly after 2000 B.C. This was an age of crisis in the
Fertile Crescent, a semicircle of densely populated land from
Egypt up north through Syria and then down the Euphrates
Valley to the Persian Gulf. The kings of Sumer and Accad had
ruled Mesopotamia for over a century, a period marked by a
Sumerian resurgence and known as the Third Dynasty of Ur
(2060–1950 B.C.). But restless people from the desert looked
enviously at the rich settled land and, at the first opportunity,
began to filter into this inviting area. The invaders were Semitic
people whom the settled population called "Amorites" (i.e.,
Westerners), and it is to these nomadic West Semitic people
that the family of Abraham belonged. We can thus explain
the mention of Abraham's family at Ur in terms of this great

Amorite movement which flooded the greater part of Northern Syria and Mesopotamia. Within a few centuries after the start of the invasion Amorite states had sprung up in such places as Babylon, Mari, Nahor, and Haran, to name but a few.

At the beginning of Abraham's story mention is made of the family journey from Ur northward to Haran. With the collapse of the great city of Ur at the hands of the Elamites it becomes quite plausible to connect this journey with a large scale migration from the ruined city to another with which it stood in some kind of political or religious relationship. The permanent associations of Abraham are not, however, with Ur, but with Haran, where the family of Abraham found itself completely at home since the whole area was now in the hands of its West Semitic kin who had pushed in from the desert. Even the names of Abraham, Jacob, and Benjamin are now known to have been used as personal names by the Amorites.

Several remarkable discoveries have helped to fill out the picture of cultural life in the Mesopotamia area, shared by Abraham and his followers, and they have also cleared up many hitherto obscure passages in the Genesis narrative. In 1925 excavations were begun by the Americans at Nuzu, a site in northeastern Iraq, not far from the modern town of Kirkuk. By the end of the campaigns, in 1931, scholars had a fairly good picture of life in this ancient center together with a wealth of data to illuminate the patriarchal narratives, some of which had often caused considerable embarrassment to the reader. At last it became apparent that Abraham was merely following the customary practice of his time when, for example, Sarah supplied him with a handmaid because she was unable to bear children. Nuzu marriage contracts even obliged a sterile wife to provide a servant who would see to it that the purpose of their marriage, children, would be fulfilled.[2] By inserting the names of Sarah and Abraham we can appreciate the parallelism in the following Nuzu document:

---

[2] C. H. Gordon, "Biblical Customs and the Nuzu Tablets," *Biblical Archaeologist*, III (1940), pp. 1–12.

Furthermore, Kelim-ninu has been given in marriage to Shen-nima. If Kelim-ninu bears [children], Shennima shall not take another wife; but if Kelim-ninu does not bear, Kelim-ninu shall acquire a woman of the land of the Lullu as wife for Shennima, and Kelim-ninu may not send the offspring away. . . .[3]

It will be recalled that the practice was repeated two generations later when Rachel gave Bilha to Jacob in order to produce offspring (Gen. 30:3). The act appears reprehensible to us, but the Patriarchs were simply following the custom of that age.

Another tablet from Nuzu provides the record of a lawsuit in which the oral blessing from a dying father to his son is upheld as legally valid, thus giving us the clue to the apparent irrevocability of the deathbed testament extorted from Isaac by the wily Jacob. These are only a few of the many parallels supplied by the Nuzu documents which confirm the antiquity and authenticity of the patriarchal account. We might also add that by the time these narratives were set down in writing the existence and meaning of these customs had been lost. And the writer could get little help from Mosaic legislation, with which he was familiar, since patriarchal custom reflected a much older and different cultural milieu. But the Hebrew historian did not take only what he understood or sympathized with, omitting what was distasteful to his sensibilities. He recorded what was in the tradition whether he understood it or not. He might touch up the form of his narrative but the substance was to be left intact. As a recent writer has put it, the history of the Patriarchs and their manner of life had already become part of what we would call an oral canon some time between the period of the events actually recorded and the time of the earliest written account.

One more discovery which has illuminated the Patriarchal Period should be mentioned. Since 1936 excavation has gone on at the city of Mari, another important Amorite settlement on

---

[3] See J. B. Pritchard, editor, *Ancient Near Eastern Texts* (Princeton: University Press, 1950), p. 220. Hereafter this important collection of translated texts will be cited as *ANET*. A second revised edition of this work appeared in 1955.

the Euphrates. It flourished in the eighteenth century B.C., and was ruled by a king with the melodious name of Zimri-Lim. Eventually the city was destroyed by an even more famous king, Hammurabi of Babylon. The most valuable discovery at Mari was the royal archives, found in Zimri-Lim's palace. They consist of over 20,000 tablets, some of them economic transactions but many of them letters from kings, officers, and ordinary people all over Mesopotamia. Among the problems with which the king had to contend were fierce, marauding nomads called *Banu-Yamina* (Sons of the South). Apparently they broke in from the desert south of the Euphrates and, like the rest of their nomadic forebears, were pressing northward into settled land. While they are not to be identified with our Israelite tribe of Benjamin, the description of these warlike troublemakers certainly squares with the picture of Benjamin as we have it in the blessings of Jacob:

> Benjamin is a ravenous wolf;
> devouring prey in the morning,
> and at evening dividing spoil.
> (Gen. 49:27)

From the letters of Mari we have our best chance of learning the dialect spoken by Abraham and his people when they were in Mesopotamia. Presumably it was a West-Semitic dialect, traces of which have already been found in the Mari letters.

After the call of Abraham, he and his family left their homeland and journeyed to the land of Canaan. Here also archaeological discovery helps us to picture their manner of life and to see them, not as shadowy figures of myth, but as real human beings in a particular historical environment. Genesis pictures the Patriarchs as moving up and down the central ridge of the Palestinian hill country, from Dothan to Beersheba. With their flocks of sheep and goats they moved from one pasturage to the other, avoiding the coastal plain and the broad valleys where fortified cities stood. It would be a mistake to think of Canaan at this time as a wild and desolate land without wealth or culture. It was precisely in this period that urban life among the Canaanites began to flourish in Palestine. In addition, the preponderant political and cultural influence throughout the area of the powerful twelfth Egyptian Dynasty is now clearly underscored by archaeological discovery.

Within the past few years Miss Kathleen Kenyon, the excavator of Jericho, has been able to tell us what this Canaanite city must have looked like when Abraham came to Palestine. Probably the most remarkable feature of Jericho was its defenses, particularly the huge plaster-faced bank or glacis surrounding the city and making it all but impregnable except to the strongest force.[4] Abraham and his associates might well have visited this town to barter or to replenish a supply of water. But it is unthinkable that the Israelites, semi-nomadic shepherds little used to the arts of urban civilization, would ever have been able to build towns like this during the Patriarchal Age. The twelfth and thirteenth chapters of Genesis record a journey to Egypt and back by the Patriarch and his family. This would entail a long trip by caravan of people carrying their household possessions and their domesticated cattle. It would demand a place where food and drink could be obtained and where men and beasts could sojourn over a fair period of time. The Negeb we have known for almost 2000 years would hardly answer such a description or meet such needs. Yet, in the summer of 1954, the American archaeologist Nelson Glueck was able to prove beyond any doubt that, in the period of Abraham, these sites which would make such a caravan journey feasible actually existed in good number in the Negeb. The journey of Abraham through the Negeb was not through an arid wasteland, but a settled area of towns and villages in which the people tended their flocks and used pottery of a very high quality. Today only heaps of stones and pottery shards remain as witnesses to what were once flourishing sites capable of sustaining life over an indefinite period of time. After seeing with his own eyes the verification of the

---

[4] See Miss Kenyon's account of the Middle Bronze city in *The Illustrated London News* for May 19, 1956, pp. 554–555.

biblical record which many were willing to dismiss as merely fanciful, Dr. Glueck could add with admiration: "In this great theological document are contained historical accounts and references and geographical and topographical descriptions which are invaluable to the student of history. Some of this material was recorded by eyewitnesses, some culled from contemporary records and still other material was long transmitted through the amazingly accurate phenomenon of historical memory before being committed to writing."[5] In the same article the author shows how his surface explorations have led to a confirmation of the military campaign described in the fourteenth chapter of Genesis. The passage mentions a line of towns which were destroyed by the Elamite king. Glueck has been able to trace a long line of such Middle Bronze I settlements which run through most of the length of Transjordan. The pottery on the surface indicates that they were destroyed in that period and never reoccupied. Few passages in the Bible have received more direct validation from an extrabiblical source.

We may close this brief look at the background of the Patriarchal Age by quoting from a contemporary (about 1900 B.C.) document which provides a good picture of what the land of Canaan was like when Abraham was wandering up and down the hill country. It is from the report of an Egyptian, Sinuhe, who was forced to flee from Egypt for political reasons and take up residence in eastern Syria. He made the acquaintance of an Amorite chieftain who gave him his eldest daughter for a wife. Such a chieftain might well have been Abraham or Jacob or Laban. The exiled official then launches into a description of his new home, though he never conceals an ardent longing to return to his beloved Egypt:

> It [Canaan] was a good land, named Yaa (in another place this is called Upper Retenu, i.e., highland country, probably including northern Palestine, southern and central Syria). Figs were in it, and grapes. It had more wine than water. Plentiful was its honey,

---

[5] Nelson Glueck, "The Age of Abraham in the Negeb," *Biblical Archaeologist*, XVIII (1955), p. 3.

abundant its olives. Every (kind of) fruit was on its trees. Barley
was there, and emmer. There was no limit to any (kind of) cattle.
Moreover, great was that which accrued to me as a result of the
love of me.[6]

ABRAHAM BELIEVED GOD

Now Yahweh said to Abraham:

"Leave your country, your kindred
and your father's house,
for the land which I will show you;
and I will make a great nation of you.
I will bless you and make your name great,
so that you shall be a blessing.
I will bless those who bless you,
and curse those who curse you.
In you shall all the families
of the earth be blessed."

(Gen. 12:1-3)

This text is one of the most important in the Old Testament for the religious history of Israel and all humanity. It is
particularly significant for the Church which sees its origins
in Abraham and claims as its rightful inheritance the legacy
of Israel. Everything which went before could be called a
preparation for this decisive entrance of God into the history
of salvation. In an undefined period of time in the distant past
a promise had been made that the victory of Satan over man
in the Garden would be reversed. The seed of the woman
would crush the enemy of human nature, but how this was
to be accomplished was left in the mysterious counsels of God.
Now the promise is repeated and a fresh beginning is made in
the history of salvation. A process is begun which would ter-
minate in that day when Christ said: "Abraham your father
rejoiced that he was to see My day. He saw it and was glad"
(Jn. 8:56). Several times later in the life of Abraham the
promise would be repeated, and the note of universalism is
never missing. The oath which God swore to Abraham and

[6] See *ANET*, pp. 19-20.

the promises He made were not meant for some insignificant West Semitic tribe living a seminomadic life in Palestine but for all men. From the loins of Abraham would come the chosen people and from them would come the Savior of the world. Lest we become uneasy about the place of the Old Testament in our theology, it is well to recall occasionally that Abraham and Moses and the prophets are not ancestors for whom we should feel obliged to apologize. This history of the People of God, from Abraham to the present, is one story. The events in Abraham's life, above all his faith, belong to the fabric of Church history. For the Church is the Israel of God and it goes back from Christ through the sages and prophets to the Covenant on Sinai and thence to the faith of Abraham.

The few verses cited above strike the keynote in the story of Abraham, the man of faith. The writer lingers with what seems to be intentional pathos on the things he is to leave — land, kindred, father's house. Consider what they meant to a Semite! And there seems to be a corresponding vagueness in describing the goal of Abraham's journey: ". . . to a land which I will show thee." Obedience under these conditions stamps the Patriarch as the great hero of faith, an example of Hebrew piety at its finest. In commenting on the Epistle to the Hebrews 11:7, Gregory of Nyssa throws into relief Abraham's journey toward God in the obscurity of faith: "It is precisely because he [Abraham] did not know whither he was going that he knew he was on the right path, for he was sure that he was not being led by the light of his own intelligence but by the will of God." He who was destined to be the Father of a great nation was asked to spend a long and unsettled life among strangers. He even had to bargain with strangers for a burial place, the only plot of land in Palestine which he seemed to be able to call his own. From all appearances he was what Max Weber called, in sociological terms, a "tolerated metic," a privileged alien who managed to get his pasture land by contract rather than by force.

Many commentators have remarked that, except for the quiet dignity of the Patriarch, we learn little about Abraham from the Genesis narrative. This is true, and the reason is that the sacred writer is absorbed in God's action on Abraham. God moves toward a man and swears to certain promises which He will carry out in the future. No obligations are imposed, no conditions are attached:

> When Abram was ninety-nine years old, Yahweh appeared to him and said, "I am God Almighty. Walk in My presence and be perfect. And I will make My covenant between Me and you, and will multiply you exceedingly." Then Abram fell prostrate, and God said to him, "This is My covenant with you; you shall be the father of a multitude of nations. You shall no longer be called Abram, but your name shall be Abraham; for I have made you the father of a multitude of nations . . ." (Gen. 17:1–5).

In this excerpt from the sacerdotal tradition there is an almost monotonous insistence on the divine election of Israel. No less than thirteen times in this chapter the word "covenant" occurs and the writer is telling us that God was binding Himself to Abraham at the same time that He made the Patriarch an instrument of His designs for mankind. Abraham could only dimly grasp the ultimate meaning of this covenant and the promises. Sufficient to believe that God would accomplish them!

There will be more to say about the covenant when we consider the place of Moses in Israel's history. In general it can be said that the covenant is a dominant idea in the story of God's dealing with man, and the free selection of Abraham rather than anyone else underlines the truth that God is not subservient to any established pattern in His action but sovereignly free in His election. Another expression of the promises to Abraham is found in a brief passage:

> "In blessing I will indeed bless you and multiply your descendants like the stars of heaven and the sands on the seashore. Your descendants will possess the gate of their enemies" (Gen. 22:17).

The divine liberality stands out in every phrase. The promises

are the gift of God, not a payment for fulfilling legal obligations. If the promises had depended on observance of the Law,
faith would have little meaning. The promises would turn out
to be a quid pro quo. Genesis assigns no reason for the choice
of Abraham, and it would be very hazardous to assume that
the choice was dictated by some excellence which Abraham
possessed from the beginning. Is it not more correct to say
that the greatness of the Patriarch is the consequence of his
election rather than its cause? His virtue consisted in his
response to grace.[7]

No one has insisted on the gratuity of Abraham's election
more than St. Paul. The Apostle recognized in the call of
Abraham the beginning of the history of salvation. Inchoatively,
at least, the great patriarchal figure heard the "Good News," and
he was not only justified by his belief in the promises but that
faith made him the prototype of all those who believe, the
"Father of the Faithful." In two of his Epistles, to the Romans
and the Galatians, Paul draws out the continuities between
the believing Abraham and the Christian who is justified by
faith and not by the works of the Law. Man's right relation
with God is not based on his own goodness and accomplishments; it is based on God's goodness and is His achievement.
This is an economy of grace which begins with Abraham and
reaches its climax in the death and resurrection of Christ.
Such an economy manifests the unity of God's design, its uni-
versality, and the continuity of the divine action in history.
It is only in the New Testament, the time of fulfillment, that
the grandeur of Abraham becomes most apparent. He has become the point of departure for the Pauline doctrine of justification; his faith is seen as a total adherence to a Person and not

---

[7] J. O. F. Murray, in Hasting's *Dictionary of the Bible*, I, 679a, brings this
out very clearly: "Since the root of all loveliness is in God, and since there
can be no goodness apart from Him, we cannot argue as if it were possible for
man to possess or develop any goodness or loveliness independent of, and so
constituting a claim on, the choice of God. We ought not, therefore, to be
surprised when we find Israel expressly warned in Holy Scripture to reject the
flattering assumption that they have been chosen on the ground of their own
inherent attractiveness."

as a purely intellectual assent. What was asked of Abraham —
that he walk before God and be perfect (*tamim*) — is asked
of the Christian who would be a true heir of the promises made
to our Father. Obedience to law in a spirit of empty legalism
does not satisfy the demands of God. What God desires is that
inner integrity, an epitome of virtues, not the least of which
is the humble acknowledgment of our own nothingness apart
from Him. The man of faith is the true Israelite called to live,
not under the constraint of law, but in the liberty of a
Christian.

MOSES

THE traveler in Rome should not pass up a visit to the Church called San Pietro in Vincoli. In the right transept of the Basilica, which goes back to the fifth century, he will find one of the most brilliant creations of Michelangelo, the statue of Moses, which forms part of the monument to Pope Julius II. On the face of Moses we can read the wrath of the lawgiver as he descends from Mount Sinai with the tablets of the Law and sees the people in idolatrous revel. The stern figure symbolizes massive strength in the service of a great and supernatural cause. This is the man who stands on the threshold of Israel's history as a nation, the faithful servant of whom God said:

> "Now hear My words:
> If there is a prophet among you,
> I, Yahweh, will make Myself known
> to him in a vision;
> I will speak to him in a dream.
> Not so with My servant Moses!
> Throughout My house is he trusted;
> face to face I speak to him,
> clearly and not in riddles.
> And the form of Yahweh he beholds."
>
> (Num. 12:6–8)

Outside of scattered references to Moses in later literature, our knowledge of the man is derived entirely from the first five books of the Old Testament. In that great work of sacred history, composed of several strands as we have already seen, Israel has left us her traditions about the man most responsible for her attaining conscious nationhood. If Abraham is the Father of his people, Moses is the Founder of the nation and her lawgiver, the representative of the people as they enter into solemn covenant with Yahweh. And there is no doubt that

Israel's deep and abiding sense of election, her awareness of a sacred destiny under a transcendent God, is the key to unlocking the secret of Israel's meaning in history. Will Herberg has pointed out:

> In the normal biblical-rabbinic view, Israel is not a "natural" nation; it is, indeed, not a nation at all like the nations of the world. It is a *supernatural* community, called into being by God to serve his eternal purposes in history. It is a community created by God's special act of covenant, first with Abraham whom he "called" out of the heathen world and then, supremely, with Israel collectively at Sinai. Jewish tradition emphasizes the unimportant and heterogeneous character of the People Israel apart from God's gracious act of election which gives it the significance it has in the scheme of world destiny. The covenant of election is what brought Israel into existence and keeps it in being, today just as truly as at Sinai; apart from the covenant, Israel is as nothing and Jewish existence a mere delusion. The covenant is at the very heart of the Jewish self-understanding of its own reality.[1]

In this period of Israelite history we find conjoined a man and a series of events, including Exodus and Covenant, and both are deeply embedded in the record which the historians have left us. This is not the same as saying that the events recounted have come to us in contemporary written documents. For at least three hundred years Yahweh's providential deliverance of His people from the bondage of Egypt was transmitted by oral recitation at sanctuaries or other places of popular assembly. Little matter that the Egyptians left no record of these incidents which undoubtedly made little impression on them. They despised foreigners anyway and were too busy living nostalgically on the memories of their own great past. But for Israel this was an event which became part of a vital, continuing tradition whose solid historical basis is unchallenged and whose influence on Israelite religious life can hardly be exaggerated. Her theology is inextricably linked with her

[1] W. Herberg, "Jewish Existence and Survival: A Theological View," *Judaism*, I (1952), p. 20.

history and often takes the form of a recital of the mighty deeds of Yahweh, the greatest of which was the Exodus. By the recitation of His great acts, the fact of God was burned into the memory of the Israelite; his liturgy was more than a simple recall of the past; it was a vital religious experience in which he relived the great event and participated in the wondrous act of deliverance. On great Hebrew feasts the young man listened to his elders recite the ancient story of the Exodus, and the very recital made him experience a solidarity with the men of old. This was the God Who had chosen Israel and revealed His Law to her.

> Later on, when your son asks you what these ordinances, statutes and decrees mean which Yahweh, our God, has enjoined on you, you shall say to your son, "We were once Pharaoh's slaves in Egypt, but Yahweh brought us out of Egypt with His strong hand and wrought before our eyes signs and wonders . . ." (Deut. 6:20–22).

THE AFFLICTION OF MY PEOPLE

The period which best fits the facts at our disposal for the time of Moses is the thirteenth century B.C. We now have a converging mass of evidence made available only in recent times by the work of archaeologists who have attacked the problem from the Egyptian and Palestinian sides. The Egypt of this period had passed the apex of its glory, even though it was, in this century, to witness the long and brilliant reign of Rameses II, the most likely candidate as the Pharaoh of the Exodus. In view of the clearly attested destruction of such centers as Lachish, Bethel, Debir, and Hazor in the thirteenth century it now appears certain that the critical phase of the Conquest of Palestine by the Israelites should be placed in the reign of Rameses' successor, Marniptah (1224–1216 B.C.), and the Exodus itself in the early part of the reign of Rameses II, probably around 1280 B.C. But we are anticipating, and should return to Moses and the society in which he was raised.

Egypt has been described as a country which was always

trying to reassert the past in a world refusing to stand still.
A great Empire, which had once extended from the Fourth
Cataract of the Nile to the Euphrates, was about to be lost to
new and powerful forces moving into the area. By the end of
the thirteenth century the Egyptian Empire would be a thing
of the past. Assyria was about to emerge again as a mighty
world power; from the west came the Sea Peoples, known in
Canaan as the Philistines; Israel had occupied part of the
land of Canaan; and the Phoenician coastal cities had already
started to become great maritime powers. Religiously it was
a time of great syncretism with Rameses himself the chief
agent in merging the gods of Egypt and Asia. Nothing shows
this more clearly than a paragraph of the nonaggression pact
which Rameses drew up with the Hittites, citing the divine
witnesses to their agreement:

> As for these words of the regulation (which) the Great Prince
> of Hatti (made) with Rameses (Meri-Amon), the great ruler (of
> Egypt), in writing upon this tablet of silver — as for these words,
> a thousand gods of the male gods and of the female gods of
> them of the land of Hatti, together with a thousand gods of the
> male gods and of the female gods of them of the land of Egypt,
> are with me as witnesses (hearing) these words.[2]

The amalgamation of Egyptian and Asiatic gods went hand
in hand with the exciting cosmopolitan atmosphere of the
Rameside capital city of Tanis in the Delta. The wealth of
Mediterranean commerce flowed into the city, beautiful Mycenaean ware from Greek cities could be purchased in its shops,
and the luxuries of Asia abounded in this proud, new capital,
named "The House of Rameses, the Great of Victories."

The Hebrews had been in Egypt a long time before the birth
of Moses, a fact firmly attested in the biblical tradition and
confirmed by our improved knowledge of Egyptian history. For
example, it is now quite difficult to separate the spectacular rise
of Joseph to a rank resembling that of a prime minister in the
Egyptian state from the Hyksos period when Egypt fell under

---

[2] ANET, pp. 200–201.

the domination of these Asiatic "Rulers of Foreign Countries" (Hyksos). But if the Hebrews prospered during the time of foreign rule, perhaps because of some relationship with the Hyksos, their position in Egypt had become desperate by the end of the four-hundred-year sojourn recorded in the Bible. The Nineteenth Dynasty became famous for its construction projects, especially in the Delta area, and nothing was more natural than that a Pharaoh should look for cheap labor among the hated Semites in their midst. The Hebrews were soon forced into labor battalions. "Accordingly, taskmasters were set over the Israelites to oppress them with forced labor. Thus they had to build for Pharaoh the supply cities of Pithom and Rameses" (Exod. 1:11). Both cities have been located by modern archaeological excavation. The first should now be identified with modern Tell er-Retabeh, covering an ancient site in the Wadi Tumilat. The second is most probably the capital of the Rameside period, already mentioned as the seat of government during this century and a site notable, even today, for its massive ruins.

The biblical tradition continues with the sad account of how the Pharaoh, worried over the increase of his miserable Israelite slaves, cruelly devised a scheme to wipe out this persecuted minority. At this critical moment the child Moses appeared, and his well-nigh miraculous escape from the evil designs of the ruler introduced a career which would culminate in the deliverance of his people from the servitude of Egypt. His name is Egyptian, meaning "to beget, bear." Some of his relatives bore Egyptian names, such as Pinehas, Hophni, and Pashur. Although Moses was apparently brought up in an Egyptian environment, he never seems to have lost contact with his suffering people. This solidarity with persecuted kinsmen together with his white-hot anger at cruel injustice was sharply dramatized in an incident which took place by the brick kilns of Egypt where the Israelites were serving in the corvée. This episode not only gives us a glimpse of Moses' character but sets in motion a train of events leading to the liberation from Egypt:

On one occasion, after Moses had grown up, when he visited his kinsmen and witnessed their forced labor, he saw an Egyptian striking a Hebrew, one of his own kinsmen. Looking about and seeing no one, he slew the Egyptian and hid him in the sand. The next day he went out again, and now two Hebrews were fighting! And he said to the man who was in the wrong, "Why do you strike your fellow Hebrew?" Then he answered, "Who has made you ruler and judge over us? Do you intend to kill me as you killed the Egyptian?" Then Moses was afraid and he thought, "This affair must certainly be known" (Exod. 2:11–14).

Moses fled to the land of Midian which lay east of the Gulf of Aqabah. From there Moses went to Sinai where he first received the divine commission. The Sinai region is known to abound in copper ore, and mines were worked there from very early times. Now the Midianites were not simply a pastoral people as is often imagined; it is highly probable that some of them worked at the mining of copper, as the name of one of their clans, the Kenites or "coppersmiths," would suggest. It was not unusual, then, for Moses to be in the Sinai area with his Kenite kinsmen when he underwent that decisive experience which transformed him into the spokesman of Yahweh. The narrative relates that Moses was shepherding the flocks of his father-in-law Jethro in the Sinai region, at the foot of the great mountain which is called Sinai in one tradition and Horeb in another. This is an awesome place and difficult of access, at the southern end of the Sinai Peninsula triangle. It consists of a great mass of granite rock some of whose peaks go up almost 8000 feet, the whole resting on a great plateau of limestone which rises above the desert. In this stark and lonely region God was about to appear to Moses, who probably brooded over the plight of his people in Egypt as he pastured the flock of Jethro. The Bible tells us that "an angel of Yahweh appeared to him in fire flaming out of a bush." Strangely enough, the bush was not consumed by the fire and Moses went over to investigate this remarkable sight. As Moses approached, God called out to him and ordered him to remove his sandals, for this was holy ground. God then identified Himself in the words,

"I am the God of your father, the God of Abraham, the God of Isaac, the God of Jacob." As frequently happened in the Old Testament, Moses was terrified at the theophany and covered his face lest he look upon God and die. The purpose of this divine manifestation was made very clear when God, proclaiming His own solidarity with the children of Israel, informed Moses what He planned to do:

> "I have witnessed the affliction of My people in Egypt and have heard their cry of complaint against their slave-drivers, so I know well what they suffer. Therefore I have come down to rescue them from the hands of the Egyptians and lead them out of that land into a good and spacious land flowing with milk and honey, the country of the Canaanites, Hittites, Amorites, Pherezites, Horites and Jebusites. So indeed the cry of the Israelites has come to Me, and I have seen how the Egyptians are oppressing them. Come, I will send you to Pharaoh to lead My people, the children of Israel, out of Egypt" (Exod. 3:7–10).

God's history is not worked out exclusively in heaven. By a mysterious condescension He has reached down to earth and chosen a man to be the instrument of His plan. Moreover, God is determined in this case to make up for any deficiencies in His servant. Moses might shrink back in fear before such a commission but God would give him authority and courage to act in His name. At this point the divine name was revealed to Moses:

> "But," said Moses to God, "when I go to the children of Israel and say to them, 'The God of your fathers has sent me to you,' if they ask me, 'What is His name?' what am I to tell them?" God answered, "I am who am." Then He added, "This is what you shall tell the children of Israel: 'I AM sent me to you'" (Exod. 3:13–15).

There has been much controversy over the meaning of this mysterious name which was revealed at the burning bush. Most satisfactory of all explanations is that which sees the word derived from the Hebrew stem *hwy*, "to become, come into existence," used in this context in the causative form and to be translated as "He who causes to be" or "He who causes to exist." This solution not only satisfies the demands of philology but dovetails perfectly with the basic Hebrew view of God as Creator of the universe, a faith which is solemnly professed at the beginning of Genesis. This is the name which the Israelite knew was too sacred to be pronounced, and the surrogate "Adonai" was used in place of the ineffable name. It was now the task of Moses to assume leadership over his demoralized people and, at the same time, to convince them that Yahweh was in their midst and that He would achieve their deliverance against all odds. This very act of salvation would reveal to them the omnipotence of Yahweh and serve as a rallying point around which national unity could be won. From that time Yahweh was at the head of His people, and it was no accident that Moses later named the altar of victory *Yahweh nissi*, "Yahweh is my banner."

OUT OF BONDAGE

Although the escape of despised foreigners from their slave labors left practically no trace in the records of Egypt, the Exodus was *the* event of Hebrew history. Apart from it the faith of Israel is unintelligible. Here was a mighty act of salvation, an event through which Israel learned the power and love of Yahweh Who had chosen this people. If you asked a Hebrew to define God he would not do it in the precise categories of the philosopher; he would simply say, "He is Yahweh, our God, Who brought us out of the land of Egypt, out of the house of bondage." About Him the psalmists sang their great hymns of praise, and the prophets spoke to the people in the name of this God Who had delivered them. Generation after generation relived in the liturgy this miracle whereby God took the side of an oppressed and insignificant company of slaves and defeated, for their sake, the greatest power in the world of that day. If the Israelite never lost the awareness that he was the member of a chosen people, it was largely due to this historical event which took place in the thirteenth century B.C. during the late imperial period of Egyptian history.

Great events which lie at the basis of a nation's history gather about them a heightened significance which grows with the passage of time. The signing of Magna Charta or the American Revolution and the Spirit of '76 are comparable events in British and American history. Such events tend to grow into symbols which become a cherished part of the national tradition. The Exodus became a symbol for the Israelite, a sign of God's providence over His people and a pledge that He always stood ready to come to their assistance. The time of the Exodus was the time of espousals, when Yahweh made Israel His bride, even though she had no special attractiveness, as the strong imagery of Ezechiel's sixteenth chapter would remind any Israelite.

If we remember that the narrative of the Exodus was not written from the standpoint of a modern historian and that the author was not interested in giving what we call a documentary version of the great event, we can more easily understand how the narrative, in the course of a long oral transmission, has taken on a heightened, epic quality which throws into relief the power and sovereignty of God. That the Exodus was an historical event is not questioned by any serious student; if it did not happen, Israel would have had no basis for her faith. But the fact is told in the manner of the Hebrew historian who dramatizes and remolds his material in order the better to glorify Yahweh, Who vanquished Pharaoh and all the gods of Egypt. The account of the plagues may be cited as an example because they illustrate the Hebrew attitude toward God and nature. Should we attempt to rationalize the marvelous events which served as warnings to the Pharaoh, there would be little difficulty in showing the Egyptian coloring of these calamities and the likelihood that they are to be explained by the operation of natural forces. But we would not be looking at the events through the eyes of the Hebrew narrator. For him there was never any doubt that God was the master of history and nature, and that He could and did use cosmic forces to accomplish His purposes. The Hebrew had no bent for analysis and no systematic knowledge of nature as a unit functioning according to regular laws. Hence he was in no position to ask whether or not a given event fulfilled our relatively modern concept of a miracle. And it does not seem that the Hebrew, even if he could, would bother to raise that question since he was accustomed to seeing the work of God in all phenomena, the ordinary as well as the extraordinary. That these great disasters which were meant to break down the defiance of the Pharaoh might be due to natural causes, in part at least, would be of slight interest to the Hebrews, since he never looked at nature apart from the God Who created and controlled it. What was significant and awe-inspiring to the narrator of the Exodus was the deliverance wrought by Yahweh, Who made use of nature just as He could make use of men to accomplish His will. It is perhaps worth repeating that the historical writing we meet in Exodus is not the coldly objective reporting of an eyewitness who has left us a purely factual chronicle. It is salvation history, a literary form which has its own laws and objectives. The writer intends to give us the substantial facts in the case along with a theological interpretation of these events. What is far more important than the details of the events is the lesson of God's transcendence, His loving care of Israel, and the confidence which should come from her realization that Yahweh was with her as He was with no other people. If we ask of the sacred writer a mirror-like reflection of the events as they actually took place and in their proper chronological order, we are asking for something which the literary form of salvation history never intended to give.

When Moses returned from the wasteland - of Sinai he assumed leadership of the oppressed community, but not before Aaron had told the people all that God had said to Moses and had performed the signs before them:

> The people believed, and when they heard that Yahweh was concerned about them and had seen their affliction, they bowed down in worship. Then Moses and Aaron went to Pharaoh and said, "Thus says Yahweh, the God of Israel. 'Let My people go,

that they may celebrate a feast to Me in the desert'" (Exod. 4:31–5:1).

The issue was joined and immediately ensued a power struggle between Yahweh and an obstinate Pharaoh in whom the Egyptians saw god, "a god by whose dealings one lives." But the outcome was never in doubt. Yahweh, through Moses, sent a series of calamities upon the obdurate Egyptians, climaxed by the death of the first-born, a catastrophe which finally broke Pharaoh's rebellious spirit:

> During the night Pharaoh summoned Moses and Aaron and said, "Leave my people immediately, you and the children of Israel with you! Go and worship Yahweh as you said. Take your flocks, as well, and your herds, as you demanded, and begone; and you will be doing me a favor" (Exod. 12:31–32).

Freed at last by Pharaoh who let them go through fear more than anything else, the unwieldy multitude set out on its journey to the Promised Land. What route did they take and where did they cross that body of water which the Hebrews called "the Sea of Reeds"? These are perennial problems but a closer study of the biblical text, coupled with recent archaeological discoveries, have brought the problems closer to a solution. Looking only at the biblical evidence, we find the following account of the journey as far as the Sea of Reeds, which should not, in our opinion, be identified with the modern Gulf of Suez, the northwestern arm of the Red Sea:

> The Israelites set out from Rameses for Succoth, about six hundred thousand men[3] on foot, not counting the children. . . .

> Now, when Pharaoh let the people go, God did not lead them by way of the Philistines' land, though this was the nearest; for He thought, should the people see that they would have to fight, they might change their minds and return to Egypt. Instead, He

---

[3] Similar literary pieces from the Ancient Near East have made it sufficiently clear that inflated figures are characteristic of this type of writing. The same is true of popular Semitic literature today as well as in ancient times. Many attempts have been made to explain these fantastically high figures. One plausible theory is that we find embedded here the Davidic census of the entire Israelite population in David's time.

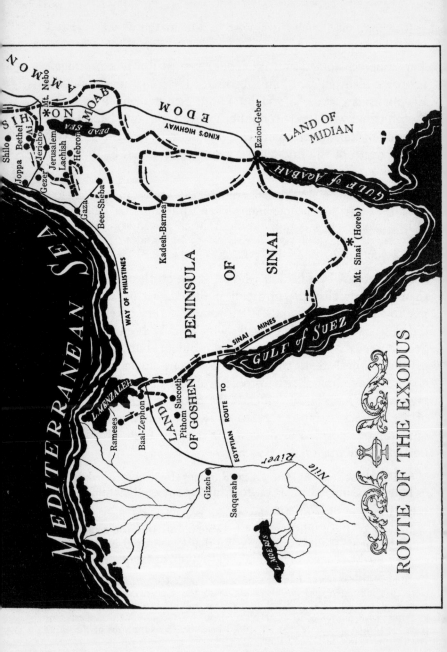

ROUTE OF THE EXODUS

rerouted them toward the Reed Sea by way of the desert road. . . .
Setting out from Succoth, they encamped at Etham near the
edge of the desert. . . . Then Yahweh said to Moses, "Tell the
Israelites to turn about and camp before Pihahiroth, between
Migdol and the sea. You shall camp in front of Baal-zephon, just
opposite, by the sea" (Exod. 12:37; 13:17–18:20; 14:1–3).

Rameses, as we have seen, was the capital of the New Empire
in the Nineteenth Dynasty, sometimes called the Rameside
Age. This city occupied the site of the ancient Hyksos capital
of Tanis, excavated chiefly by the French archaeologist, Pierre
Montet. Succoth lies about thirty miles to the southeast of
Rameses, and it was situated in the Wadi Tumilat at the site
of modern Tell el-Maskhutah. It appears that the Israelites
went in this direction to avoid running into the strongly fortified Egyptian positions on the direct road to Palestine. From
there it would appear that the Israelites turned northward, in
loop fashion, camping at Baal-zephon, located near modern Tell
Dephneh (ancient Daphne of the Greeks). Here Jeremiah was
taken by his captors after the destruction of Jerusalem in 587
B.C. (Jer. 43:7–9). The actual crossing of the Sea of Reeds was
made in an area not far from Rameses, probably at the southern
part of modern Lake Menzaleh. The construction of the Suez
Canal altered the topography of this region so that it is no longer
possible to locate the exact spot where the Israelites crossed
and the Egyptians met disaster.

It will be recalled that almost immediately after the mass
of Israelites set out from Goshen, the Pharaoh and his servants
relented of their permission to depart. With a strong, mobile
force of chariotry the Egyptians began their pursuit of the fleeing Israelites. Few narratives have more dramatic qualities than
this episode of deliverance. On the day before the crossing, the
people had cowered in fear at the sight of the approaching
Egyptians in their war chariots. But it was at this very moment,
when they were caught between the impassable sea and the
powerful army of a Pharaoh bent on returning them to captivity,
that the power of Yahweh saved them from certain disaster.

The Israelite was never to forget this night of miracle when God intervened as his savior:

> Then Moses stretched out his hand over the sea and Yahweh swept back the sea by a strong east wind all through the night, and turned the sea into dry land and the waters were divided. Then the sons of Israel went into the midst of the sea on dry ground, the waters being walled up to their right and to their left. The Egyptians pursued after them; all Pharaoh's horses, chariots and horsemen went after them into the midst of the sea. . . .
> Then Yahweh said to Moses, "Stretch out your hand over the sea, that the waters may rush back upon the Egyptians, upon their chariots and horsemen." . . . When the waters rushed back, they covered the chariots and horsemen of Pharaoh's entire army which had followed them into the sea. Not a single one was saved (Exod. 14:21–23, 26–28).

When the Hebrews had seen the power of the Lord, their enthusiasm carried them away and they broke out into song. It seems more likely that the tradition which connects this hymn of triumph with Miriam is correct. In any case, it is one of the oldest sources we possess for this period and it was set down in writing not long after the event commemorated. In this stirring song of faith and exultation, which compares favorably with the Song of Deborah, we hear one of the earliest expressions of Israel's faith in her deliverer, Yahweh:

> So the prophetess Miriam, Aaron's sister, took a tambourine in her hand, while all the women went out after her with tambourines, dancing; and they sang this song to Yahweh:
>
> "Let me sing to Yahweh, for He is gloriously triumphant; horse and rider He has cast into the sea.
> My might and my defense are Yahweh,
> He has saved me.
> He is my God, Him I praise;
> the God of my father, I extol Him!"
>
> (Exod. 15:1–2)

Once in the Peninsula of Sinai the Israelites headed due south until they came to the traditional site of Mt. Sinai. Here we have arrived at a decisive turning point in their history.

BEHOLD, I AM MAKING A COVENANT

Arrived at Mt. Sinai, Moses and the people prepared to cement, by solemn covenant, that union with God which had begun with Abraham. All the details of the narrative conspire to heighten the solemnity of the scene and the majesty of God, Who was about to conclude a pact with one people from among all the nations. The idea of covenant dominates the whole religious life of Israel, for it is the unique source of her privileges and responsibilities. The word for covenant is *berit*, and it already appears in cuneiform writing as *beritu* a century before the time of Moses. It is very likely that the word has a connection with Accadian *biritu* meaning "fetter, bond." Covenants were made between men or tribes or nations before the time of Moses, so we have to do with the adaptation of a well-known legal form to a religious use, with the changes necessary in such an adaptation.

The covenant with Israel was no legal bargain entered into between equals. Through the covenant Israel took upon herself specific obligations which were a grateful return of obedience to the benefactor who had delivered her from Egypt. No such obligations were imposed upon Yahweh, although it was assumed that He would protect and bless His people if they remained faithful to Him according to the terms of the covenant. What is demanded and why become clear in the opening words of God to Moses at Sinai:

> While Israel was encamped here in front of the montain, Moses went up the mountain to God. Then Yahweh called to him and said, "Thus shall you say to the house of Jacob; tell the Israelites: You have seen for yourselves how I treated the Egyptians and how I bore you up on eagle wings and brought you here to Myself. Therefore, if you hearken to My voice and keep My covenant, you shall be My special possession, dearer to Me than all other people, though all the earth is Mine. You shall be to Me a kingdom of priests, a holy nation. That is what you must tell the Israelites" (Exod. 19:3–5).

As the consecration of a priest sets him apart from the common, secular interests of life, so Israel, by her summons to holiness, was marked off from all the other nations. But this separation gave no cause for narrow self-complacency and contempt for the rest of men. Yahweh had a universal purpose in mind when He made the choice. Israel, His people, was to worship in love and obedience and in doing so to be a source of blessing to all nations. The promises made to Abraham were not canceled out by the election of Israel, nor was the universal character of her vocation in the least diminished. Ever since the covenant at Sinai the great ideal of being a "light to the Gentiles" was implicit in Israel's election. And when the prophets later brought a message of doom because of Israel's infidelities, they made it clear that, in repudiating her obligations, she was more sinful than the Gentiles whom she was imitating and whose gods she was serving.

Recent studies of covenant forms in Israel and other ancient countries from the same broad area have considerably illumined the character of the Sinai Covenant and the relations it presupposed and established between the two covenanting members.[4] The closest parallel discovered up to the present is provided by the suzerainty treaties concluded between the Hittite king and his vassals. A number of these treaties have been preserved in the archives of the Hittite capital, and a legal analysis of the form and pattern of these covenants turns up striking parallels with the Sinai Pact. These treaties were concluded between the Hittite king and a subject nation, the purpose being to provide mutual support for both parties, although the form was unilateral and the stipulations were binding only upon the vassal. Nothing in the treaty was done to infringe upon the sovereignty of the king. In return for his oath, in which the vassal pledged obedience, he could put firm reliance on the benevolence of the sovereign and could trust that the king would protect him from the aggression of other states. In a good number of specific points the Israelite covenant form

---

[4] See especially the excellent study of G. E. Mendenhall, "Covenant Forms in Israelite Tradition," Biblical Archaeologist, XVII, 3 (1954), pp. 50–76.

follows the pattern of the Hittite suzerainty treaty. "In effect, then, each clan became a vassal of Yahweh by covenant — and at the same time bound to each other in a sacred truce. No clan was sovereign, and at the same time, the terms of the covenant left each clan free to regulate its internal affairs so long as the religious covenant obligations were protected."[5] Comparative studies have thus provided examples of covenant forms which are earlier than the Mosaic Covenant and the Decalogue in which obedience was enjoined by Yahweh on the tribes and then solemnized by an oath. Most important of all, the resemblance of the Sinai Covenant to a suzerainty treaty sets in its proper light the relation between the two partners of the covenant. It was not a bargain hammered out between equals and involving mutual obligations, but the initiative of a sovereign Lord Who bound a group of people to Himself in obedience and fidelity.

Since the covenant forms the basis of Israelite life as a nation, it is necessary to dwell for a moment on that virtue to which each member of the covenant pledged himself. *Hesed* is the word the Hebrew used to describe that mutual manifestation of loyalty expected of those united in a *berit*. This is one of the most important religious terms in the Old Testament, and it is unfortunate that no single English word gives us a satisfactory translation of what the Hebrew meant by *hesed*. It is sometimes rendered as "mercy" or "loving kindness" or "steadfast love" and it is all of these and more, since for the Old Testament it expressed the essential element of the bond which should exist between God and men. In the New Testament the word which corresponds most closely to *hesed* is *agape*, which is obviously a key word in the theology of the New Testament. We would drain out much of its meaning if we restricted the word *hesed* to a legal meaning as though it provided the groundwork for a legal contract and nothing else. It goes far beyond this, to meanings we associate with grace and unowed generosity. As applied to Yahweh, the word cer-

---

[5] *Ibid.*, p. 64.

tainly referred to the loyalty to His promises in the covenant
and His readiness to help the people He had chosen. But
Israel was a stiff-necked nation and broke the covenant continually. There was no obligation on God's part to maintain
the covenant; yet He did so. As a result, ḥesed, as an attribute
of God, denoted His boundless mercy and grace, going far
beyond the requirements of a legal contract. Those who showed
ḥesed to one another were bound together in a warm, personal
relationship such as we see in the friendship between David
and Jonathan. If God showed ḥesed in His dealing with Israel
He also demanded the same virtue from them as participants
in the covenant. It was to be shown not only to God but also
to his fellow man who likewise stood in a covenant relation
with God. In one sense it meant sharing in a virtue which
Yahweh had already manifested; this was a return, made in
loving devotion, for the love first shown by God for Israel.
The ideal of Israelite piety is summed up in the word ḥesed.
He was the pious, the devoted man, the one who has shown
covenant loyalty toward God and man. On Sinai God revealed
to Moses that He was a God of ḥesed, but also one Who would
not let sin go unpunished.

> Thus Yahweh passed before him [Moses] and proclaimed,
> "Yahweh, Yahweh, a merciful and gracious God, slow to anger
> and rich in kindness [ḥesed] and fidelity, continuing His kindness
> for a thousand generations, and forgiving wickedness and crime
> and sin; yet not declaring the guilty guiltless, but punishing chil-
> dren and grandchildren to the third and fourth generation for
> their fathers' wickedness" (Exod. 34:6–7).

Before this self-revelation of the God Who has covenanted
with Israel out of unmerited love and yet Who must mete out
punishment to His sinful people Moses could only bow down to
the ground and prostrate himself in worship.

MOSES MY SERVANT

Every attempt to estimate the personality and work of Moses
runs into the difficulty that our written sources, while numerous

and unanimous in centering attention on Moses, are not contemporary with the figure they describe. This certainly does not mean that any effort to portray the man is doomed to failure, for even if our written sources are relatively late, they rest upon ancient traditions orally transmitted for many generations. Unwillingness to accept this evidence from the living traditions of a people would be wholly unwarranted. The past counted for very much in the mind of the Israelite, and he was never allowed to forget that Israel had enjoyed an heroic age in which one man stood out above all others. It was during this age that a new nation emerged, and the Hebrew tradition is unanimous that Moses was the founder of that nation. In the same era the religion of Israel took form as a covenanted society in possession of a *torah* which revealed the purposes of Yahweh and the obligations which this new community assumed upon entering the covenant. It is misleading to think of this *torah* as little more than a collection of laws which the Israelite was bound to observe; this obscures the truth that *torah* meant primarily a teaching which involved a very personal relation between God and His people. *Torah*, as a teaching or body of doctrine, directed men toward God and, even though it contained much civil and cultic legislation, it may more properly be classed as a rule of life by which Israel might fulfill her vocation to be a holy nation.

We need not insist that the Law, in all its details, goes back to the time of Moses, but few today would deny that the substance of this complex legislation stemmed from the man whom Israel venerated as the lawgiver. Before modern discoveries changed the whole picture, scholars of an earlier generation could confidently assert that a collection of Hebrew laws such as we have in the Covenant Code (Exod. 21–23) was an anachronism. Now it has become clear that the civil and criminal legislation of Israel fits in with the social institutions of her neighbors and that the cultural background of this covenant legislation lies in the second millennium B.C. and not in the period of the monarchy. The recovery of codified Mesopotamian and Hittite law has made it certain that the background of the Mosaic Code is the Middle and Late Bronze Age (2000–1200 B.C.) and not the later Iron Age. We have long known about the Code of Hammurabi and the parallels to the later Law of Moses.

In addition to Hammurabi's Code we now have the Sumerian Code of a king of Isin, the Laws of Eshnunna, and the law codes of the Hittites and Assyrians, all older than the Mosaic Code. There is no need to assume that the Hebrews borrowed directly from this earlier legislation, since the social, political, and especially religious conditions were different in Israel. Still, as far as can be determined, these conditions fit the time when Moses lived better than any later period. Thus we have no good reason to suspect the validity of the strong Hebrew tradition which assigns the function of lawgiver to Moses. From Sinai, then, came in substance both the Ten Commandments and the Covenant Code, both through the mediation of Moses. Finally, it was the same man who had heard the voice of God on the mountain who solemnly ratified the covenant with the people in a formal ceremony:

> Moses then wrote down all the words of Yahweh and, rising early the next day, he erected an altar and twelve pillars for the twelve tribes of Israel at the foot of the mountain. Then, having sent some of the young Israelites to offer holocausts and sacrifice young bulls as peace offerings to Yahweh, Moses took half of the blood and put it in large bowls; the other half he splashed on the altar. Taking the Book of the Covenant, he read it aloud to the people, who answered, "All that Yahweh has said we will heed and do." Then he took the blood and sprinkled it on the people, saying, "This is the blood of the covenant which Yahweh has made with you in accordance with all these words of His" (Exod. 24:4–8).

Over and above his function as lawgiver, Moses was the designated leader of his people, the man providentially raised up at a critical moment of history and endowed by God with those qualities which distinguish the leader. To no man did the Israelites believe that they owed more, and in their memories

of Moses, embedded in the sacred writings, they revealed the
extent to which his personality had influenced and molded their
national life. Great men have always left a personal mark on
the people they led, some for good and others for evil. As God's
spokesman and interpreter of His will and purpose, Moses came
to a demoralized group of slaves in Egypt and, after their
deliverance, brought them into covenant with the same Yahweh
Who had appeared to him in the burning bush. The record
shows that he was capable of great outbursts of anger over either
injustice or the folly of his stiff-necked countrymen. But his love
for this people and his devotion to the charge laid upon him
by God were like a consuming fire which purged his diffidence
and human weakness. It is a rare leader who will offer his life
for his own people. But we have a touching scene in which it
is recounted how Moses stood as the intercessor for the people
whom Yahweh would destroy because of their idolatry:

> On the next day Moses said to the people, "You have com-
> mitted a grave sin. I will nevertheless go up to Yahweh; perhaps
> I may be able to make atonement for your sin." So Moses went
> back to Yahweh and said, "Ah, this people has indeed committed
> a grave sin in making a god of gold for themselves! O, that You
> would only forgive their sin! If You will not, then strike me out
> of the book that You have written" (Exod. 32:30–32).

God would not let Moses die; he would have to live with this
people and continue to lead them until they arrived at the
land which God had promised to give them as an inheritance.
Instances of Moses' interceding for the people could be multiplied, and all of them show that tender and loving side of a
stern and wrathful man. Many times he is pictured as standing
between the guilty, terror-stricken Hebrews and the wrath of
God which was about to break out upon them. But God had
revealed His compassion to Moses, and he knew that God's
love for His people was stronger than His wrath. God had come
to Moses in the thunder and smoke of Sinai and had laid upon
Moses the heavy burden of leading this rebellious people, but
Israel could depend upon Yahweh's *ḥesed* which alone explained

His choice of Israel. Tradition has left us a many-sided picture of this great religious genius — quick to anger, slow of speech, courageous to the point of doing battle with Pharaoh, powerful in works, living by the command of God, pleading alone before God, bearer of his people, and capable of transforming these recalcitrant Hebrew tribes into the Israel of God. But none of these qualities fully explain the lasting impression Moses has made upon the history of salvation. It is only at the close of the story of Moses that the sacred writer gives us an appraisal which is in any way satisfying. He lived in the presence of God and his mission in life was to be obedient to that divine will:

> Since then no prophet has arisen in Israel like Moses, whom Yahweh knew face to face. He had no equal in all the signs and wonders Yahweh sent him to perform in the land of Egypt against Pharaoh and all his servants and against all his land, and for the might and the terrifying power which Moses showed in the sight of Israel (Deut. 34:10–12).

O TRULY BLESSED NIGHT

The annual celebration of the Passover, whose liturgy retells the gracious acts of Yahweh, stamped the Exodus on the memory of every Israelite. Psalms 78 and 105 (Hebrew text), inspired by the memory of these stirring days, were probably part of the temple liturgy which helped to keep alive the sacred traditions of the people. But Israelite faith did not live only in the past. It possessed a unique and persistent hope in a better day to come, which it pictured under various forms or symbols. Since the Israelite had already experienced one great deliverance through the favor of Yahweh, what was more natural than to express this conviction of a future age of blessing in terms of a second Exodus under the leadership of a new Moses? In other words, the past event, constantly renewed in the consciousness of the people, began to give form to this hope for future salvation along the lines of the historical Exodus of the thirteenth century. This expression of the future in terms of the past is particularly evident in the second part of Isaiah where the return of the exiles from the Babylonian Captivity is seen as a new Exodus and hence as a new and even greater manifestation of Yahweh's glory and redeeming love. On Sinai His majesty was revealed in thunder and smoke and lightning, as nature herself acknowledged His sovereignty; in this new Exodus from Babylon all flesh was to see His glory, as God once more stepped onto the stage of history. In Isaiah 40 the imagery of return is drawn almost entirely from the Exodus narrative.

The influence of the Exodus, as the primary and typical act of salvation, did not cease with the Old Testament. The hopes of Israel have found their fulfillment in Christ, and so it is not at all surprising that the writers of the New Testament, themselves children of Israel, saw Christ in the light of Moses and His work of redemption in the light of the Exodus. This perceived relation between two events is the basis for what is known as "typology," whereby certain significant persons, events, or things in the Old Testament prefigure a similar but greater reality in the New. Typological exegesis consists in the study and exposition of these correspondences between the two Testaments, concluding that some of these relations of type and fulfillment have been willed by God. The continuities between both are not haphazard since the prefigurative character of the Old Testament is nothing else than the divine preparation for God's definitive intervention in history.

The Gospel of Matthew, ever alive to the theme of fulfillment, has proclaimed the Good News through the image of a New Exodus under a new Moses, Christ. In the Sermon on the Mount, charter of the Kingdom of God, Christ is presented as a second Moses giving the New Law which does not destroy but fulfills the Old Law. The Law of Israel according to the spirit is indeed revolutionary and makes tremendous demands upon those who enter the Kingdom, but it is not wholly divorced from its antecedents in the Old Law. What the prophets and the lawgivers of ancient Israel prepared has now been fulfilled by the Son of God. In transforming the Law of Moses, Christ changed its spirit more than its formulation. Matthew has organized the sayings of Jesus into five great discourses, using as his pattern the Five Books of the Law of Moses. The ten miracles narrated in Chapters 8 and 9 are the antithesis of the ten plagues of Egypt. The miracles are acts of salvation performed for the new people of God, as the plagues were acts of judgment against the oppressors of His people in the former dispensation. In the mystery of the Transfiguration both Matthew and Mark present Moses and Elijah, representing the Law and the Prophets, as witnesses of the divine glory with which the Son of Man is invested, as He prepares for the "exodus" in His redemptive passion and death.

In the Epistles of St. Paul there are almost forty references to the Exodus as a preparation for the New Exodus of salvation under the new Moses:

> For I would not have you ignorant, brethren, that our fathers were all under the cloud, and all passed through the sea, and all were baptized in Moses, in the cloud and in the sea (1 Cor. 10:1-2).

St. Paul is not recalling the events of the Exodus for their own sake or merely because his readers were fond of hearing again the story of God's mighty deeds in the past. "Now all these things," Paul reminds them, "happened to them as a type, and they were written for our correction, upon whom the final age of the world has come." As a Jew, Paul must have realized that he was personally involved in the Exodus from Egypt, for the ancient liturgy reminded each generation that it went out of bondage with its ancestors. But now Paul was a Christian and he could hardly find a better way to express the ineffable mystery of his own redemption than by seeing it as a New Exodus under Jesus, his Saviour. A new and profounder dimension was added to the deliverance from Egypt when it was interpreted as a prefiguration of the new and universal liberation from the bondage of sin.

The Israelite shared in the experience of the Exodus by circumcision, through which he was aggregated to the chosen people. This was his "baptism in Moses," as Paul calls it.

Similarly, the Jewish proselyte could, by baptism, become one with the Exodus generation and he could be said to have crossed the Red Sea with the Israelites. The member of the New Israel, in Paul's thought, must also undergo baptism by which he is incorporated in the new Moses and becomes a sharer in the great act of Christian deliverance, the passion and death of Christ. In the Epistle to the Romans Paul dwells at greater length on this incorporation with Christ and membership in the new people of God. By baptism the Christian has crossed the Red Sea and has emerged as a new being since he has now participated in the Exodus of Christ's passion and death:

> Do you not know that all we who have been baptized into Christ Jesus have been baptized into His death? For we were buried with Him by means of baptism into death, in order that, just as Christ has arisen from the dead through the glory of the Father, so we also may walk in newness of life (Rom. 6:3-4).

These are a few of the ways in which the writers of the New Testament interpreted the mystery of salvation in the light of the Exodus. The same mercy and love were at work in both events. What God had accomplished in Egypt and the wastes of Sinai through His servant Moses, He would accomplish in the New Exodus through His only-begotten Son. Israel has not honored Moses only because of his human achievements or because he was richly endowed with talents of personality and character, but because he was a man united with God. No prophet ever had a greater sense of the presence of God. His work was significant insofar as he acted as God's accredited representative, imparting the word of God to his people. As the self-effacing executor of the divine purpose, Moses achieved his true greatness. On the foundation laid by Moses the structure of Christianity was built; and its cornerstone, Christ, prefigured in Moses, appeared as both Servant and Son of God. What had been begun with Moses on Sinai was completed in Christ, the leader of the New Israel to the Promised Land.

JOSHUA AND THE CONQUEST

After Moses, the servant of Yahweh, had died, Yahweh said to Moses' aide Joshua, the son of Nun: "My servant Moses is dead. Now make ready to cross the Jordan here, along with all the people, into the land which I will give to the children of Israel" (Josh. 1:1–2).

FROM earlier references to the man, it was no surprise that Joshua should be commissioned by the Lord to finish the work begun by Moses. In the preceding books there are five references to Joshua, all indicating a close relationship between Moses and the young military leader. To meet the Amalekite attack on Israel at Rephidim, Moses ordered Joshua to round up a fighting force and lead it in battle (Exod. 17:8–9). At Sinai, Moses brought his servant Joshua up to the mountain when God gave the tablets of stone on which the laws were written (Exod. 24:13). Joshua remained as a custodian of the Tent of Meeting where God had spoken familiarly with Moses (Exod. 33:11). Out of mistaken zeal for his master's honor Joshua complained about the prophesying of Eldad and Medad, only to have Moses remind him that it is not for man to determine upon whom the spirit shall rest. "Are you jealous for my sake? Would that all of Yahweh's people were prophets, that Yahweh would put His spirit upon them!" (Num. 11:29.) Finally, the divine commission came explicitly to Joshua shortly before the death of Moses. "And Yahweh commissioned Joshua the son of Nun and said, 'Be strong and of good courage; for you shall bring the children of Israel into the land which I swore to give to them: I will be with you'" (Deut. 31:23).

These are the preliminary notices which we have concerning the Israelite chieftain before he appears, in full command of Israel, in the book of Joshua. Because the book finishes the story begun in the first five books of the Old Testament, some scholars prefer to look upon it as the last of a six-volume work. They would search for traces of the four main traditions which went into the composition of the Pentateuch, but it must be said at once that there is nothing like unanimity in the documentary analysis of the book. Other scholars are very skeptical about the possibility of finding the four traditions, JEDP, in the book of Joshua.

There is another way of looking at the book in relation to the other historical books. Beginning with the book of Deuteronomy and continuing through the books of Samuel and Kings we have an extended history of Israel from the moment when the Israelites were about to take possession of the land to the time of the Exile in the sixth century B.C. This historical work has a recognizable uniformity of style and viewpoint, the latter being centered in establishing a relation between obedience to law and national prosperity. This was the choice of the two ways presented to Israel, the way of life and the way of death:

> And if you obey the voice of Yahweh your God, carefully obeying all His commandments which I command you this day, Yahweh your God will set you high above all the nations of the earth. And all these blessings shall come upon you and overtake you if you obey the voice of Yahweh your God (Deut. 28:1–2).

To this Deuteronomic tradition, which is very early in its material but relatively late in its final editing, the book of Joshua belongs. The author is not a chronicler but is writing salvation-history which combines the record of events with a theological interpretation of this history. The conquest of the land was the work of the Lord, a jealous God who would tolerate no rival, and the people must respond by having nothing to do with the gods of other nations. If Israel trusted the Lord wholeheartedly and obeyed His commands she could expect to live happily in the newly-won land. From her history, the author was saying, she could learn much about the nature of God and what He demanded of the people with whom He had entered into covenant.

That the book is suffused with the spirit and theology of the Deuteronomic tradition does not diminish one whit its historical value. The more that is known about this period the greater becomes the scholar's respect for the ancient material embodied in the narrative which, like the Pentateuch, must have been orally transmitted for many generations before it was set down in written form. It is quite possible that this epic of conquest was recited to pilgrims who came to such early sanctuaries as Shechem and Gilgal for the celebration of annual feasts. The liturgy, as we have noted, was one of the most effective instruments for keeping alive the remembrance of what Yahweh had done for this people and what He, in turn, expected from them. We will have gained a much more realistic view of the transmission of Israel's sacred literature when we see it as the task of a living tradition which cherished and preserved this holy legacy from the past. It is quite anachronistic, and out of keeping with ancient custom, to picture this transmission in purely literary terms as if writing were as widespread and essential then as it is now.

The book of Joshua is centered on the military hero, but was not written by him. It opens with the children of Israel still on the opposite (east) bank of the Jordan, mourning the death of Moses but fired with enthusiasm to be on with the business of taking possession of the land which Yahweh had promised to give them. It was an extraordinary land which the Israelite warrior saw as he stood on the plateau of Moab and looked to the west. In the far distance was the endless expanse of the Mediterranean. Along the shores of the sea was a coast line unbroken from Egypt to Carmel, but the coastal plain, with its rich soil, offered attractive possibilities for the cultivation of vineyards and the raising of crops. The hill country stood out like a great ridge splitting the whole land vertically and broken only here and there by broad valleys such as the Plain of Esdraelon. From the rocky summits of the hill country the land fell rapidly to the east until the great trench of the Jordan was reached. In this steaming valley, over 1200 feet below sea level, lay one of the first and greatest prizes for the Israelite soldiers, the city of Jericho. As the newcomer looked out on this scene from the heights of Moab, over 3000 feet above the level of the sea, it must have seemed like a very rich and fertile land which he was about to invade. It was a land of startling contrasts as well. In a matter of a few hours one could go up from the jungle-like marshes of the Jordan to the cool highlands of the central hill region. He could look down at the dark blue waters of the Dead Sea, lowest body of water in the world; a moment later he could glance northward and see the snow-covered summit of Mt. Hermon where the cedar flourished. To eyes which had looked for years on the sandy wastes of the Sinai Peninsula this must indeed have seemed like a land "flowing with milk and honey."

Under their new leader, Joshua, the Israelites stood poised and ready to advance westward against the land. On this occasion Yahweh repeated the assurance of victory once given to Moses:

> "No one can withstand you while you live. I will be with you as I was with Moses: I will not abandon nor forsake you. Be firm and steadfast, so that you may give this people possession of the land which I swore to their fathers I would give them. Above all, be firm and steadfast, taking care to observe the entire Law which My servant Moses enjoined on you. Do not swerve from it either to the right or to the left, that you may succeed wherever you go" (Josh. 1:6–7).

How have the historian and the archaeologist filled out the picture left by the sacred writer? How have they amplified and documented a number of hints dropped in the narrative of this book? Why does the modern scholar esteem so highly the reliability of the biblical report even when he knows that the writer was not interested simply in a factual and thoroughly detailed record of exactly what happened? To answer these questions we must turn again to the modern discoveries which have added so much to our knowledge of this crucial period.

FOR THE LORD FOUGHT FOR ISRAEL

For several centuries the land of Canaan had been under the control of Egypt. Although local autonomy was not entirely destroyed, Egyptian rule was harsh and rapacious. From the evidence supplied by the Amarna Letters, sent to the Egyptian court at Amarna in the fourteenth century by Egyptian vassals in Canaan, there was almost constant unrest and rebellion on the part of the native population. Egypt was forced to build fortresses throughout Palestine, forerunners of the sturdy police posts erected by the British during the time of the Mandate. A particularly bothersome group is mentioned very often in these letters. They are the Habiru who turn up in the Near East at numerous places during the second millennium B.C. It would be an oversimplification to identify these Habiru completely with the Hebrews of the Bible, but it now seems more than likely that there is a definite relation between the Israelites and this broad group made up of diverse ethnic elements without the close family and tribal ties we find among the Israelites.

To establish some kind of an equation between the warlike Habiru and the biblical Hebrews it is necessary to put together several bits of evidence scattered throughout the early history of Israel. In the first place, it should be recalled that the Patriarchs secured a foothold in Palestine only along the central ridge of the hill country. They are never associated with the more heavily populated coastal plain nor did they dwell in the rest of the Palestinian lowland already occupied by the strongly entrenched natives, the Canaanites. But they found the hill country which was thickly wooded and where there were few large and fortified settlements admirably suited to the pasturing of their flocks. When need arose, they even fought for possession of this area, as is clear from the account about the battle at Shechem, told as a story of revenge for the wrong done to an Israelite maiden. If the central ridge in the hill country was under the control of the Hebrews not only in the time of the Patriarchs but centuries later as well, we have an explanation for the strange omission in the record of fighting by the incoming Israelites under Joshua in the central hill country. What now seems very likely is that Joshua had no need to conquer this area since it was already populated by people, the descendants of the Patriarchs, with whom the Israelites enjoyed a kinship. Israel had to fight for territory in other parts of Palestine; here, it seems that matters were settled by treaty between two groups who recognized a blood tie between themselves even though they had not lived together for many centuries.

If this theory proves to be correct, there will be further reason for holding that not all the Israelites went down to Egypt in the time of the Patriarchs; consequently, it was not all the Israelites who took part in the Exodus. Some of them, it would appear, never left Palestine, and in the thirteenth century they were able once again to unite with their own group by covenanting with the invading Israelites under Joshua. At least a century before the invasion, the Amarna Letters tell us of rebellious groups of Habiru in the region around Shechem, and it is very tempting to connect them with the Hebrew descendants of the men who settled this area in late patriarchal times. What is far more certain is that the Habiru of the Amarna Letters, for various reasons, should not be identified with the Hebrews who invaded Palestine in the thirteenth century. Chronology is not the only factor which argues against associating the two groups; in their manner of life, mode of warfare, and purpose in fighting, the two must be kept distinct.

This brings us to the major contribution which archaeology has made to the period of the conquest. Few epochs in the history of Israel have received comparable illumination from this science. The first service performed by the archaeologist was to settle the date of the invasion under Joshua. The Israelites chose to assault the land of Canaan from the eastern side of the Jordan, and started northward along the old route known as the "King's Highway" which bisected the kingdoms of Edom,

Moab, and the territory of Sihon, king of the Amorites whose capital was at Heshbon. Since the king of Edom refused permission to traverse his territory and it was likely that the king of Moab would follow the same policy, the Israelites moved northward along the western edge of Edom and then turned eastward, proceeding along the River Zered which separated Edom and Moab.

Whatever obscurities still remain in the itinerary, the biblical narrative leaves no doubt that Edom, Moab, and Sihon's land were settled areas, with definite boundaries and a form of government recognized by the Israelites. This is the area where Professor Nelson Glueck conducted surface explorations for over ten years and came up with the conclusion that this southern part of Transjordan was not settled before the thirteenth century B.C. Previous to this time the people of this area lived a nomadic life without settled boundaries or clearly defined administration. Then, beginning with the thirteenth century, towns began to appear in this locality, among them Heshbon and Jazer. The only period, accordingly, which can fit the biblical record and archaeological evidence is sometime during the thirteenth century, but not earlier, when the nomadic conditions of southern Transjordan would hardly suit the indications given by the biblical account of the operations in this area.

Once the Israelites had secured a permanent foothold on the eastern side of the Jordan, in Gilead and Bashan, they were ready to launch an attack against their primary objective, the land of Canaan, on the western side of the Jordan. In the book of Joshua this campaign is visualized as a three-pronged attack against central, southern, and finally northern Palestine, with Joshua everywhere leading the victorious forces. Not a few scholars are wont to take this story of one smashing triumph after the other with a grain of salt; they eagerly point to the first chapter of the book of Judges where one can read about a slow, piecemeal conquest of the land, with victories matched by reverses. Here, they would claim, was the true picture of what happened. The account in Joshua was nothing but the typical exaggeration of an oriental historian bent on glorifying a local chieftain, Joshua. The conquest as described in Joshua was therefore to be dismissed as having little or no foundation in fact, and reliance was to be placed solely on the version given in the opening chapter of Judges. Each tribe was forced, by hard struggle, to secure its own portion in the land, and the picture of a united group sweeping all before it was so much fancy.

Time and the accumulation of new evidence have changed this pessimistic assessment of the Joshua narrative. To begin with, an attentive reading of the story makes it very clear that the victory in Palestine was not as total as a hurried reading might suggest. Even after the three successful campaigns were terminated much remained to be done. The coastal plain, the valley of Esdraelon, strongholds like Bethshan and Jerusalem still remained in the hands of the native population. Jerusalem would not be conquered and occupied permanently until the time of David. On the other hand, the violent destruction in the thirteenth century of a good number of Canaanite cities squares very well with the account of remarkably successful campaigns by Joshua at the very beginning of the invasion. It now seems that the accounts in Joshua and Judges can be reconciled by referring them to two stages in the conquest of the land. Joshua reports the initial victories won under the leadership of Joshua while Judges reflects the slow and gradual occupation of the country by wresting it from natives who put up stubborn resistance before they were dislodged. We noted that the campaigns of Joshua were carried out in three stages, based on the geography of the land. In each of these phases we can now point to an important Canaanite center taken and destroyed by the Israelites in the thirteenth century.

For the penetration into the central hill country, the first objective of the invading force, it would be natural to begin with Jericho, the first settlement to fall before the onslaught of the Israelites. Unfortunately, the latest and most scientific excavations conducted at this ancient site by the English archaeologist, Kathleen Kenyon, have proved very disappointing as far as the Jericho of the Israelite period is concerned. This period would fall in that division of ancient chronology known as the Late Bronze Age (1500–1200 B.C.).[1] The depredations of time and weather in the Jordan valley have left practically no traces of remains from the Late Bronze Age. Earlier and erroneous interpretations of archaeological remains at Jericho have now been corrected, but that has left us with only the negative conclusion that no traces of the walls of the Late Bronze city remain. The city which Joshua took has been washed away by the winter rains or swept away by the hot winds which blow through the valley.

The territory in the vicinity of Bethel and Ai would be the next logical target for a force seeking control of the central highlands. The book of Joshua describes the sacking of Ai in great detail but is silent about the capture of Bethel. Here is a case where excavation has left the biblical scholar with a puzzle rather than a solution. For the archaeologist has discovered that Ai was destroyed about 2400 B.C. and, except for a small occupation in 1000 B.C., abandoned for all time. On the other hand, there is clear evidence for a violent destruction of Bethel in the thirteenth century, at the very time when we would expect the army of Joshua to have assaulted the city. How explain the biblical account describing the overthrow of a city which had not been occupied for over a thousand years while making no mention of the fall of Bethel which the archaeologist dates to the period of Joshua? This is admittedly a difficulty, and only a probable solution can be offered. The opinion which offers the fewest difficulties is one which claims that the story of Bethel's fall was transferred to the neighboring town of Ai (a name meaning "the ruin"). There is no reason to question the fact that a devastating blow was struck in the Bethel-Ai area, as both the Bible and archaeology relate. The theory of transfer is a probable one and it is a phenomenon for which parallels could be found elsewhere in historical writing.

[1] Kathleen Kenyon, *Digging Up Jericho* (London: Ernest Benn, Ltd., 1957).

Pushing into Judah the Israelites did not make frontal assaults on such strong points as Gezer and Jerusalem, but reduced the surrounding towns which served as outposts for the hill country of Judah. The most important of these was Lachish, and we are told that Joshua took it; the archaeologist fully confirms the destruction of this powerful city-state in the thirteenth century. Swinging south the Israelites took, among other places, the town of Debir; again archaeology offers its own independent witness to the catastrophe which overtook the town in the second half of the thirteenth century. The last phase of the campaign against Canaan brought Joshua into the north country, the area of Galilee, whose most powerful city was Hazor. "At that time Joshua, turning back, captured Hazor and slew its king with the sword; for Hazor formerly was the chief of all those kingdoms" (Josh. 11:10). Since 1955 there have been four major archaeological campaigns at the impressive site which, at one time, sheltered a population of 40,000 people, an unusually large number for any Palestinian settlement. In one of the supervised areas, the excavators, under the direction of Professor Yigael Yadin, former Chief of Staff of the Israeli Army and now one of Israel's leading archaeologists, found clear evidence for the destruction of Hazor in the thirteenth century.[2] For each of the three major areas, therefore, where the Israelites waged campaigns, the archaeologist has found evidence for the destruction, usually by fire, of native strongholds. Lachish, Bethel, Eglon, Debir, and Hazor are only some of the towns which offer their testimony to the onslaught of the Israelites in the thirteenth century.

Pharaoh Marniptah was the successor of Rameses II, who was, as we noted, the Pharaoh of the Exodus. It was during the reign of Marniptah that Egypt, for the first time in many centuries, was threatened with invasion from the west by a group of warriors known as the Sea People. The Pharaoh met the foe at the western frontier of Egypt and routed them. On this occa-

---

[2] See the preliminary reports of Professor Yadin in *The Illustrated London News* for April 14, 1956, pp. 298–301, and December 8, 1956, pp. 990–993.

sion he set up a victory stele or monumental slab with an inscription commemorating his victory. On this stele we have the first reference to Israel outside the Bible:

> The Canaanite land is despoiled with every evil.
> Ashkelon is carried captive; Gezer is conquered;
> Yanoam is made as though it did not exist.
> The people of Israel is desolate, it has no offspring;
> Palestine has become a widow for Egypt.

By the use of linguistic symbols the Egyptians were able to distinguish between nomadic and sedentarized people, and in this victory hymn the word "Israel" is followed by the signs indicating that they were a group as yet unsettled in the land. The date of the stele is about 1220 B.C. and it provides further evidence that the Israelites were in Palestine at that time although they had not, as yet, fully settled in this new land which they were eventually to occupy as their home.

In the Israelite battle for possession of the land we are confronted with a practice, the ḥerem, or "ban," which underscores the imperfection of Old Testament morality. According to this custom, which belonged to the law of holy war, whole populations of conquered cities were exterminated as a kind of gigantic offering to the deity who had made the victory possible. The practice was widespread among the Semitic peoples; and one ruler, Mesha of Moab, has left on his stele the record of how he had "devoted" or massacred men, women, and children of captured towns to the honor of his god. There are indications in the biblical tradition that the Hebrews did not carry out this policy of extermination, as a religious act, with all the thoroughness which some texts might suggest. The practice, inhumane though it seems to us who are taught to live according to the standards of Christian morality, should not be judged apart from its context in the ancient Semitic world. Nor should it be forgotten that the Israelites were convinced that their destiny demanded the utter destruction of any people or things which threatened the purity of their monotheism. Subsequent history was to demonstrate what would happen to the religion of Yahweh when Hebrew and Canaanite freely mixed in society. Worth considering also is the possibility that the stern law of ḥerem as found, for example, in the book of Deuteronomy, represents a later and uncompromising attitude of the Hebrew toward Canaanite religion rather than an actual command given the Israelites at the time of the conquest. Without in the least condoning a practice which was barbarous and shocking when carried out to the letter, the ḥerem again reminds us that God did not create a nation of moral and intellectual supermen in order to work out His purposes. He took men as they were, with all their faults and wrong ideas, their weaknesses and ignorance. These imperfect men were the instruments by which the history of salvation would be worked out. We might see in this a very instructive example of using "the weak and contemptible things of this world to confound the strong." And our modern record of brutality and cruelty in war gives us little right to be smug about the imperfect morality of the Hebrews. Coming closer to home, our early colonists along the eastern seaboard frequently treated the natives of the new Canaan pretty much as the Israelites of old had treated the Canaanites. The Indian Wars of the seventeenth century provide many uncomfortably close parallels to the ḥerem.

The problem of Old Testament morality involves the whole question of how God deals with man. Even when God chooses a man for a religious task, He does not suddenly erase the moral and intellectual limitations which are inevitably present at a certain stage of man's development; the man is not, in virtue of God's election for a specific work, removed from his environment which is conditioned by the period of history in which he lives and the level of education which has been attained. David does not become a St. Francis de Sales. God takes man as He finds him and builds upon that material with all its shortcomings and imperfections. Father H. J. Richards has some excellent things to say on this point:[3]

---

[3] H. J. Richards, "The Word of God Incarnate," *The Life of the Spirit*, XIII (August–September, 1958), p. 98.

Here is man as he is, as we know him to be, in all his weakness. And here is God as He is, not an abstract Prime Mover or First Cause, but a God who is interested in men of flesh and blood, a father who bends down to appeal to his wayward children. If we had had the job of inspiring this book, of laying out a blueprint of the sort of thing that God's Word should speak to us, what a strange mixture we should have turned out of speculative theology and hot-house piety. And how very inhuman we would have made it.

We do not mean by this that God is indifferent to the moral conduct of man nor that He ever ceases to elevate the imperfect ideals of the men He has chosen. This is evident from the Old Testament where there is demonstrable progress in the knowledge of God and what He demands. God educates His people. If we want a parallel to the ways of God with Israel we need go no farther than the dealings of God with the individual soul. God can still make use of us despite our sins and failures. Our own weakness does not prevent God from calling us to higher perfection and that very call neither confirms us in sanctity nor allows us to forget that it is God Who works the good in us, often in spite of our human frailty. In judging the morality of the Old Testament and its limitations, which are obvious, nothing is more salutary than to look into our own hearts; the story of what God has done with me is, for the most part, the story of His dealing with mankind.[4]

Though he built upon the firm foundations laid by Moses, the achievement of Joshua was not an insignificant one. After the death of Moses on Mt. Nebo there fell to this warrior chieftain the onerous task of welding a relatively small group of seminomads into an effective fighting force capable of taking possession of the land promised to them by their God. More than that, and this is one of the most important of Joshua's accomplishments, once in the land, he was able to unite all the tribes, whether or not they took part in the invasion, into a unity cemented by their common worship of Yahweh. It is

---

[4] On this question see the article by Fr. L. Johnston, "Old Testament Morality," *Catholic Biblical Quarterly*, XX (January, 1958), pp. 19–25.

even likely that as early as the time of Joshua the process of assimilating some of the Canaanites had already begun. The book of Joshua closes with an impressive covenant ceremony at the ancient sanctuary of Shechem. After reciting the mighty deeds of Yahweh in favor of His people and especially how He had delivered them from the servitude of Egypt, the old warrior bids them turn their backs on the idols of the past and serve God Who had delivered them. After the people made their choice, Joshua, in the last recorded act before his death, led them into a solemn reaffirmation of the covenant:

"Now, therefore, fear Yahweh and serve Him completely and sincerely. Cast out the gods your fathers served beyond the River and in Egypt, and serve Yahweh. If you are not willing to serve Yahweh, decide this day whom you will serve, the gods your fathers served beyond the River or the gods of the Amorites in whose country you are dwelling. As for me and my house, we will serve Yahweh. . . ." Then the people promised Joshua, "We will serve Yahweh, our God, and obey His voice."

So Joshua made a covenant with the people that very day and made statutes and ordinances for them at Shechem, which he recorded in the Book of the Law of God. Then he took a large stone and set it up under the oak which was in the sanctuary of Yahweh. And Joshua said to all the people, "This stone shall be our witness, for it has heard all the words which Yahweh spoke to us. It shall be a witness against you, should you wish to deny your God." Then Joshua dismissed the people, each to his own inheritance (Josh. 24:14–15, 24–28).

SAUL, THE FIRST KING

BIBLICAL tradition and archaeology agree that the military successes of Joshua were only the prelude to stubborn local fighting between the Israelites and the natives they sought to dispossess. The tribes were anxious to settle down in the newly won territory, but initial victories, important though they were for obtaining the necessary foothold, did not by any means bring a period of uninterrupted peace. The evidence is all to the contrary, especially in the traditions preserved in the book of Judges and in the results from excavated Palestinian mounds of that period, many of which show three and four destructions in a relatively short space of time. All our information points to the time of the Judges as one of chaotic struggle with victory and defeat following in quick succession. Nothing can sum up more tersely the existing anarchy than the remark which closes the book of Judges: "In those days there was no king in Israel; everyone did what he thought best."

One of the factors which goes a long way toward explaining the early triumphs of Joshua is the strong cohesion of the Israelites when they launched their attack against western Palestine. The years in the desert under the tutelage of a personality like Moses had formed them into a more or less compact group with common ideals and a strong sense of national unity. The religion of Yahweh, setting them apart from those who worshiped many gods, not only united them but gave them a fervor in war which more than compensated for their technical weaknesses. In the time of the Judges this religious influence was practically the only means of assuring any kind of unity among the tribes. During this critical era the tribes were bound together in a rather loose confederation which was essentially religious in character, since it was centered at one of the great sanctuaries

and symbolized by the Ark of the Covenant which rested at
Shilo. This was the central shrine around which the tribes
united and were able to achieve some measure of common
action.

But there were centrifugal forces constantly operating against
even this small measure of unity. In the first place, the geographical structure of Palestine has always been a deterrent to
unity. Galilee is separated from the hill country of Ephraim
by the broad valley of Esdraelon, and no Israelite battle force
of that period could withstand the onslaughts of Canaanite
chariotry which controlled the plain. Ephraim and Judah to the
south were separated by the transverse wadies and deep passes
which ran east and west along the ridge of the hill country and
effectively cut the country up into districts, sometimes even
linguistically. Added to the divisive character of the terrain was
the even more serious obstacle of diminished zeal for Yahwism,
the one great binding force of the tribes, once contact was
made with the gross but very appealing religion of Canaan.
From this time there would be an unceasing struggle between
those who slipped into native paganism and the stanch followers of Yahweh who refused all compromise with the gods
of Canaan. A sign of the times was the appearance, as early as
the time of the Judges, of proper names with Baal as one of
the elements. This suggests that there might have been some
syncretism between Yahweh and Baal, but the loyal follower
of Moses, who taught the people that Yahweh was a jealous
God, knew that the true son of Israel could have no truck with
Baal. We shall see later how this religious problem reached a
crisis in the time of Elijah.

Operating against the disintegrating forces of geography and
a weakening in their Yahwism was the peril which the young
nation faced from formidable enemies in the land of Palestine. To the south, the Philistines, who had invaded the country
in force barely fifty years after the Israelites took Jericho, were
compactly organized into a union of five cities (a pentapolis)
along the coastal strip south of Joppa. Further immigration

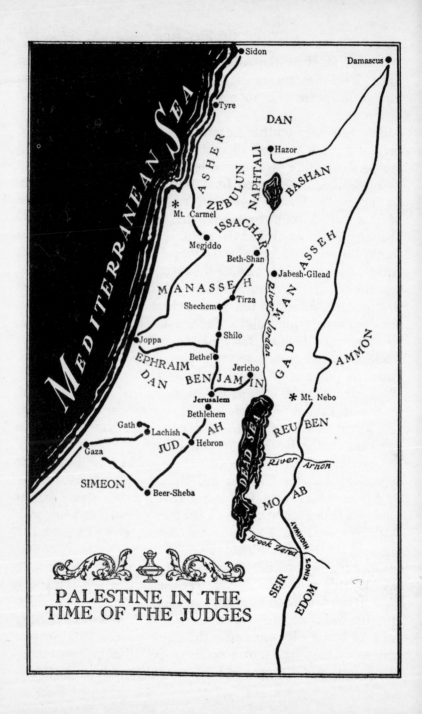

PALESTINE IN THE
TIME OF THE JUDGES

from the Aegean area increased their numbers and soon the Philistines were fanning out into other parts of Palestine, notably the inviting lowland known as the Shephelah, as well as the Negeb. Wherever the Philistines went they left a distinctive type of pottery easily identified by the archaeologist. It was made according to models proper to the Aegean world, as is clear from the striking similarity between this ware and the Mycenaean pottery discovered on the island of Cyprus. Its characteristic features include a series of graceful spirals and geometric designs to which are added highly stylized paintings of swans pluming themselves. But the Philistines were busy with the arts of war as well as with ceramics. The archaeologist has uncovered traces of their depredations in the territory of Judah and Ephraim, where they sacked such towns as Debir, Shilo, and Beth-Zur. An interesting passage in the first book of Samuel helps to explain why the Philistines were able to hold the upper hand over the Israelites until the liberation under Saul and especially David, who threw off the Philistine yoke once and for all:

> Now there was no smith in the land of Israel; for the Philistines said: "For fear that the Hebrews would make themselves swords or spears." But all the Israelites went down to the Philistines so that each one could sharpen his plowpoint, his mattock and his axe. And he had to pay a pim [2/3 of a shekel] for the plowpoints and the mattocks, and a third of a shekel for the sharpening of the axes and for setting the goads. So when the day of battle came there was neither sword nor spear in the hand of any of the people who fought with Saul and Jonathan . . . (1 Sam. 13:19–22).

This notice underlines the handicaps under which the Israelites challenged the Philistines, who held a monopoly on the working of iron, even for agricultural purposes. Once they learned how to work iron, the Philistines introduced the technique into Palestine but jealously guarded the secret and thus preserved their control of the iron industry. It was only at the time of Saul and David that the Israelites were able to break this monopoly and to begin using iron on a large scale.

While the Philistines were undoubtedly the greatest menace
to the security of the Israelites, grave danger also came from
the Canaanite strongholds in the north which had survived the
first wave of conquest led by Joshua. Fortress cities such as
Bethshan and Megiddo constantly menaced the young nation
in its formative period. The memory of what must have been
a typical skirmish in the north is preserved in that precious gem
of ancient Israelite poetry, the Song of Deborah. Put down in
writing only a short time after the incident it narrates, this
thrilling piece vividly re-creates for the reader the perilous times
of the Judges along with the exaltation of a people for whom
Yahweh fought. As an historical source for this critical period
the Song of Deborah is unsurpassed, even though its archaism
in language and imagery have baffled generations of scholars:

> Of chiefs who took the lead in Israel,
>   Of noble deeds by the people who bless Yahweh,
> hear, O kings! Give ear, O princes!
> I will sing my song to Yahweh,
> my hymn to Yahweh, the God of Israel.
>
> O Yahweh, when You went out from Seir,
>   when You marched from the land of Edom,
> the earth quaked and the heavens trembled,
>   yea, the clouds sent down showers.
> Mountains trembled before Yahweh,
>   the One of Sinai,
>   in the presence of Yahweh, the God of Israel.
>
> In the days of Samgar, son of Anath,
>   in the days of Jael, caravans ceased;
>   and wayfarers went by roundabout paths.
> The peasantry ceased in Israel,
> they ceased until thou didst arise, Deborah,
> until thou didst arise, a mother in Israel. . . .
>
> The kings came and fought,
>   then fought the kings of Canaan,
> at Taanach by the waters of Megiddo.
> spoils of silver they took not;
> From the heavens fought the stars,

from their courses they fought against Sisera.
The Wadi Kishon swept them away. . . .

Thus may Your enemies perish, O Yahweh!
But all Your friends be as the sun rising in his might!
(Judges 5:2–7, 19–21, 31)

Against two such redoubtable foes as the Philistines and the Canaanites the loosely organized Israelites, held together only by a weakening religious bond, were open to attack from all sides. Whatever leadership they had during this time was entrusted to men who were called "judges," not because they acted solely as magistrates, but because they were believed to be endowed with divine gifts of wisdom and valor. Max Weber coined the phrase "charismatic leaders" to describe them because of the special outpouring of the divine spirit which took possession of them. This was Israel's heroic age when only men who stood out above their fellows could hope to check the disintegration of the nation.

GIVE US A KING

An Israel beset on all sides by well-organized foes could not indefinitely depend on leaders who arose spontaneously to deliver the people from their oppressors. The hand of the Philistines lay heavier and heavier upon the land until the culminating blow was struck about 1050 B.C., when the sanctuary of Shilo was destroyed and the Ark fell into the hands of the enemy. There followed a generation of humiliating subjection to the Philistines, and then one man, whom the prophet Samuel anointed as king over Israel, intervened decisively in her history. It was a fateful moment, as subsequent events were to prove, but a more stable form of government was absolutely imperative if Israel was ever to enjoy any security in Palestine.[1]

---

[1] The first book of Samuel has left two traditions about the origins of kingship, one favorable and the other opposed. Many scholars believe that the tradition opposing the institution reflects the thinking of a later age when Israel had become disillusioned with its kings and disgusted with their abuses of the sacred office. This is a solidly probable solution, but it is also possible that

The aged prophet must have meditated long upon the series of disasters which had overwhelmed his people before taking the step of anointing a leader who could rally the tribes and provide the unity they so desperately needed.

What sort of man was Saul, the first to be anointed king over Israel? Here is one of the great tragic figures of Old Testament literature. Ultimately, he became a rejected leader, but even in his dismal failures it is not hard to discern the elements of greatness in the man. He first appears as a man in the prime of life working for his father, a wealthy Benjaminite by the name of Kish. ". . . and he had a son whose name was Saul, a handsome young man. There was not a man among the people of Israel more handsome than he; from his shoulders upward he was taller than any of the people" (1 Sam. 9:2). Besides his sheer physical stature there was an unmistakable impression of dignity and reserve in Saul, in the beginning at least. Before this meeting Samuel had learned from God that Saul was the man to save his people from the Philistines. On the day after this meeting Samuel took a vial of oil and poured it upon the head of Saul, saying: "Has not the Lord anointed you to be prince over His people Israel? And you shall reign over the people of the Lord and you will save them from the hand of their enemies round about" (1 Sam. 10:1).

No sooner had Saul left Samuel than God gave a new heart to this consecrated leader; he was turned into another man. At this moment the biblical tradition describes Saul's encounter with the prophets, fiery zealots for the cause of Yahweh, who roamed about the countryside in bands and, with music and dancing, worked themselves into a frenzy of religious enthusiasm. This is the first mention in the Bible of the bands of

---

both views existed simultaneously at the time of Saul's anointing. It is not farfetched to hold that Samuel himself was at first opposed to the idea of the monarchy since he believed that God alone was to be Israel's king and then, realizing that it was God's will that Israel should have a king, set about to find the right man, anointed him and then enthusiastically presented him to the people. "Do you see him whom Yahweh has chosen? There is none like him among all the people."

prophets, and it is very likely that, at just this time, the second half of the eleventh century, ecstatic prophetism began in Israel. Thanks to this movement there was a renewal of zeal for the religion of Yahweh, and by the time of David Yahwism was perhaps stronger than it had ever been since the time of Moses:

> And they came to Gibeah and behold, a band of prophets came to meet him (Saul); and the spirit of God possessed him, and he prophesied in their midst. And when all who knew him formerly saw that he prophesied with the prophets, the people said to one another, "What has come over the son of Kish? Is Saul also among the prophets?" And a man from that place answered, "And who is their father?" Therefore it became a proverb, "Is Saul also among the prophets?" (1 Sam. 10:10–12.)

The spirit of the Lord, as powerful in its effect as it is unpredictable in its coming, had taken possession of Saul and he returned to his home at Gibeah, there to await the beginning of his life's work. Almost immediately an incident occurred which marked him as the leader and popular hero. The people of Jabesh-gilead had been humiliated by the Ammonites, and messengers brought the news to the town of Gibeah. Returning from the fields, Saul heard the wailing of the people. Once again, the spirit of Yahweh descended upon Saul and he acted swiftly and decisively. Taking his yoke of oxen, he cut them in pieces and sent the mangled flesh throughout Israel, saying, "Whoever does not come out after Saul and Samuel, so shall it be done to his oxen." Here was a man worthy to lead Israel and capable of uniting the tribes in a worthy cause. The victory was complete and the Ammonites were annihilated. In triumph the people brought Saul to the sanctuary of Gilgal and publicly proclaimed him king:

> And all the people went to Gilgal, and there they made Saul king before Yahweh in Gilgal. There they sacrificed peace offerings before Yahweh, and there Saul and all the men of Israel rejoiced exceedingly (1 Sam. 11:15).

The success in relieving Jabesh-gilead gave the Israelites a lesson in their own strength when united solidly behind a dynamic and courageous leader. Selecting a small army of three thousand men, Saul now prepared to deal with Israel's most dreaded enemy, the Philistines. The campaign of liberation began with the slaughter of the garrison at Geba. This was followed by a victory at Michmash; and then ensued a long period of skirmishes between Saul and the Philistines, who never regained their hold on the country until the great battle at the end, when Saul and his sons were killed at Gilboa. 1 Sam. 14:52 sums up the situation in a sentence: "There was war with the Philistines all the days of Saul." The turning point in Saul's career is connected with another victory, this time against the Amalekites. Ordered by Samuel to carry out the ḥerem against Agag, the defeated king of the Amalekites, Saul disobeyed and spared both Agag and the choice animals of his flock. For this act Samuel appeared before Saul and pronounced the sentence of divine rejection in the famous passage:

> Does Yahweh take as great delight in burnt
>   offerings and sacrifices,
> as in obeying the voice of Yahweh?
> Behold, obedience is better than sacrifice,
> and to hearken than the fat of rams.
> For like the sin of divination is rebellion,
> and stubbornness is like iniquity and idolatry.
> Because you have rejected the word of Yahweh,
> He has rejected you from the kingship.
>
> (1 Sam. 15:22–23)

WHAT MORE CAN HE HAVE EXCEPT THE KINGDOM?

From the moment of this break with Samuel a marked change came over Saul. "The spirit of Yahweh departed from Saul and an evil spirit from Yahweh tormented him." Up to this time he had been wholly absorbed in the responsibilities thrust upon him by kingship. In the fury of battle and the exhilaration of temporary successes the defects in his character did not come to the fore. Now there set in a steady deterioration which is described with remarkable vividness in the biblical record. The dark moods of depression and despair came upon Saul with greater frequency; fits of insane jealousy drove him to rash and murderous acts. The court attendants at Gibeah were alarmed at the steady decline of the king and sought to counteract his morbidity by bringing a skilled musician to Saul, hoping that the songs of the lyre would soothe the disturbed king. The young musician was David of Bethlehem, who immediately won the heart of Saul. The latter insisted that he become a permanent member of the royal court. Professor Albright excavated the "palace" of Saul at Gibeah, which proved to be quite unlike anything we associate with a royal dwelling. It was rather the stronghold of a rustic chieftain, solidly built with roughly dressed stones and protected at its vulnerable points by sturdy towers. The palace of Saul, as it is now known through archaeology, somehow suited the character and temper of this resolute and energetic ruler who was nevertheless unable to fight off the dark impulses which preyed upon him:

> And David came to Saul, and served him. And Saul loved him very much, and David became his armor-bearer. Then Saul sent to Jesse, saying, "Let David remain in my service, for he has found favor in my sight." And whenever the evil spirit from God came upon Saul, David took the lyre and played it with his hand; and Saul was refreshed, and was well, and the evil spirit left him (1 Sam. 16:21–23).

But the musician was also a warrior, eventually winning command over Saul's small standing army. Both of them threw themselves wholeheartedly into the fight against the Philistines and came off with many victories. It was while returning from one of these triumphs that the Israelite women, in typical Oriental fashion, came out to celebrate the slaughter of the Philistines in song and dance, as Miriam and her followers did when the children of Israel had crossed the sea unharmed. This action is represented in the biblical tradition as the first break between Saul and David, now recognized as the two popular heroes:

When they were returning home, and David was coming back from slaying the Philistine, the women came out from all the cities of Israel, singing and dancing, to meet King Saul, with timbrels, songs of joy, and musical instruments. And the women sang joyfully to one another,

> "Saul has slain his thousands,
> but David his ten thousands."

And Saul was very angry, and this saying was very displeasing to him; and he said, "They have given to David ten thousands, but to me they have given thousands; and what more can he have except the kingdom?" And Saul eyed David from that day on (1 Sam. 18:6–8).

Obsessed with a jealous hatred of David, the tormented king set about to destroy him. Driven from the court, David was forced to go into hiding. Finally, his plight became so serious that he sought refuge among the Philistines, in the city of Gath. Eventually, David gathered about him a band of outlaws like himself, fleeing from place to place as Saul pursued the fugitives relentlessly. During this hectic chase an incident took place which shows both the magnanimity of David and the greatness of Saul in admitting his own guilt. David had managed to trap Saul but spared his life. He then revealed his identity to Saul and tried to induce him to change his ill-advised course of action. The old love of Saul for David was reawakened and, on this occasion at least, Saul honestly faced up to his own weakness and blundering:

When David had finished speaking these words to Saul, Saul said, "Is this your voice, my son David?" Then Saul lifted up his voice and wept. And he said to David, "You are more just than I; for you have repaid me with good, whereas I have repaid you with evil" (1 Sam. 24:17–18).

There cannot be the slightest doubt that Saul really loved David, but his affection was smothered by the suspicions and jealousies which upset his mental balance. His repentance and remorse over his folly could not last long. Saul was soon pursuing David again.

With David out of the way, and even for a time enlisted in their ranks, the Philistines launched one more great attack on Israel. This time it was centered on the plain of Esdraelon at the foot of Mt. Gilboa, where the Israelites mustered their army to await the onslaught. Saul was seized with fright and, on the eve of battle, went in disguise to the Witch of Endor, one of the mediums whom he had formerly tried to drive out of Israel. Popular tradition has painted in unforgettable colors the meeting between Saul and Samuel, brought back from Sheol. The message of Samuel was a verdict of doom: "Yahweh has turned from you and become your enemy." In a paroxysm of fear Saul fell prostrate on the ground and all his great strength left him. Before the battle started he was a beaten man. The Philistines overwhelmed the outnumbered Israelites and slew the sons of Saul. They pressed on to take the king but Saul, fearing to be captured alive and brought back in disgrace to Philistia, fell upon his own sword and ended his tragic life. On the following day, when the Philistines found Saul and his three dead sons on Mt. Gilboa, they cut off Saul's head and hanged his body on the wall of Bethshan.

The first book of Samuel closes with a touching incident of gratitude on the part of the people whom Saul had saved at the beginning of his reign. The citizens of Jabesh-gilead never forgot the brave man who had delivered them in their hour of peril. Having heard the news that Saul was dead, the men of Jabesh-gilead set out under cover of darkness and moved north along the thicket-infested valley of the Jordan. Arrived at Bethshan, they performed the last act of reverence for their deliverer by taking down the disfigured bodies of Saul and his sons and burying them in their own land. But it was David, the man who was hunted by Saul for so many years, who spoke the valedictory of all Israel over the fallen hero. There is every reason to believe that this dirge, one of the world's great pieces of lyric poetry, was composed by David himself during his lamentation:

Thy glory, O Israel, upon thy high places is slain!
How have the mighty fallen!
Tell it not in Gath,
publish it not in the streets of Ascalon;
lest the daughters of the Philistines rejoice,
yea, the daughters of the uncircumcised exult.

O mountains of Gilboa,
let neither dew nor rain come upon you,
nor welling-up of the deep!
For there the shield of the mighty was defiled.
the shield of Saul, not anointed with oil. . . .

Daughters of Israel, weep for Saul,
who clothed you in scarlet,
who put ornaments of gold upon your dress.
How have the mighty fallen
in the midst of the battle!

Jonathan upon thy high places lies dead.
I am distressed for you, my brother Jonathan;
very dear have you been to me;
your love to me was wonderful,
surpassing the love of women.
How have the mighty fallen,
and the weapons of war perished!

(2 Sam. 1:19–27)

DAVID AND THE GOLDEN AGE

WITH Saul's death David was now in a position to assume the kingship. His days of outlawry in the cave-pocked hills of Judah finished, he immediately turned his attention and great energies to the crisis facing the young kingdom. The Philistines were more strongly entrenched than ever after the victory at Gilboa; a new and more astute leadership was the need of the hour. And David acted with that skill and decisiveness which were to characterize his public life. Directing his steps to Hebron, a sanctuary long revered because of its associations with Abraham, he made it clear to his fellow countrymen that he had broken once and for all with the Philistines in whose ranks he had once fought. The men of Judah came to Hebron and anointed David as their ruler; at the same time, the commander of Saul's broken army, Abner, had taken a son who had survived the massacre at Gilboa and brought him across the Jordan to Mahanaim, the capital of Gilead. Every tribe from Benjamin northward pledged allegiance to Ishbaal, Saul's son, so that it could be said that he was "king over all Israel."[1]

For all practical purposes, the land was divided into two Kingdoms, in the north and south, with the odds all in favor of David eventually gaining control of both regions. For seven and a half years David reigned in Hebron, and the time was marked by long and bitter skirmishes between the houses of David and Saul. Typical of this border warfare is the incident

[1] Ishbaal means "Baal exists" or, less likely, "Man of Baal." It does not necessarily mean, however, that the parents of the child had apostatized and now served Baal since the word *baal* was sometimes used as an appellative for Yahweh. It is interesting to note, however, that later writers substituted *bosheth* ("shame") for *baal*, so that the son of Saul became known as Ishbosheth. The substitution reflects the Israelite abhorrence of anything connected with Canaanite religion, especially when the danger of syncretism was ever present.

described in 2 Sam. 2:12–17. Joab, nephew of David and general of his army, appears as the adversary of Abner, the sponsor of Ishbaal. The encounter at the pool of Gibeon was more like a tournament than a battle but, in any case, the forces of Joab beat the men of Abner. It was on this occasion that Abner earned the undying hatred of Joab who eventually killed the North Israelite general just after he had promised to hand over the remnant of Saul's Kingdom to David.[2]

In a struggle between David and the weak Ishbaal the outcome could never be in doubt. Once Abner was put out of the way by the treachery of Joab, two officers murdered Ishbaal in the hope that they could thus win the favor of David. Not by such means was David to take over the inheritance of Saul. Ishbaal was an innocent, though ineffectual, man and there was nothing to be gained by his death. The murderers of the pathetic young pretender would earn the same reward as the man who claimed that he had killed Saul and then boasted about the deed. David said to the two assassins:

> "When one reported to me, 'Behold, Saul is dead,' and thought he was the bearer of good tidings, I took and slew him at Ziklag. This was the reward I gave him for his news. How much more, when wicked men have slain a just man in his own house upon his bed. Shall I not require his blood at your hand and destroy you from the earth?" Then David gave orders to his young men, and they killed them, cut off their hands and feet, and hanged them beside the pool at Hebron. But they took the head of Ishbaal and buried it in Abner's tomb at Hebron (2 Sam. 4:10–12).

---

[2] In the summer of 1956 an American expedition, led by Professor James B. Pritchard, began excavations at Gibeon, modern El Jib, about eight miles northwest of Jerusalem. Not only did they discover and completely excavate the great rock-cut Pool of Gibeon but they found a remarkable spiral stairway leading from the bottom of the well down 82 feet through the rock to a subterranean spring. Little wonder that the Gibeonites in the Bible are called "carriers of water" when it is seen that a thirsty citizen was obliged to walk up and down over 150 steps for a drink of cold spring water. From the debris clogging the great Pool the archaeologists have put together much of the city's history in biblical times. For preliminary reports of the work, see J. B. Pritchard, in *The Illustrated London News* for October 27, 1956, pp. 695–698, and March 29, 1958, pp. 505–507.

JERUSALEM—CITY OF DAVID

The elders of Israel, realizing now that their only hope lay in David, assembled in Hebron and proclaimed him king by acclamation. The eyes of the king of all Israel now turned northward to that imposing stronghold which would forever after be known as the City of David. It was the fortress city of the Jebusites, strategically located on the ridge of the hill country about 2500 feet above sea level. Although it was easily defended except on the north, there were other, nonmilitary reasons which led David to choose Jerusalem as his capital. Politically it would have been impossible to select a more neutral place. It had no history of clan struggle since it had always been a Canaanite city. Moreover, its very location between the jealous factions of north and south gave good reason to believe that, of all localities, this would be the least objectionable to the tribes who probably would not tolerate the elevation of one tribe to a hegemony over the rest. Added to this, David conquered the city with his own men and he could look upon it as a personal acquisition as well as the seat of his government. After fortifying the already redoubtable fortress, David began to organize his new state, probably on the lines of Egyptian models which must have been well known to him. The "recorders" and "scribes" of the Davidic bureaucracy have excellent Egyptian parallels, and an institution such as the thirty-man bodyguard or elite corps which David set up is now known to have existed in Egypt. Even more important, from a religious and national viewpoint, David brought the Ark of the Covenant, symbol of Yahweh's presence among the people, to the city, thus making it the religious center of the kingdom. Tradition has recalled in great detail the procession led by David naked except for a small linen apron (the Ephod) and how he danced mightily before the Ark, only to be scorned by Michal, his wife:

> When the Ark of Yahweh entered the City of David, Michal the daughter of Saul looked out of the window, and saw King David leaping and dancing before Yahweh; and she despised him

in her heart. Then they brought in the Ark of Yahweh, and placed it inside the tent which David had pitched for it; and David offered burnt offerings and peace offerings before Yahweh (2 Sam. 6:16–17).

By such measures as described above, Jerusalem had become under David more than the political center of the new and united state. It was the earthly dwelling place of Israel's true King, Yahweh of hosts.

No city, Athens and Rome included, has ever meant more to its people than did Jerusalem to the pious Israelite. It was the very embodiment of the national spirit and a symbol of its hopes; Yahweh had chosen to place His name there. In the light of the central place which Jerusalem holds in the hearts of all Israelites it is indeed a strange twist of fate that, so far, the modern excavator has not been able to discover a wall, or ruin, or artifact which can with certainty be dated to the time of David. The turbulent history of the Holy City, together with continuous occupation up to the present, has effectively preserved the secrets of David's capital.

The messianic hope of Israel, one of the richest currents of thought and aspiration, occasionally took the form of a restored Jerusalem to which the nations of the world would come for blessing. Psalmist and prophet recalled the glory of the city under David and his son Solomon, and they could hardly find a better image of God's final intervention in history than that of a procession of the nations to holy Mt. Sion. Nowhere is the Israelites' deep affection for Jerusalem more beautifully expressed than in Psalm 87. God has established Sion as a mother and the nations boast that their names appear on the family register:

> His foundation is on the holy mount;
> Yahweh loves the gates of Sion
> more than all the dwelling places of Jacob.
> Wondrous things are said of you,
> O city of God!
> I mention Rahab and Babylon
> among those who know Me,

Behold, Philistia, Tyre, along with Ethiopia —
"this one was born there."
And of Sion it will be said:
"One and all were born in her,"
for the Most High has established her.
Yahweh notes down as He records the people,
"This one was born here."
Singers and dancers alike shall proclaim,
"All my springs are in you."

(Ps. 87:1–7)

To be sure, in the Songs of Sion, the psalmist is thinking
primarily of the actual center of Davidic royalty, the Jerusalem
of his day and the Temple where these Songs were sung as part
of the liturgy. But the Old Testament, as a book of hope, moves
ahead to the future; there is in its pages an aspiration to something better, to a fulfillment of what is imperfect. Mt. Sion
itself is bathed in the distant but very mysterious light of the
messianic hope. The author could not see this fulfillment with
the clarity of those who live in the new dispensation, but there
is general agreement that the Church, in its militant phase as
well as in its triumph, is present inchoatively in these hymns to
the glory of Sion. When the psalmist, for example, sings of
the deliverance of Jerusalem from an enemy, it would be a
superficial exegesis to interpret this solely as a definite historical
event, without reference to a much wider, messianic perspective.

St. John, in the Apocalypse, saw a vision of a new heaven
and a new earth. This would be the time of consummation,
when all things have passed away, and God is all in all. Among
the symbols used to communicate this vision John chose the
idea of the New Jerusalem, coming down from heaven like a
bride adorned for her husband. The Old Jerusalem, where once
the glory of God had dwelt in the Temple, lay in ruins, ploughed
under by the Roman armies. But the destruction of Jerusalem
and its magnificent Temple brought to an end the first act of
world history, the age of Israel. The old order was yielding
place to the Church, the New Israel which continued its march
through history and carried within it the assurance of ultimate

4*

triumph. Between the New Jerusalem and the Old there was the relation of reality and symbol, of fulfillment and prefigurement. Both Christian and Jew could understand with little difficulty the luminous vision of St. John, who epitomized the Christian triumph in the story of two cities:

> And I saw no temple therein. For the Lord God almighty and the Lamb are the temple thereof. And the city has no need of the sun or the moon to shine upon it. For the glory of God lights it up, and the Lamb is the lamp thereof; and the kings of the earth shall bring their glory and honor into it. And its gates shall not be shut by day; for there shall be no night there. And they shall bring the glory and the honor of the nations into it. And there shall not enter into it anything defiled, nor he who practises abominations and falsehood, but those only who are written in the book of life of the Lamb (Apoc. 21:22–27).

I WILL MAKE YOUR NAME GREAT

David was the last of the great charismatic leaders in Israel and the first to establish the hereditary principle in the kingship. The Israelites, for almost two centuries, had become accustomed to government according to the charismatic principle, following a leader upon whom the spirit of Yahweh had descended. It was, accordingly, no easy task to establish an hereditary monarchy, much less to regulate the succession where two or more claimants were scheming for the throne. The Court History of David (2 Sam. 9–20 to 1 Kings 1–2), a priceless historical document, gives us a vivid, eyewitness account of the intrigue which went on in the court of Jerusalem, with special attention to the treacherous defection of Absalom and the abortive revolt which he hoped would win him the throne. Even as David lay dying in the palace, one of his sons, Adonijah, was plotting to obtain the kingship which had been conferred on Solomon at the express command of David. Despite this innovation in the manner of ruling all Israel and the obstacles thrown up against its realization by his own flesh and blood, David succeeded in establishing once and for all the principle of hereditary rule.

Kings had ruled in Mesopotamia and Egypt for over a thousand years before the reign of David. If there was anything distinctive in Israelite kingship, then, it must not be looked for in the institution itself but in the form which it took in Israel. From the Hebrew viewpoint the king was no incarnation of a god as he was in Egypt; nor was the king a servant chosen by the assembly of the gods and dependent upon their whims and favors. The Hebrew idea of God as absolute, transcending all phenomena of nature, saved them from embracing an ideal of kingship which would have been indistinguishable from that of Egypt or Mesopotamia. The Hebrew was not wont to blur the distinctions between the human and the divine — his king was a man among men who, even if he stood in a special covenant relation to Yahweh, was nevertheless a man under the judgment of Yahweh and responsible to Him for his actions as king.

Let it suffice to recall the sin of David with Bathsheba and the rebuke of Nathan the prophet. The incident illustrates not only the weakness of David but his willingness to admit his guilt. "I have sinned against Yahweh," confessed David when confronted by the fearless Nathan. The action taken by Nathan in going directly to the king and accusing him of the adultery and murder brought the king back to his senses and the realization that he was answerable to God for his conduct just as was any other Israelite. No one could arrogate to himself absolute authority, even if it were royal authority he wielded. Men like Nathan and Elijah, to name only two, saw to it that the despotic principle, "the king can do no wrong," never secured a permanent foothold in Israel. A highhanded disregard of human rights might appear here and there, but there were never wanting bold spokesmen of the Lord, vindicating the supremacy of God's law regardless of the personal risk involved. Kingship had its advantages, but the Israelite seems never to have forgotten that it was during the sojourn in the desert, a kingless period, that Israel had enjoyed something like an ideal relationship with Yahweh.

Was it possible to maintain the covenant idea during the royal period and incorporate the same idea into the institution of kingship? It was one of the great achievements of the Davidic era that kingship in Israel was conceived as a covenant between Yahweh and David. With this covenant went the promise of an eternal dynasty, which would issue eventually in a world-wide kingdom of peace and justice.[3] The setting for this covenant and the accompanying promise are connected with David's expressed desire to build a suitable house for Yahweh. Having already provided himself with a house of cedar, David felt ashamed that Yahweh still abóde in a tent, and he confided to Nathan his plan to erect a temple for the Ark. On this occasion Yahweh revealed to David the fact that Solomon would build the Temple but that David's piety would nevertheless receive its reward in the promise of an eternal dynasty:

> Thus speaks Yahweh of hosts:
> "It was I Who took you from the folds,
> from following the sheep,
> to be prince over My people Israel.
> I was with you wherever you went,
> cutting your enemies down before you;
> and I will make your name great,
> like that of the great ones of the earth. . . .
> Yahweh will make you great,
> Yahweh will make a house for you.
> When your days are ended,
> and you sleep with your fathers,
> I will raise up for you a descendant,
> the offspring of your body,
> and I will establish his kingship.
> It is he who shall build a house for My name,
> and I will establish forever the throne of his kingship.

---

[3] In a previously mentioned study, entitled "Covenant Forms in Israelite Tradition," G. E. Mendenhall pointed out that the Covenant with David, extended to later kings, was patterned on the Covenant with Abraham rather than on the Covenant with Moses. The latter imposed specific obligations on the Israelites. In a real sense, then, the Covenant with David could be considered the fulfillment of the Covenant with Abraham. See the *Biblical Archaeologist*, XVII, 3 (1954), p. 72.

I will be a father to him,
and he a son to Me.
If he acts wickedly I will chastise him
with the rod of men,
with blows of the sons of men.
But My covenant-love shall not be taken from him,
as I took it from his predecessor.
Your house and your kingship shall endure forever before Me,
your throne is established forever."

> (2 Sam. 7:8–16; for parallel versions of this
> Oracle, see Psalm 89 and 1 Chron. 17)

Hope for a coming Messiah is one of the constant themes of Old Testament theology. It is a wide hope, expressed in many forms, of which one of the most common is to picture the Messiah as a king of David's line, in whose person the promises made to David are fulfilled. This is called royal messianism, and the foundation of this particular form of the messianic hope rests on the Oracle cited above. An echo of this promise is found in "the last words of David," where the everlasting covenant is recalled, along with the high ideal of justice associated with the house of David, eternally covenanted with the God of justice:

> "He who rules men with justice,
>   rules in the fear of God;
>   he is like the morning light when the sun rises . . .
>   that makes the grass grow from the earth after rain.
>   Is not my house thus with God?
>   For He has made an everlasting covenant with me,
>   wholly ordered and secured;
>   will He not bring forth
>   whatever I need and want?"

> (2 Sam. 23:3–5)

Many other allusions to the Oracle of Nathan served to stamp the time of David as Israel's Golden Age. God had promised Abraham that a great nation would come from his loins and many an Israelite must have seen in the Kingdom of David the realization of that ancient promise. An unprecedented era of peace, unity, and security had come to people whose ancestors had known little else than the chaotic period of the Judges and the harrowing insecurity of Philistine domination.

But if the promise attached to the covenant was eternal, the prosperity of Israel under David and Solomon was not destined to endure. The harsh realities of history must have served as a corrective against the tendency to identify the promise of the covenant exclusively with an earthly Israel which grew more and more accustomed to looking back upon the "good old days" of David and his son Solomon. The division of the Kingdom in 922 B.C., the destruction of North Israel in 721 B.C., and the sweeping away of Judah in 587 B.C., forced men to look beyond the nation they had known to an ideal state or kingdom which God would bring into existence at some future time. This was the messianic hope — for a kingdom won not by war and oppression but a kingdom of peace and justice to which all men would come and submit to the reign of God. Once the actual Kingdom of Judah ceased to exist and the tiny remnant had gone into the Babylonian Exile, men still hoped for a new David, a Prince of David's line. The spirit of God would rest upon Him as it had upon David, but this King would not establish His rule by military stratagem. The warrior Prince could also be pictured under the image of a small child:

> For a child is born to us,
> a son is given to us.
> Upon his shoulder dominion rests.
> They name him Wonder-Counsellor, God-Hero,
> Father-Forever, Prince of Peace.
> His dominion is vast
> and forever peaceful,
> from David's throne, and over his kingdom,
> which he confirms and sustains
> by judgment and justice,
> now and forever.
> The zeal of Yahweh of Hosts will do this!
>
> (Isa. 9:5–6)

Thus was Israel's hope for the Messiah tied to the line of

David and anchored in the oracle which Nathan spoke to him. This hope was indeed a mighty one, since it was able to survive all the blows which fell upon the Kingdom. It would seem that God wanted to teach this people, so often tempted to national pride, that the Messiah would not come to a nation mighty and powerful but to one tried in the fire. Out of that purging fire would come a Remnant, purified of national delusions, and this Remnant or "New Israel" would inherit the promises. To this Israel "according to the spirit" the Messiah, in all His humility and lowliness, would come, and in His coming, the hoped-for Rule of God would begin.

SWEET SINGER OF ISRAEL

The Hebrew word for "psalms" is *tehillim*, meaning "songs of praise." The 150 religious poems which make up the book of Psalms cover practically the whole range of religious experience. For this reason it is unwise to group all the psalms under any one category; still, in a deeper sense, it may be said that God is so central to all the psalms that they are all hymns of praise to His goodness, power, and mercy. Both Jewish and Christian traditions agree in attaching the name of David to the Psalms. Few scholars would, however, today maintain that David personally composed all the hymns in the Psalter, but it would be a serious blunder in the other direction to consider the tradition as purely fictitious and without foundation. The more we learn about the times of David and Solomon, about ancient poetry in Israel and the surrounding countries, about the antiquity of writing, the greater is our respect for the tradition which associates the book of Psalms with the "sweet singer of Israel."

It must not be forgotten that David was an extremely gifted man. Besides his talents in warfare there is no doubt that he was a skilled musician and that he was capable of composing poetry of the highest order. The man who composed the Lament over Saul and Jonathan reached a level of lyrical composition rarely attained in the ancient (or modern) world. The author of the book of Chronicles, writing about 400 B.C., credits David with the organization of the musical guilds which supplied singers for the Temple. Many scholars have taken this bit of evidence with a grain of salt and have placed the formation of these guilds in the post-exilic era. Today it is recognized that there is nothing inherently improbable about the tradition and, while the picture is not altogether clear, there are good indications that the Chronicler was reporting a perfectly reliable historical tradition rather than fabricating out of whole cloth a fanciful picture of David the musician. Semites carrying their musical instruments appear on a tomb in Egypt which goes back to the nineteenth century B.C. Egyptian records often make mention of Canaanite music and there are numerous representations of Canaanite musicians and instruments on the frescoed walls of Egyptian tombs. There is even one biblical tradition which attributes the founding of musical guilds to pre-Israelite, Canaanite families.[4] Positive proof, apart from the Bible, is not yet at hand that David certainly organized the first musical groups in his new Kingdom. For the present it is enough to have shown that music, temple and otherwise, went back to pre-Israelite times and was especially associated with the native population of Palestine, the Canaanites.

On the question of Davidic authorship, it may be helpful to remind ourselves occasionally that the ancient Hebrews may not have meant the same thing as we do by the term "author" of a book. When they spoke of the Mosaic authorship of the Pentateuch or the Davidic authorship of the Psalms, or the Solomonic authorship of wisdom literature, it would seem that they did not use the word "author" in the precise, modern sense to which we are accustomed. The ancient Israelite preferred to group large segments of his sacred literature under well-known names such as Moses, David, and Solomon, without intending to affirm that every line of this literature was written by the

---

[4] The evidence for this may be found by combining the information given in 1 Kings 4:31 with that of 1 Chron. 2:6 where the founders of these guilds are called "Ezrahites," i.e., members of pre-Israelite families.

man to whom it was attributed. The Hebrew shied away, as far as possible, from anonymity when it came to his sacred writings which he knew had been written under divine inspiration. It was known that, in the past, the spirit of God had worked through men like Moses, David, and Solomon. What could be more natural, then, than to place sacred writings, though written much later, under the patronage of men who were renowned for having written this kind of sacred literature in the past? This is a much broader and vaguer usage of authorship than ours, but there are advantages in coming to terms with this ancient Semitic custom. It shows us how the Hebrews expressed the important truth that certain literary compositions were sacred or inspired without committing us to the untenable position that the literature was written entirely by this or that man under whose patronage it had been placed. In his Presidential Address to the Twentieth General Meeting of the Catholic Biblical Association, Father Roderick A. F. MacKenzie, S.J., dwelt at some length on this important distinction between the ancient and modern ideas of "authorship."

Authorship, in this (ancient) usage, is obviously something much vaguer than our modern literary concept — with which, however, for better or worse, our doctrine of inspiration is closely connected. The inspired authors envisaged by the Vatican Council and by *Providentissimus* [the Encyclical of Leo XIII on Sacred Scripture] are literary authors in the modern sense, not authors in that ancient sense, which is practically the same as "patrons." Up to a point, we see the same concept at work in the New Testament, for which tradition claims, in general, apostolic authority — i.e., authorship in the older sense. It is true, the somewhat more self-conscious and "modern" outlook of the hellenistic world has preserved the names of two of the literary authors of written Gospels — Mark and Luke. Yet tradition has preserved also the apostolic authority which covered them, Mark's Gospel being under the aegis of Peter, Luke's under that of Paul. Had the Old Testament point of view still obtained, the Church would probably now refer to St. Peter as the author of the second Gospel, and St. Paul as the author of the third. I suspect in fact that that is pretty much the relation of St. Matthew to the first

Gospel, which is otherwise anonymous. Some similar connection, of patronage or approbation, might account for the eastern tradition which has associated — so strangely, as we think — the name of St. Paul with the Epistle to the Hebrews.

This concept of authority expressed as authorship is a precious and valid part of tradition. But, as I said, it seems to have no immediate connection with the charism of inspiration. It is hard to conceive that Moses could be in any way an *inspired* author of, say, Deuteronomy or the Law of Holiness, if these, as literary units, did not exist till centuries after his death.[5]

The religious poems of the Psalter were composed at various stages of Israel's history, from the time of David, and perhaps even earlier, to the post-exilic period, though it is doubtful that any of our psalms were written after the fourth century B.C. Modern research has practically ruled out the possibility that any of the psalms were composed in the Maccabean Age. Many of the psalms were written with a view to using them in the liturgy of the Temple, but this should not be interpreted as meaning that all the psalms were cultic in their origin. It would be truer to say that the psalms were the product of the worshiping community of Israel, from the earliest times to the period of the Second Temple. They are filled with the thought of God and of His all-pervading activity in nature, the history of His people, and the individual soul. Scarcely a single idea about God is absent from these sacred songs, which cover the whole range of Israelite religious experience, whether it be that of the individual before his God or the commuity offering its collective praise or thanksgiving.

In the modern study of the Psalter two contributions, not wholly unrelated, stand out above the rest. The first is the epoch-making work of Hermann Gunkel, who in his elaborate commentary on the Psalms (1926), proposed for this very diverse religious poetry a classification which still holds the field and appears in most commentaries on the Psalms. Seeking to find the "setting in life" (*Sitz im Leben*) or the situation

---

[5] R. A. F. MacKenzie, "Some Problems in the Field of Inspiration," *Catholic Biblical Quarterly*, XX (January, 1958), pp. 4–5.

which best accounts for the composition of a given psalm, Gunkel proposed a scheme embracing five major types of psalms, to which he added five minor categories. His five main types, with examples of each, represent a serious effort to discover the living historical factors which accounted for the composition of these religious poems.

1. *Hymns:* Psalms 8, 19, 29, 98, 104, 115, etc. These were originally intended for choral or solo performance in public worship.[6]
2. *National Laments:* Psalms 44, 74, 79, 80, 83. The setting of this type is some national adversity which threatened the whole community and not just some individual. The psalm represents the public display of grief and the plea that Yahweh will avert the calamity.
3. *Royal Psalms:* Psalms 2, 18, 20, 21, 45, 72, 101, 110, 132. They are concerned with the Israelite king but often provide the point of departure for a messianic development. They should be dated before 587 B.C., the end of the Davidic monarchy. Gunkel looked for the immediate occasion of these psalms in such events as the enthronement of a king, a royal wedding, the eve of the king's departure for battle, or the celebration of his return.
4. *Individual Laments:* Psalms 3, 5, 6, 7, 13, 25, 26, 57, 59, 140, etc. They express the cry of the individual to God. He is in great distress, surrounded by enemies, and only God can deliver him.
5. *Individual Songs of Thanksgiving:* Psalms 30, 32, 34, 41, 66, 92, 116, 118, 138. The individual worshiper proclaims his gratitude to God for a favor received. Many of these psalms would be recited in the Temple, and the recitation was often accompanied by a sacrifice or some other cultic action.

Allowing for some measure of arbitrariness in locating psalms under this or that category, it is safe to say that this approach

---

[6] In citing from the book of Psalms, I follow the numbering of the Hebrew text.

to the Book has initiated a new era in the study of the Psalms. There is hardly a single modern commentary on the Psalms which does not show the influence of Gunkel's pioneer work.

The second major contribution of modern scholarship to the study of the Psalter consists in the rediscovery of the ancient Near East and the consequent enrichment of our knowledge of the world from which the Old Testament came. Now it is possible to study the Israelite poet against the background of the vast world in which he lived and which exercised an influence on his way of thinking and expression. Gunkel had always insisted on the necessity of comparative studies for appreciating the poetry of Israel, but he could hardly have suspected the huge mass of new material which has revolutionized the scholar's knowledge of the biblical world. Before these discoveries, the Psalms, and other parts of the Old Testament, were at the mercy of critics who felt free to emend the text or even, in some cases, to rewrite whole psalms in order to bring them into line with some favorite postulate. The purpose of these comparative studies, made possible by the discoveries, is not to rob the Old Testament of its originality nor to question the unique values of its theology nor to build up facile equations between the Old Testament and earlier or contemporary literature among Israel's neighbors. Quite the contrary! Placing the Psalter in its historical context of place and time has not only clarified many obscurities in Old Testament poetry, but demonstrated again the gulf which existed between the religious thought of Israel and that of her neighbors.

For purposes of comparative study, the most important discovery, by far, has been that of the Ugaritic literature from the mound of ancient Ugarit (modern Ras Shamrah). For the past twenty years this site on the northern coast of Syria, about twenty-five miles south of the Turkish border, has been yielding an immense amount of new material, especially literary, which has revolutionized our knowledge of Canaanite culture in all its aspects. The literature from Ugarit is predominantly poetic, and epic in form. The literary pieces were written in a hitherto unknown alphabetic script, employing cuneiform signs, and dating from about 1400 B.C. Canaanite literature from this site is thus earlier than any extant Hebrew poetry. While much of the Ugaritic material has already been published and studied very carefully, a great deal remains to be done, particularly in applying this new material to biblical poetry. When the task has been finished, it will be seen that the wholesale emendations of the past were entirely unwarranted and that the text of the Psalter has been transmitted with far greater fidelity than scholars of another generation believed. Many strange words and phrases in the poetry of the Bible stand to be clarified, as some have been in studies which have already appeared. The parallelism of Hebrew poetry, its best-known and most characteristic feature, is now seen to be of Canaanite origin. The Hebrews did not balk at borrowing music from the Canaanites; and they felt no misgivings about taking over the metric forms, style, imagery, and other features of this poetry. The Hebrew poet, with his all-pervading belief in Yahweh, was able to assimilate these formal elements of pagan poetry without in the least compromising his own strict monotheism.

Professor H. L. Ginsberg, one of the leaders in Ugaritic studies, has shown how Psalm 29, for example, is a Hebrew adaptation of an old Canaanite hymn in honor of Baal. The imagery of the psalm is filled with reminiscences of Canaanite poetry; and its geographical setting is proper, not to Palestine as we might expect from a Hebrew writer, but to Phoenicia or modern Lebanon. Even more striking is a passage from Ugaritic literature encouraging Baal who is about to fight with another god:

> Lo, thine enemies, O Baal, lo, thine enemies wilt thou smite,
> Lo, thou wilt cut off thy foes.

With this compare the following passage in Psalm 92:

> Lo, thine enemies, O Yahweh, lo, thine enemies shall perish;
> all evildoers shall be scattered.

Without changing the style or phrasing, the Hebrew psalmist

substitutes Yahweh for Baal and changes the "enemies" of the Ugaritic to the "evildoers" of the psalm. Hebrew monotheism has no place for gods with whom Yahweh must fight; only the wicked, the "workers of iniquity," are the enemies of God! Many more examples could be adduced to show how this discovery of Ugaritic literature has aided the scholar in his interpretation of biblical poetry. Further study can only confirm and add to the far-reaching parallels in style, concepts, and word-patterns between Ugaritic and Hebrew poetry. The religious significance of the Psalter will not be diminished in the slightest by these studies; instead, it will be no small gain to see more objectively the background, with all its good points and weaknesses, against which the one true God spoke to man and summoned him to union with Himself.

ookings Tel: 0990 33

ation
...und on page 90. **AA** *AA Ferry Guide Ratings – information supplied by the 1996 AA Passenge*

...cility.

. KING OF NDINAVIA

Amsterdam (IJmuiden)
7 – 24 Mar '98 only)
...ide rated ★★★★ '96

m.s. PRINCESS OF SCANDINAVIA

Harwich/Newcastle to Gothenburg
AA Ferry Guide rated ★★★★★ '96

m.s. ADMIR SCANDINA

Newcastle to Ha
Newcastle to Amsterda
(25 Mar – 31 Oct '
Harwich to Ha
(4 Nov '97 – 14 Mar
AA Ferry Guide rated ★

ookings Tel: 0990 3

ELIJAH, TROUBLER OF ISRAEL

THE prophet Elijah enters suddenly and unexpectedly in the narrative of the Old Testament. The account of this indomitable fighter for Yahweh against the menace of Canaanite religion is found in 1 Kings 17–19, 21 and 2 Kings 1–2, forming a cycle of traditions which interrupt the regnal histories of Israel and Judah. The traditions about Elijah first circulated orally in the Northern Kingdom of Israel where he carried on his prophetic activity. Judging from the excellent classical prose style of the Hebrew narrative it would seem that the oral period of transmission was relatively short. 800 B.C. would be a plausible date for the writing down of this material. It is a characteristic of oral tradition to select and heighten outstanding events in the life of a national hero without falsifying the historical situation described. As for the Elijah cycle, the later historian of Israel would be immeasurably poorer without these dramatic narratives which so vividly re-create the religious crisis of the ninth century.

The description of the lonely figure on Carmel, standing against the frenzied prophets of Baal, tells us more about the religious struggle which convulsed the Northern Kingdom than chapters of conventional historical narrative could. With Elijah and his successor, Elisha, a period of prophetic activity came to a climax, to be followed within a century by men upon whom the same spirit of Yahweh rested but who, fortunately, left us written records, often in literary masterpieces, of their prophetic activity. Elijah and Elisha were not "writing prophets," but men of deeds whose work was reminiscent of great predecessors like Samuel and Nathan. But the differences between these men of action and the writing prophets must not be exaggerated. Amos and Isaiah of the following century were the true spiritual descendants of Elijah and Elisha, conscious of the same office as "spokesmen of Yahweh" and moved by the same zeal to keep the religion of Yahweh free from any taint. Both classes of prophets, though in different ways, played the same essential part in what we might call the "Age of Conflict." Professor Albright summarized this relation very pointedly when he wrote:

> If we want to know how Elijah and Elisha reacted to the evils of the ninth century, we have only to read what Amos, Hosea, and Isaiah said in the eighth, though they may have expressed themselves differently.[1]

THE SEEDS OF CONFLICT

The reigns of David and Solomon have always been celebrated as the Golden Age of Israel, when north and south were united in one strong and prosperous Kingdom. But it would have required no extraordinary astuteness to read the signs of the time as early as the days of Solomon. Hardly had the Temple been erected when Solomon opened the Holy City itself to the inroads of pagan religions. Urged on by his foreign wives, Solomon went so far as to erect cult centers for alien gods, thus exposing the religion of Yahweh to the dreaded danger of syncretism to which the people proved altogether too prone. The editor of Kings sadly commented:

> When Solomon grew old his wives turned away his heart after other gods; and his heart was not wholly true to Yahweh his God, as was the heart of his father David (1 Kings 11:4).

After the division of the Kingdom in 922 B.C., the northern leader, Jeroboam I, sought to consolidate his position by weaning his people away from the religious center of the once united Kingdom, Jerusalem. To this end Jeroboam established shrines at Bethel and Dan, the two geographical extremities of his own territory and centers to which religious traditions had long been attached. The "golden calves" which he set up at both sanctuaries have often been misunderstood as grossly pagan represen-

---

[1] W. F. Albright, *From the Stone Age to Christianity* (New York: Doubleday Anchor Books, 1957), p. 306.

tations of Yahweh under the form of a young bull. On the face
of it, we have good reason to doubt that the rebel in the north
would have broken so drastically and effectively with the religious traditions of the past and thus put in immediate jeopardy
his newly established Kingdom. It has now become quite certain
that Jeroboam was far more sensitive to ancient Israelite traditions than was once suspected. In reality, his action at Bethel
and Dan went back to the Mosaic era when Aaron, the brother
of Moses, fashioned a golden statue of a young bull as a pedestal on which was enthroned the invisible God of Israel. Evidence
for this widespread conception of a deity enthroned upon a
young bull is steadily mounting. Sumerians, Canaanites, Arameans, and Hittites represented their gods, especially the great
storm-god of the ancient Near East, as standing upon the back
of powerful young bulls or enthroned above these animals. Even
though the action of Jeroboam in setting up these young bulls
went back to earlier and orthodox practice, the danger was ever
present of seeming to countenance syncretistic aberrations which
threatened the purity of Israelite faith. There is no need to insist
on the inherent peril of Jeroboam's bold measure, taken at a
time when Israel was about to enter a life and death struggle
with Canaanite Baalism, a religion already long familiar with
this conception of the young bull as the visible pedestal of the
divine storm-god Baal.

To the threat of religious contamination from their neighbors was added the political instability of the Northern Kingdom. Not until the reign of Omri was there anything like
dynastic rule, since plotting and assassination continually dis-
rupted the country after the death of Jeroboam I. The throne
was finally won by a vigorous and energetic ruler, Omri, who
was not only able to hand the kingship down to his grandsons,
thus re-establishing the dynastic principle, but ruled Israel so
effectively that the mighty Assyrians referred to his kingdom as
"the House of Omri." The author of the book of Kings is
extremely reticent about his achievements, being satisfied with
informing us that he built the new capital of Samaria (about

870 B.C.) and that "he did evil in the sight of Yahweh, in fact more evil than all who went before him" (1 Kings 16:25). The famous Mesha Stele of the Moabite king gives a glimpse of his military activity in reconquering Moab and exacting tribute from that country. The transfer of the capital from Tirzah to the magnificent new site of Samaria was not only an act of great political sagacity comparable to David's choice of Jerusalem for his new capital; it meant a new orientation of Israel's policy toward Phoenicia, then enjoying great commercial prosperity, rather than toward Damascus and the east.

Economically sound though this policy might have been, it opened the way to further religious abuses, above all when Omri cemented his friendly dealings with Phoenicia by marrying off his son Ahab to the daughter of a Tyrian king, Ittobaal. No marriage alliance in the history of Israel was ever to have such disastrous consequences as the one between the crown prince, Ahab, and the Tyrian princess, Jezebel.[2] Far from adopting the religion of her husband, Jezebel, with her own Tyrian retinue, set about the practice of her native religion in a "house of Baal," built on the Hill of Samaria. Under their very eyes the Israelites could now see foreigners celebrating the liturgy of the Tyrian divinities, Baal-Melcarth and Asherah.

At this point we should give some attention to the religion of Canaan, which pious Israelites found so repulsive and against which Elijah and the later prophets inveighed unremittingly for over two centuries. Before the age of modern discovery our knowledge of Canaanite religion was largely derived from the Old Testament. With the sensational discovery of the Ras Shamrah literature, beginning in 1930, the study of this religion entered an entirely new phase. The epic compositions and rituals of Ras Shamrah make it possible now to compare the

---

[2] The economic advantages of this match are obvious. Political and military considerations seem also to have played a part. The Aramean King Ben Hadad, inveterate foe of Israel, was cultivating the Phoenicians, and Omri felt it necessary to strengthen his ties with the powerful Phoenicians by this union of the two royal houses. While both Omri and Ahab profited from the move, the alliance ultimately pulled down the dynasty in a frightful blood bath.

stern and uncompromising monotheism of Israel with the very
sensual religion of ancient Canaan. The leader of the Canaanite
pantheon was El, a remote, cosmic figure who was said to dwell
at the "Source of the Two Deeps" where the lesser gods were
forced to go when they wished a favor from the father and ruler
of the gods. The goddess Ashirat (better known as "Asherah"
in the Old Testament) was El's wife, though her relations to
the other well-known goddesses Astarte and Anath are quite
complex. All three were certainly connected with the fertility
rites which were a prominent feature of Canaanite religion. The
most dynamic figure among the gods was Baal, the great storm-
god of the pantheon. In the tablets of Ugarit he is styled "The
Exalted, Lord of the Earth" and later, the "Lord of Heaven"
(*Baalshamem*). When thunder crashed in the heavens it was
said to be the voice of mighty Baal. All fertility, of the soil or
the womb, was due to him; when, as we read in the Baal epic,
Baal succumbed to Death (*Mot*), famine and sterility ravaged
the land. Once Death was vanquished by the fierce warrior
goddess Anat, then Baal, the giver of life, was restored and there
was once again fertility in the land. By such myths in
gods and goddesses play the leading parts, did Canaanites
explain the succession of rainy and dry seasons in the land of
Canaan.

Since agriculture was the chief occupation of the Hebrew
settlers in the new land, it should cause no surprise to learn that
they were influenced by myths which were closely related to
the changing seasons of the agricultural year. Fervent religious
leaders would, as expected, be repelled by the gross aspects of
Canaanite fertility cults, but they faced a real struggle to keep
the general run of Hebrews from contamination by the religion
of the indigenous population. Archaeologists have turned up
many small statues of Canaanite goddesses of fertility in their
excavations of Israelite settlements, providing telling evidence
of the encroachments made by Canaanite nature worship on
the religion of Yahweh. Polytheism must have won many a
victory over the monotheism which Israel inherited from her

ancestors, just as a coarse materialism carries a strong popular appeal in our own day. In addition, the material culture of Canaan, far surpassing anything which the Israelite could offer in the arts of music, poetry, and architecture, added to the fascination of a sensuous polytheism which exploited all these arts in its religious worship.

ELIJAH THE TISHBITE

With dramatic suddenness appeared the prophet who was destined to stem the tide of pagan syncretism in Israel and to stand for the ancient religious traditions which Moses had bequeathed to his people. Like Moses before him, Elijah knew that Yahweh was the Lord of transcendent majesty Who would tolerate no rivals. The abhorrent religious movement, pursued by Jezebel and tolerated by the weakness of Ahab, was an abomination in His sight. The first commandment of the Decalogue had explicitly forbidden the worship of other gods, and Israel's history had shown how severely Yahweh dealt with those who violated this commandment. From his home in the wilderness across the Jordan, Elijah boldly appeared in the presence of the vacillating Ahab with his first message:

As Yahweh, the God of Israel, lives, before Whom I stand, neither dew nor rain shall fall in these years, except by my word (1 Kings 17:1).

So abrupt was his appearance and brief his message that some have thought that the original introduction to the career of Elijah has been lost. But this is to miss the dramatic force of his coming upon the scene as the bearer of God's word. Lightning-like appearances and disappearances are characteristic of the man and clothe him with a mysterious quality which seems very appropriate to this man of God. The battle was joined between the champion of Yahweh and the ruthless queen who would stop at nothing in her ardent proselytizing for the Tyrian Baal.

At the command of Yahweh, the prophet fled from the

domain of Ahab, who probably planned to retaliate against the man responsible for bringing such a serious drought on the land. After several years, during which God providentially cared for His messenger, Elijah was told by God to present himself before Ahab, now grown desperate because of the famine in his country. The king and Obadiah, the chief steward who had protected a hundred prophets of Yahweh from the fury of Jezebel, had set out in opposite directions looking for enough food and water to keep the animals alive. While Obadiah was busy in his search, Elijah suddenly appeared before him and ordered him to tell Ahab that Elijah had been found. Knowing how quickly and mysteriously a man of God could be spirited away and hidden from a vengeful king, Obadiah refused to carry the message until Elijah solemnly swore that he would surely meet Ahab. The encounter between the two and the challenge issued by the uncompromising Elijah are vividly described by the sacred writer:

> When Ahab saw Elijah, the King said to him, "Is it you, O troubler of Israel?" And Elijah answered: "I have not troubled Israel, but you have, and the house of your father as well, because you have forsaken the commandments of Yahweh and followed the Baals. Now therefore summon all Israel to me at Mount Carmel, and the four hundred and fifty prophets of Baal and the four hundred prophets of Asherah, who eat at the table of Jezebel" (1 Kings 18:17-19).

Ahab immediately accepted the challenge and there followed one of the most dramatic scenes in all literature. The narrative has been praised as a matchless piece of dramatic prose; far more important is the portrait of a man's faith by which he stood alone against an entrenched paganism and singlehandedly brought a nation back to the service of the one God. The account is written up in the style of popular traditions with that heightening which gives color and vitality to the action. With all allowances being made for obscurities which still exist, no reader can fail to hear the authentic voice of Israelite prophecy calling the people back to their first loyalty — the God

of Israel. This was the fight which the prophets, from Elijah
to the time of the Exile, had to wage against the seductions
of Canaanite religion. It was no time for halfhearted compro-
mises which the indifferent make so easily; tolerance might
have its place, but this was the hour for vigorous decision:

> And Elijah came near to all the people and said, "How long
> will you keep shifting from one leg to the other? If Yahweh is
> God, follow Him; but if Baal, follow him." And the people
> answered him not a word (1 Kings 18:21).

Then began the contest in which each party was to prepare a
sacrifice but without setting fire to it. Jezebel's minions were to
call upon Baal to kindle the sacrifice and Elijah would call upon
Yahweh. The multitude assembled on Mt. Carmel to witness
the contest could then judge who was the true God. As the
prophets of Baal performed their ritual dance about the altar
and gashed themselves with ecstatic abandon, Elijah poured out
his scorn upon these raving prophets of Baal:

> They took the young bull which was given them, prepared it,
> and called upon the name of Baal from morning until noon,
> crying, "O Baal, answer us!" But there was no voice and no
> answer. And they limped about the altar they had built. And
> at noon Elijah mocked them with the words, "Cry aloud, for
> he is a god; he is either musing or has gone aside, or he is on a
> journey, or maybe he is asleep and must be awakened." And they
> continued to cry aloud, and cut themselves after their custom
> with knives and lances, until their blood gushed out. When noon-
> time had passed they raved on until the offering of the evening
> sacrifice, but there was no voice; no one answered, no one paid
> attention (1 Kings 18:26–29).

In contrast with this shocking frenzy, the prophet of Israel
quietly rebuilt the broken altar of Yahweh where sacrifice had
once been offered. After preparing the victim and placing it
on the wood, Elijah prayed to the God of Abraham, Isaac, and
Jacob to enkindle the sacrifice in order that the people might
return to God. Immediately the fire of God came down from
heaven and consumed the victim, the altar, and even the water
which had been poured out in the encircling trench:

And when all the people saw this, they fell upon their faces and cried: "Yahweh, He is God; Yahweh, He is God!" But Elijah said to them, "Seize the prophets of Baal; let not one of them escape." And they seized them; and Elijah took them down to the brook Kishon, and killed them there (1 Kings 18:39-40).

The wholesale slaughter of the false prophets may shock our sensibilities but the swift and drastic action, another instance of the ḥerem, should be judged against the crisis which faced Elijah's people. No half-measures would do, and Elijah undoubtedly considered the extermination of the prophets a necessary means to preserve his people from the abominations of Canaan. Israel and Canaan represented two entirely different ways of life, the one a strict and pure monotheism along with a severe code of morals, the other a sensuous polytheism around which had grown up a repellent mythology and gross moral aberrations. A fusion between the two would have spelled disaster for Israel by degrading her lofty beliefs and high standard of conduct.

BEFORE WHOM I STAND

The temporary character of Elijah's victory served notice that Israel's struggle against paganization would be a ceaseless one. Jezebel was not the sort of woman who would let go unpunished the killing of her prophets. The daughter of Ittobaal, king and priest of Tyre, she belonged to a house which produced an Athaliah and a Dido. Such a woman was not to be deferred from her program of implanting a foreign religion on the Hill of Samaria and providing ministers for her pagan worship. A momentary defeat at Mt. Carmel only stirred her up to vow vengeance upon the man who had slain her prophets of Baal:

Ahab reported to Jezebel all that Elijah had done, and how he had killed the prophets with the sword. Then Jezebel sent a messenger to Elijah, saying, "So may the gods do to me, and more besides, if I make not your life as the life of one of them by this time tomorrow." Then Elijah was afraid, and he arose and fled for his life, and came to Beersheba, in the territory of Judah, and left his servant there. But he himself went a day's journey into the wilderness, and finally sat down under a broom tree; and he begged to die, saying, "It is enough; now, O Yahweh, take away my life; for I am no better than my fathers." And he lay down and slept under the broom tree; and behold, an angel touched him and said, "Arise and eat." And he looked, and behold, at his head there was a cake baked on hot coals and a jar of water. And he ate and drank and lay down again. And the angel of Yahweh came a second time, and touched him, saying, "Arise and eat, else the journey will be too much for you." And he arose, and ate and drank, and in the strength of that food he walked forty days and forty nights to Horeb, the mount of God (1 Kings 19:1–8).

This is a very different picture from that of the triumphant Elijah racing before the chariot of Ahab in the plain of Jezreel. As a royal herald he had come to announce the victory of Yahweh and the reawakening of faith on the part of king and people. But the weak Ahab had hardly arrived at his winter residence when he notified Jezebel of all that had happened at Mt. Carmel. The victory of Elijah was thus short-lived, and it is not surprising that Jezebel's threat, fortified by a solemn oath, not only forced Elijah to flee for his life but made him despair of any permanent success against this fanatical enemy of Yahweh. In a fit of depression he set out for the desert wilderness of the south where he prayed for death as a release from what seemed to be a fruitless mission. At this low point of his life he was given miraculous strength to push on to the sacred mountain.[3] It was here that Moses, the first of the prophets, had spoken with Yahweh face to face. Standing at the mouth of the cave, as Moses had stood in a cleft of the rock, Elijah would now receive a revelation which would confirm what he had already done and strengthen him for the work which lay ahead. Here, in a great upheaval of nature, Yahweh appeared to Elijah. There are many theophanies in the Old Testament in which Yahweh appears as the Lord of the storm; before

[3] In the Elohistic and Deuteronomic traditions the mountain is called Horeb; in the Yahwistic and Sacerdotal traditions it is called by the more familiar name of Sinai.

Him the mountains quake and the hills melt; the thunder is His voice, He sends forth lightning and numbers the clouds in His wisdom. All the phenomena of nature are signs of His presence, but with none is He identified as were the nature-deities of Canaan. In a mighty wind, earthquake, and fire, Yahweh passed by — but He was in none of these. The elements are the heralds of Yahweh but none of them can contain Him. In the midst of this great storm and at the sound of the "still small voice," Elijah covered his face with his mantle and came out of his cave to stand once again before Yahweh and await His revelation:

> And behold, a voice came unto him, saying, "What are you doing here, Elijah?" Then Elijah answered, "I have been zealous for Yahweh, the God of hosts; for the people of Israel have forsaken Your covenant, thrown down Your altars, and slain Your prophets with the sword; and I, even I only, am left; and they seek my life, to take it away." And Yahweh said to him, "Go back to the wilderness of Damascus; and when you come there, you shall anoint Hazael as king over Syria; and Jehu, the son of Nimshi, you shall anoint as king over Israel; and Elisha, the son of Shaphat, you shall anoint as prophet in your place. And him who escapes from the sword of Hazael shall Jehu slay; and him who escapes from the sword of Jehu shall Elisha slay. Yet will I leave seven thousand in Israel, all the knees which have not bowed to Baal, and every mouth which has not kissed him" (1 Kings 19:13–18).

Elijah no longer considered his cause hopeless. Not only did Yahweh send him back to the struggle against Jezebel and her followers, but He promised that a faithful remnant, a nucleus which kept faith with Yahweh, would escape the divine wrath and help to turn the tide against the enemies of Israelite religion. When the strengthened prophet returned from his meeting with Yahweh at Horeb, he realized that the task could not be performed in his own lifetime. A disciple, one who would have a portion of his spirit, should take up the work of purifying Israel. Elisha was the man, and Elijah found him in the field plowing with twelve yoke of oxen. As he passed by, Elijah cast his mantle over him and the young disciple, bidding farewell to his parents and offering a sacrificial meal with the people, rose up and followed Elijah and ministered to him. Years later he was known as the one "who poured water on the hands of Elijah."

The disciple was destined to instigate the rebellion which ended in the bloody extermination of the house of Ahab; but, before that, an incident in the ministry of Elijah caused this prophet to pronounce judgment upon the royal house. The murder of Naboth and the confiscation of his vineyard, both engineered by the unscrupulous Jezebel, were atrocious perversions of justice and sealed the doom of Ahab's line. Naboth had a piece of property which adjoined the royal estate in Jezreel. Since the plot of ground was an inheritance from his forefathers, Naboth knew that it was not a purely private possession but belonged to the whole family and to those still unborn. Ancient custom forbade the alienation of such property and consequently Naboth refused the offer of Ahab to purchase the land. Ahab accepted the refusal with anything but good grace. Returning to his palace, he sulked childishly. When Jezebel learned the reason for his vexation she immediately set out to solve the problem with characteristic vigor and ruthlessness. Using the royal seal, she sent letters to the elders and nobles of Jezreel, ordering them to condemn Naboth on a trumped-up charge supported by two witnesses. The innocent man was stoned to death and Jezebel could now report to Ahab, "Arise, and take possession of Naboth's vineyard, which he refused to sell to you, for Naboth is not alive, but dead" (1 Kings 21:15). Ahab went down to Jezreel to take over his new property only to meet Elijah, bearing a message from the Lord. "Have you found me, O my enemy?" cried Ahab; and the reply came, "Thus says Yahweh: 'Have you murdered and also taken possession? . . . In the place where dogs licked the blood of Naboth, shall dogs lick your own blood'" (1 Kings 21:19).

The historian knew that the real target of Yahweh's wrath

was Jezebel, who was solely responsible for this outrageous crime of murder and theft. He describes Ahab's repentance, which was probably sincere, and which moved God to mitigate the condemnation and postpone the judgment until after the death of the king:

> And when Ahab had heard these words, he tore his garments, and put sackcloth on his flesh, fasted, and went about depressed. And the word of Yahweh came to Elijah the Tishbite saying, "Have you seen how Ahab has humbled himself before Me? Because he has humbled himself before Me I will not bring the evil in his days; but in the days of his son I will bring the evil on his house" (1 Kings 21:27–29).

In Jehu's bloody massacre of Jezebel and the whole royal house the prophecy of Elijah was fulfilled. The one true God, before whom Elijah stood, would not let go unpunished the crimes of the wicked.

The final scene of the Elijah cycle is presented in a manner worthy of the man. From a literary standpoint alone, the story has few equals in the Old Testament. It is told with a richness of symbolism and with an imagination which is both exalted and restrained. The prologue describes the itinerary of Elijah and Elisha from Gilgal to Bethel, then to Jericho and finally across the Jordan which is parted by the mantle of Elijah. Three times Elijah tells Elisha to leave him, but the younger man persists in following the venerable prophet:

> And once they had crossed [the Jordan] Elijah said to Elisha, "Ask what I may do for you, before I am taken from your midst." And Elisha said, "I beg of you, give me a double portion of your spirit." And he said, "You have asked a hard thing; but if you see me when I am being taken from you, it shall be done to you; but if you do not see me, it shall not be done." And while they were talking, behold, a fiery chariot and horses of fire separated the both of them. And Elijah went up to heaven in the whirlwind. And when Elisha saw it he cried out, "My father, my father! the chariots of Israel and its horsemen!" And he saw him no more (2 Kings 2:9–12).

Thus did tradition remember the passing of Elijah from this

earth without experiencing death. The man of fire, whose coming and going resembled the whirlwind, left only his mantle to the prophet who would take up his task. It is not surprising that Malachi, longing for a new intervention of God in history, should point to this man as the precursor of that day:

> Behold, I will send you Elijah the prophet before the coming of that great and terrible Day of Yahweh. And he will turn the hearts of fathers to their children and the hearts of children to their fathers, lest I come and smite the land with a curse (Mal. 3:23–24).

AMOS

IN THE middle of the eighth century B.C. there appeared on the scene the first of the writing prophets. As men of God they were conscious of a call from Yahweh to act as "watchmen over Israel." Amos headed a succession of spiritual leaders whose published oracles have been preserved for posterity in the Canon of prophetic writings, and whose vocation was to make the people of Israel as worthy as possible of God's great purpose for them. For Israel was meant to be the People of God, that holy community which began with the call of Abraham and would culminate in the definitive reign of God over the whole world. In Christ the faith of the prophets would find its fulfillment. What else does the New Testament mean when it proclaims with such urgency that "the time is fulfilled," except that in the death and resurrection of Jesus the decisive event in the history of salvation has been accomplished, that the purpose of God has been realized? Among those privileged men who received the word of the Lord and who sought to keep Israel faithful to her vocation stands Amos of Tekoa. This is how he described his divine call to bring a message of judgment to an Israel blinded by its ephemeral prosperity:

> I was not a prophet, nor a son of a prophet: I was but a shepherd and a dresser of sycamore trees, when Yahweh took me away from the flocks and gave me this command: "Go, prophesy to My people Israel" (Amos 7:14-15).

Were it not for Amos the obscure Judean village of Tekoa would no longer be remembered by the student of the Old Testament. It was located about six miles to the southeast of Bethlehem on the western edge of that parched and forbidding wasteland known as the Wilderness of Judah. Life at Tekoa was hard and comforts were nonexistent, but at least there was the luxury of solitude where a man might open up his soul to God. On the solitary heights of this barren plateau, surrounded on three sides by limestone hills, Amos tended his flocks with the other shepherds of Tekoa, supplementing his meager income by the seasonal work of puncturing the fruit of the sycamore trees. Undoubtedly, the bleak surroundings in which he lived and worked left their mark on the message he brought to the Northern Kingdom. He had seen the cart laden with sheaves, had heard the lion growling over its prey, and had watched the poor shepherd bring the remnants of a slain sheep to the owner as proof that the animal had been killed by a lion. The snare set for the birds was a familiar sight, as were the searing wind and the mildew which blighted the standing crops.

The four visions described in 7:1–9 and 8:1–2 probably came to him before he set out for the north with his message of judgment, and they should, accordingly, be read as part of the preparation for his vocation. The visions follow the cycle of the seasons and strikingly illustrate how the common events of a man's everyday life could be transformed into moving spiritual experiences. The Hebrew prophets had an uncommon gift for bringing the two worlds of material and spiritual realities into a dynamic unity. The first vision came in the spring as the latter rains were bringing the crops to their full growth. This was the season when attack by the locusts would be disastrous:

> Thus the Lord God showed me: behold, there was a swarm of locusts in the beginning of the shooting up of the latter growth. This was the latter growth after the king's mowing. After they had finished devouring the grass of the land, I cried,
>
> > "O Lord God, forgive, I beg You!
> > How can Jacob stand?
> > He is so small!"
> > Yahweh repented of this;
> > "It shall not be," said Yahweh.
>
> (Amos 7:1–3)

Summer came and with it another vision in which Amos saw
Yahweh about to destroy the land with a great conflagration:

> Thus the Lord God showed me: behold, the Lord God was
> calling for a judgment by fire, and it devoured the mighty deep
> and ate up the land. Then I said,
> "O Lord God, forgive, I beg of You!
> How can Jacob stand?
> He is so small!"
> Yahweh repented of this;
> "This also shall not be," said Yahweh.

(Amos 7:4–6)

A third vision, of a plumb line, brought home to Amos the
certainty that Yahweh was about to measure crooked Israel with
the plumb line of His judgment:

> He showed me: behold, the Lord was standing beside a wall
> built with a plumb line, and in His hand was a plumb line.
> And Yahweh said to me, "What do you see, Amos?"
> And I replied, "A plumb line." Then Yahweh said,
> "Behold, I am putting a plumb line
> in the midst of My people Israel;
> I will never pass them by again;
> the high places of Isaac will be made desolate,
> the sanctuaries of Israel will be destroyed,
> and I will rise up against the house of Jeroboam
> with a sword!"

(Amos 7:7–9)

The final vision, during the autumn, played upon the words
for "summer fruit" (qayits) and the "end" (qets). The basket
of summer fruit was a sign of the end:

> Thus the Lord God showed me: behold, a basket of summer
> fruit. And He said, "What do you see, Amos?" And I said, "A
> basket of summer fruit." Then Yahweh said to me,
> "The end has come upon My people Israel,
> I will never pass them by again."

(Amos 8:1–2)

There is something of the divine pathos in the words "My
people," for God never let rebellious Israel forget that she had

been drawn into a covenant with her Founder and that she owed Him love and obedience. Her sins were not the violation of some impersonal law, but a refusal of that covenant-love which cemented the union between Yahweh and His people. Following the visions, in which the inevitability of punishment was revealed to Amos, God called him to the prophetic office with the peremptory charge: "Go, prophesy to My people Israel."

Amos left his sheep in the sparse thickets and the dark ravines of the Wilderness of Judah, set out for the north and, after a journey of about thirty miles, came to Bethel, one of the great religious centers of the Northern Kingdom. It was here that Jeroboam I, king of ten tribes after the division of the Kingdom, had set up a shrine with an elaborate cult in order to keep his subjects from returning to Jerusalem and the Temple of Solomon. The strategy must have worked, for worshipers flocked in great numbers to the new religious centers. As Amos walked into the sacred precincts of Bethel he must have made a strange impression on the carefree and complacent crowds milling about the sanctuary. It was close to the year 750 B.C., and the occasion was probably the annual autumn Feast of the New Year which was celebrated with great solemnity by the people. But before we listen to the message brought by this austere and solitary man it will be necessary to describe very briefly the situation in Israel at the time of the prophecy.

WHO FEEL SECURE ON THE HILL OF SAMARIA

During the long and brilliant reign of Jeroboam II (786–746 B.C.), the Kingdom of Israel attained the height of its prosperity and prestige. Expanding its territory to the north and south through military victories and gaining control of important trade routes, wealth poured into the country, but especially into the hands of the upper classes. The victories of Israel's armies made the people forget the humiliations of the past as well as the threats of the future. Assyrian forces had withdrawn from the west because of internal strife at home, and Israel took full advantage of this respite in Assyria's remorseless march to empire. It seems incredible to us that Israel, even though flushed with temporary prosperity, could have failed to foresee the eventual reckoning with the mightiest military power of that age. Within a generation after the prophecy of Amos, the Assyrians would resume their southern penetration into Palestine and destroy once and for all the proud capital of Samaria. So far had Israel's smugness blinded her to the realities of a world in which she could never hope to stand up against a first-class power!

The increase of wealth brought a rise in the material standard of living, as the excavation of Israelite sites in this period amply demonstrates. At Samaria, for example, the excavated remains of the impressive palace complex, the rich ivory inlay of the sumptuous furniture, and the famous Ostraca of Samaria, throw new light on the indictment brought by Amos against a luxury-loving and greedy people. The newly acquired wealth was not evenly distributed among the whole population, but only increased the disparity between rich and poor. The merchant class, thriving on the trade with nearby Phoenicia, could afford to copy the practice of Syrian royalty in building summer and winter houses and in surrounding them with pleasant vineyards. Their callous disregard for the poor went unpunished, for the debtor in those days was at the mercy of his rapacious creditor:

> Because they sell the just for silver,
>   and the poor for a pair of shoes —
> they who trample the head of the poor
>   into the dust of the earth,
> and turn aside the way of the meek;
> a man and his father go to the same maid,
>   so as to profane My holy name.
>
> (Amos 2:6–7)

Amos spoke out fearlessly against these ruthless exploiters of the poor who sought in vain for redress from Israel's venal judges:

> Therefore, because you trample upon the poor
> and exact from him large shares of wheat,
> houses of hewn stone you have built,
> but you will not live in them;
> lovely vineyards you have planted,
> but you will not taste their wine!
> For I know your many crimes,
> and your grievous sins —
> you who afflict the just, and take bribes,
> and brush aside the poor man at the gate.
>
> (Amos 5:11–12)

But it is for the sleek, carousing women of Samaria that Amos saved his most powerful invective. They drove their husbands on to provide more luxuries, without a thought for the poor who would be ground into the dust to provide more adornments and rich food for their entertainment. The prophet is unsparing in his condemnation of this evil and draws a vivid picture of the fate which awaited the pampered wives of Samaria's successful businessmen. When the city was taken they would be dragged out like cattle and their corpses left to the scavengers.

> Hear this word, you fat cows of Bashan,
> who dwell on the Hill of Samaria,
> who oppress the helpless, who crush the poor,
> who say to their husbands, "Bring, and let us drink!"
> The Lord God has sworn by His holiness
> that, lo, the days are coming upon you,
> when they will drag you away with hooks,
> yes, the very last one of you with fish hooks.
> Out through the breaches shall you go,
> every woman straight before her;
> and you shall be thrown on a dung heap!
> The utterance of Yahweh.
>
> (Amos 4:1–3)

Amos has often been called the "Prophet of Social Justice," but the reader must not forget that the prophet appeared at Bethel as the bearer of God's word and not as a sociologist or an economist. The sins of the Northern Kingdom constituted rebellion against God Who had made man in His image and expected men to show, in their treatment of their poorer and more defenseless brethren, the mercy and loving kindness which He had shown to Israel. Amos judged the conduct of these men, not by some rationally constructed code of ethics, but by his vision of Yahweh. His social consciousness was a corollary of his faith, and the voice which thundered denunciation was not that of an indignant social reformer nor that of a peasant attacking the vices of the city; it was the authentic voice of Yahweh proclaiming that cruelty to their fellow men was not breach of a code but rebellion against a Person. Far from being some new doctrine to which the people of Israel would have to be educated, it was as old as the Mosaic period. What Amos said God demanded found embodiment in the Law of Moses which regulated the relations of man to man and warned the Israelite that he could not "walk with God" unless his love extended to his fellow man as well as to God. The prophets were not innovators. They sought to restore an order which was in danger of being overturned by human wickedness.

If social conditions in the Northern Kingdom were bad, the state of religion was not much better. As far as externals went there could be no complaint. The cult-centers were thronged with worshipers, the feasts were scrupulously observed, hymns of joyful confidence welled up from the sanctuaries where countless sacrifices were offered. The confident assurance of Yahweh's good pleasure was in the air and it suited the temper of these prosperous times, unclouded by any misgivings about the future. But was this true religion? Could this smug complacency and national pride pass for the service of God Who demanded justice more than burnt offerings and made His own peculiar care the poor and the oppressed?

"To seek Yahweh" is a Hebrew way of expressing man's obligation to do God's will. This meant something more than pilgrimages to their shrines and the offering of sacrifices to ensure the continuance of material prosperity. It would be a caricature of Israelite religion, as it had been handed down since the time of Moses, to think of Yahweh as an automatic provider of good things once the proper rites had been performed. When it is said that the prophets were opposed to sacrifice we must be very clear on what they opposed. Sacrifice is an external sign of man's complete dependence upon God and a means of acknowledging His complete sovereignty over us. It is the visible expression of an authentic interior spirit. But if there is no interior disposition accompanying the external rite it becomes an empty form, a sign which does not signify. The invisible roots must be there, or it becomes nothing more than an act of hypocrisy and self-deception. It is the abuse and not the institution of sacrifice which draws down the wrath of the prophets. To the worshipers at Bethel who believed that they could buy God's favor and protection from their enemies by going through empty forms at a sanctuary, Amos issued his warning:

> Seek good and not evil,
> that you may live;
> so may Yahweh, the God of hosts,
> be with you as you claim!
> Hate evil and love good,
> and let justice prevail at the gate;
> then it may be that Yahweh, the God of hosts,
> will take pity on the remnant of Joseph.
>
> (Amos 5:14–15)

The religious condition of the Northern Kingdom is nowhere better exemplified than in the interpretation Amos gave to an Israelite article of faith which went back to the earliest times. This was the belief that history was moving toward a goal, a divine intervention in the affairs of men by which Yahweh would rout the forces of evil and usher in an age of happiness. Since Yahweh had already decisively broken into the history of Israel and had proved that nature and men were but instruments of His purposes, there was no reason to question this ultimate and definitive coming of Yahweh. This hope for the future took on various forms, but one of the most familiar was found in the notion of the Day of Yahweh. At the time of Amos there was a widespread popular belief that the Day was not far off and that it would bring Israel its hour of triumph over all her enemies. The phrase was a catchword among the people, making them insensible to the danger which loomed on the horizon. It revealed the shallow optimism which went hand in hand with their mechanical forms of piety. Many Israelites felt that they had particular claims on Yahweh, that the covenant relationship insured victory over their foes even though they could forget the responsibilities of the covenant and the stern demands of Yahweh Who would hold them to account for their wickedness. Popular fancy pictured this Utopian future as a day of light, the glorious sunrise of their history when the victory of Israel would inaugurate the unending era of her pre-eminence over the nations. It was an exhilarating thought, and it added to Israel's sense of security the further assurance that her time of national exaltation was at hand. Amos believed in the Day of Yahweh, but it was quite different from the one envisioned by this self-centered people. It was indeed a day of judgment, not only upon the pagan nations, but especially upon the people He had chosen. The day would be one of moral judgment when Israel would be called to account for her oppression of the poor, her sinful luxury, and her false and hollow worship. Imagine the shock of these self-satisfied worshipers when they heard Amos describe the Day of Yahweh as a dreadful visitation of God, a day of national defeat and disgrace, the complete reverse of popular expectations:

> Woe to you who desire the Day of Yahweh!
> Why would you have the Day of Yahweh?
> It is darkness and not light;
> as if a man fled from a lion
> and a bear met him;
> or entered a house and rested
> his hand against the wall,
> and a serpent bit him.

> Is not the Day of Yahweh darkness,
> and not light,
> and gloom, without any brightness?
> > (Amos 5:18–20)

It was to a society which was morally sick that Amos brought
his message of judgment. Pride in their temporary military victories, the steady increase in material wealth, a religious life
which put Yahweh at the service of their own avarice, a per-
verted notion of the nation's inviolability, all had conspired to
blind Israel to its true vocation as a covenanted people destined
to prepare the way for the establishment of God's Kingdom.
The times called for a man whose profound faith in the sovereign rule of God had given clarity to his vision and the
courage to announce that Israel was a nation under judgment.

THE LORD WILL ROAR FROM SION

Yahweh had called Amos from tending his flocks at Tekoa
and commissioned him to announce the impending doom to
the House of Israel. It was not through any private inspiration
that he took up this onerous task, but because the Lord had
taken possession of him. Like the other prophets, Amos was
conscious of a divine mandate which he could not refuse; and,
in the prophecy itself, he has left a few lines which describe
Yahweh's power over him. These were his credentials:

> Surely the Lord God will do nothing,
> without revealing His plan
> to His servants, the prophets.
> A lion has roared;
> who will not fear?
> The Lord God has spoken;
> who will not prophesy?
> > (Amos 3:7–8)

The same inner necessity which is found between cause and
effect existed between the word of God and the prophecy of
His servant. Any personal distaste for the prophetic mission,
especially when it centered around a message of condemnation,

was a secondary matter; the divine compulsion overrode natural reluctance and the sense of one's unworthiness. This divine mastery over His elected prophet strikingly illustrates the intertwining of the divine and human in prophecy; we have, in the case of Amos, a simple and untrained man who had no other preparation for his strange vocation than a deep faith in and unquestioning obedience to God.

The theme of judgment is introduced by a series of oracles against the neighbors of Israel. It is easy to imagine the throngs at Bethel enthusiastically seconding the imminent doom of enemies such as the Arameans of Damascus whose kings, Hazael and Ben-hadad, humbled Israel in war:

> Thus says Yahweh:
> "For three transgressions of Damascus,
>   and for four, I will not revoke the doom,
>   for they threshed Gilead
>   with threshing sledges of iron.
> And I will send fire upon the
>   house of Hazael
> and it will consume the
>   strongholds of Ben-hadad.
> I will smash the bar of Damascus,
>   and cut off the ruler from the plain of Aven,
>   and him who holds the sceptre from Bit-Adini;
>   and the people of Aram shall be exiled to Kir."
> > The utterance of Yahweh.
> > (Amos 1:3–5)

This is followed by oracles against the Philistines, Phoenicians, Edomites, Ammonites, and Moabites, all of whom, at some time or other, had been enemies of Israel. In concrete and forceful imagery Amos pronounced judgment against them for violations of moral laws universally recognized. Israel was not the only nation accountable to Yahweh for its conduct; for He is the Lord of history and even though He had chosen one nation as His own possession and marvelously delivered it from bondage in Egypt, He nevertheless brought the Philistines from Caphtor (Crete) and the Arameans from Kir. It is no denial of Israel's unique relationship to God when we recognize that the destinies of all nations are subject to His control and that God enters positively and actively on the stage of universal history. This is a basic teaching of the prophets, but one which many of their narrow and chauvinistic countrymen were reluctant to admit.

Amos would have had a satisfied and grateful audience if his message of impending catastrophe had gone no farther than the walls of Tyre and the strongholds of Moab. It was the business of certain professional prophets to feed the fatuous popular optimism by predicting prosperity for Israel and disaster for her enemies. Underlying these execrations of enemies may have been the ancient Semitic belief in the dynamic power of the word to accomplish what it foretells. But Amos was not a professional searching for handouts in return for happy omens. The flaming sword of justice did not stop at the borders of Judah and Israel. With dramatic suddenness Amos recites the indictment of the divided Kingdom and smashes the complacency of the worshipers at Bethel:

> Thus says Yahweh:
> "For three transgressions of Judah,
> and for four, I will not revoke the doom,
> for they have rejected the law of Yahweh,
> and His statutes they have not observed,
> their lies have led them astray,
> in paths walked by their fathers.
> Therefore I will send fire upon Judah,
> and it will consume the
> strongholds of Jerusalem."
> Thus says Yahweh:
> "For three transgressions of Israel,
> and for four, I will not revoke the doom. . . ."
>
> (Amos 2:4-6)

Besides their inhuman oppression of the poor, or it might be better to say, concomitant with it, the superficially religious Israelites had made a mockery of Yahwism by introducing, in imitation of the Canaanites around them, sacred harlots to their shrines. Religion had turned into another outlet for their own selfish gratification, and in a form which was an abomination to God. These were the people whose ancestors had entered into a sacred covenant with Yahweh at Mt. Sinai, and this relation had become the cornerstone of Israel's existence. It was not an insurance policy against the consequences of the divine wrath. If they had deluded themselves into believing that their privileged position had dispensed them from the responsibilities which went with election, they still had to reckon with Amos, reporting the word of Yahweh:

> "You only have I known
> of all the families of the earth;
> therefore I will call you to account
> for all your iniquities."
>
> (Amos 3:2)

This was the answer to anyone who thought he could manipulate the deity in his own favor and use the fact of covenant-relationship as a pretext for evading divine punishment. It is so easy for the self-righteous to fashion a God Who punishes only their enemies!

God's sovereignty over His people has not been exercised with the cold indifference of one who rules but does not love. Of course, the mysterious and tender love of Yahweh for His people is nowhere as prevalent or evident in Amos as it is in Hosea. The latter prophecy expresses the covenant relation between Yahweh and Israel in terms of wedded love. Still, Amos recalls episodes of their history in which God punished them only that they might return. Love was at the bottom of it. Amos was given a vision of God in which He was working, not only in the great deliverances of the people, as had long been recognized, but also in the reverses of history which were but another aspect of God's concern for His people. If they could not be won by the blessings for which they constantly prayed, then let them be brought back to their senses by the disasters they feared!

Looking back on the long road traveled by Israel, the prophet Amos saw that chastisement was not God's final word, but a means of winning back His people. God speaks directly in these oracles and the refrain "yet you did not return to Me" not only points up the pathos of Israel's folly but gives a glimpse into the saving purpose of God's visitations. It was only because their obduracy had reached the point where they failed to recognize the presence of God in either blessing or curse that Yahweh had no choice but to pronounce the inevitable doom.

> "It was I who gave you cleanness of teeth in all your cities,
>   and lack of bread in all your places,
>   yet you returned not to Me."
>   The utterance of Yahweh.
> "I also withheld the rain from you
>   when the harvest was still three months away;
>   I sent rain upon one city,
>   but no rain upon another;
>   one field would receive rain,
>   but the field which had no rain withered. . . .
>   I devastated you as God devastated
>   Sodom and Gomorrah,
>   and you were like a brand
>   plucked from the fire;
>   still you returned not to Me."
>   The utterance of Yahweh.
> "Therefore, this will I do to you,
>   O Israel;
>   because I will do this to you,
>   prepare to meet your God, O Israel!"
>
>   (Amos 4:6–7, 11–12)

The Day of the Lord, from the awesome viewpoint of Amos, was but another way of expressing this inevitable meeting in judgment between Yahweh and His impenitent people.

It is difficult to say what effect the prophesying of Amos had on the Northern Kingdom. No record has been left of any large-scale conversion or any public acts of penance; as far as we know, the unwelcome stranger, having delivered his message, returned to the Wilderness of Judah and resumed his work as a herdsman. Fortunately, we have the eyewitness evidence of official reaction in the person of Amaziah, the priest of Bethel. There was a head-on clash between the spokesman of God and the frightened official of a religion which had sacrificed its interior strength to mere external show. The immediate reaction of Amaziah was to rush a message to Jeroboam, accusing the newcomer of subversion.

> Amos has conspired against you in the
> midst of the house of Israel;
> the land is not able to bear
> all his words.
>
> (Amos 7:10)

But the visionary had to be dealt with on the spot, and Amaziah ordered Amos out of the sanctuary with the contemptuous implication that Amos was just another professional prophet ready to sell his services for bread. The eyes of all the people were fixed on the protagonists of this encounter. In a few phrases which summarized his whole life, the prophet testified that he knew nothing about the techniques of the professional prophets; he was simply a man upon whom the spirit of the Lord had rested and he was only delivering the message entrusted to him. It was the Lord Who took him from following the flock and the Lord Who ordered him to prophesy. Even the dreadful fate he was about to pronounce upon Amaziah was not the outpouring of a vindictive foe, matching banishment with banishment, but a revelation from God that Amaziah was to share in Israel's doom.

> Now therefore hear the word of Yahweh. You say, "Prophesy not against Israel, and preach not against the house of Isaac." Therefore thus says Yahweh:
>> "Your wife will be a harlot in the city,
>> and your sons and daughters will fall by the sword,
>> your land will be measured out with the line;
>> in an unclean land you will die,
>> and Israel will go into exile far from its land."
>
> (Amos 7:16–17)

The prophecy of Amos ends with a magnificent oracle of
hope in which the divine wrath seems to be consumed in His
love. The authenticity of this passage has been questioned by
eminent scholars on the ground that its note of hope is inconsis-
tent with the tone of the rest of Amos' message. Other scholars,
unwilling to admit that Amos is merely a prophet of doom
without hope for the future, and pointing to the sudden alter-
nations between threat and promise which appears to be a
characteristic of the prophetic style, assign these verses to
Amos. This is not the place to rehearse the pros and cons of
the debate, but one suggestion is in order. Whether or not
this oracle of hope was composed by Amos, whether it belongs
to the eighth or the sixth century B.C., the fact remains that
it is consistent with Amos' vision of God as the Lord of history Whose last word is salvation and not destruction. Even
if we grant that the oracle was inserted later in the collection
of Amos' prophecies, the inspired editor knew that the promise
of a day in which Israel's fortunes would be restored did not
contradict that earlier vision of the Day "which is darkness and
not light." The same Yahweh who had struck them down and
destroyed their cities would, under other circumstances, again
prove His sovereignty over events and restore His people to
their heritage:

> "On that day I will raise up
> the fallen hut of David;
> I will wall up its breaches,
> raise up its ruins,
> and rebuild it as in days of old;
> that they may conquer the remnant of Edom,
> and all the nations that bear My name."

>> The utterance of Yahweh
>> Who will do this.

> "Behold, days are coming,"
> says Yahweh,
> "when the ploughman will overtake the reaper,
> and the treader of grapes him who sows the seed;

sweet wine will drip down the mountainsides,
   and all the hills will overflow with it.
I will restore My people Israel;
they will build up their ruined cities
   and dwell in them again.
They will plant vineyards and drink their wine,
   set out gardens and eat their fruit.
I will plant them in their own land,
   never again will they be plucked up
   out of the land which I have given to them.
Yahweh, your God, has said this."

(Amos 9:11–15)

ISAIAH OF JERUSALEM

THE greatest of Israel's prophets exercised his ministry during the reigns of four kings of Judah, as we are informed by the first verse of the prophecy:

> The vision which Isaiah, son of Amos, had concerning Judah and Jerusalem in the days of Uzziah, Jotham, Achaz, and Hezekiah, kings of Judah.

Adding together the length of these reigns we see that the work of Isaiah spanned a period of at least forty years, during which the doom pronounced by Amos on the Northern Kingdom came to pass in the destruction of Samaria (721 B.C.). It is not certain when Isaiah died, although there is a late Jewish legend that he was put to death under the reign of Manasseh (687–642 B.C.). What is certain is that the lifetime of Isaiah covered the first great age of the classical prophets, among whom he stood out for the sheer power of his faith and the beauty of his poetry. Isaiah, for example, was still a young man when Amos uttered his white-hot denunciations at the North Israelite sanctuary of Bethel; he was a contemporary of another Judean prophet, Micah, who spoke his message in Jerusalem though, strangely enough, there is no evidence that the two ever met. Hosea was prophesying in the north at the same time, trying to communicate to a wayward and uncomprehending people the infinite compassion of Yahweh.

Of Isaiah's personal life we know very little, and he has left no autobiographical record comparable to the "Confessions" of Jeremiah. From the scant evidence provided in the book we know that Isaiah was married to a woman whom he designates as *hannebi'a* (the prophetess), and that she bore him two sons who were given the symbolic names of "A remnant shall return" and "Swift the spoil, speedy the plunder," each a sign of the divine purpose. It is likely that all of his prophetic activity was exercised in Jerusalem, the city which Yahweh loved despite its infidelities and which was envisioned as the spiritual center of the world to which men would come to share the blessings of the Messianic Era. In a beautiful passage, repeated by the prophet Micah, Isaiah expressed his calm faith in the trumph of God's Kingdom as the goal toward which Israel's turbulent history was moving:

> This is what Isaiah, the son of Amos, saw concerning
> Judah and Jerusalem. In days to come,
> the mountain of Yahweh's house
>   shall be established as the highest mountain
>   and raised above the hills.
> All nations shall stream toward it:
>   many peoples shall come and say,
> "Come, let us ascend Yahweh's mountain,
>   let us go to the house of the God of Jacob,
>   that He may instruct us in His ways,
>   and we may walk in His paths."
> For from Sion shall go forth instruction,
>   and the word of Yahweh from Jerusalem.
> He shall judge between the nations,
>   and impose terms on many peoples.
> They shall beat their swords into plowshares
>   and their spears into pruning hooks.
> One nation shall not raise the sword against another,
>   nor shall they train for war again.
> O house of Jacob, come,
>   let us walk in the light of Yahweh!

(Isa. 2:1-5)

This majestic vision of the prophet is all the more remarkable when set against the perils which threatened to destroy forever the Holy City and to crush the hopes centered in the dynasty of David. Jerusalem faced irrevocable doom but its destiny transcended military defeat. Some had falsely interpreted her future in terms of national glory, but the true prophet knew that Jerusalem's unique vocation was to lead all men to a knowledge of the one God. This done, all might dwell in peace together.

Since he was both the spokesman of Yahweh and a counselor of Judean kings, the oracles of Isaiah are best appreciated when we know something about the historical events with which they are so closely related. For Isaiah spoke to the men of his time and never removed himself from the crises which faced his people in the second half of the eighth century B.C. The shadow of impending destruction lay over the land and the very existence of both Israel and Judah was at stake; the times called for a man who would interpret for his contemporaries God's sovereign control over history which, in those days, appeared to be the highroad to annihilation.

At the outset of Isaiah's prophetic career the entire Near East was just beginning to feel the impact of a reinvigorated Assyria, once again resolutely set on the path of world conquest. It is enough to read the boastful inscriptions of the Assyrian kings to realize how the presence of the mighty Assyrian armies could strike terror into the hearts of people. Here is the way one king described his warfare against a coalition of Aramean states which stood in the way of Assyrian long-range plans for control of both Asia Minor and Egypt:

Hani from Sam'al, Sapalulme from Hattina, Ahuni, man of Adini, Sangara from Carchemish put their trust in mutual assistance, prepared for battle and rose against me to resist. I fought with them [assisted] by the mighty power of Nergal, my leader, by the ferocious weapons which Ashur, my lord, has presented to me, [and] I inflicted a defeat upon them. I slew their warriors with the sword, descending upon them like Adad when he makes a rainstorm pour down. In the moat [of the town] I piled them up, I covered the wide plain with the corpses of their fighting men, I dyed the mountains with their blood like red wool. I took away from him many chariots [and] horses broken to the yoke. I erected pillars of skulls in front of his town, destroyed his [other] towns, tore down [their walls] and burnt [them] down.[1]

---

[1] See ANET, p. 277.

Confronted by the colossus of Assyria, the Kingdoms of Israel and Judah, their years of prosperity already behind them, were about to be drawn into the vortex of world history. This was to be a mighty test of Israel's faith in Yahweh Who had thus far preserved and guided the people He had formed after delivering them from Egypt, the leading power of an earlier age. Would the God of Israel prove mightier than the gods of Assyria? Was the test to be one of sheer military strength, with the true God proving His claims by armed victory? Many Israelites undoubtedly phrased the struggle in those terms, but spiritual leaders like Isaiah were to give a different interpretation to historical events now rapidly changing the old familiar patterns of life. Humiliation and defeat were judgments of God upon a faithless people, and not the capitulation of Yahweh before the superior power of Assyria's gods. When Assyria had played its part in the divine scheme of things, it too would fall swiftly and completely before a more powerful nation. Only in Palestine was this voice of prophecy heard and only there was it said that God was the Lord of history and that He was using the events of history, terrible though they might be, for His own purposes. In a certain sense, the historically insignificant countries of Israel and Judah, dwarfed by the rising power of Assyria, appeared in the prophetic oracles as the center of world history. The king of Assyria was an instrument in Yahweh's hand, just as later Cyrus would be called His "anointed."

At the beginning and end of his public life Isaiah was obliged to face two major crises involving the threat of subjugation to Assyria. The first was related to the rise of Tiglath Pileser III, who appears in the biblical record as Pul (2 Kings 15:19). In 743 B.C. this conqueror who proudly bore the title of "The legitimate king, king of the whole world, king of Assyria, king of all the four corners of the earth," moved southward against the states of Syria and Palestine. The goal was the rich land of Egypt, but it was necessary first to secure control of the land which served as a bridge between the great Empires of Mesopotamia and Egypt. Israel's breathing spell of peace and prosperity

under Jeroboam II had come to an end, and his successor,
Menahem, was soon put under tribute to the powerful and
energetic Assyrian ruler. Tiglath Pileser is also remembered for
having begun the policy of systematic deportation of conquered
populations, hoping thus to nip any resistance movement in
the bud. The lands were quickly resettled by those on whose
loyalty the conqueror could count and they were incorporated
into the Assyrian dominions as provinces.

Israel chafed under the heavy demands made by the Assyrian
overlord; and a leader of the anti-Assyrian faction, Pekah, seized
the throne after murdering the son of Menahem. Uniting with
the Aramean state of Damascus, faced with the same threat
from Assyria, the new coalition sought to enlist the support of
the Southern Kingdom of Judah, as yet untouched by foreign
rulers and relatively stable after the long and prosperous rule
of Uzziah. The king was Ahaz (735–715 B.C.) who, immediately
upon ascending the throne, found himself the target for the
pressure tactics of Pekah and his Aramean ally, Rezin of
Damascus. They threatened to depose him and put a usurper
on the throne of David.[2] That the allies meant business became
clear when the combined armies began to push southward in
the direction of Jerusalem. At their approach "the heart of the
king and the heart of the people trembled, as the trees of the
forest tremble in the wind." One course lay open to the frightened Ahaz and it was to prove disastrous. Against the advice
of Isaiah he appealed to Tiglath Pileser for help, and the
Assyrian was only too glad to seize the opportunity of intervention. It is from this period that the famous Emmanuel
oracles of Isaiah come, as the prophet tried in vain to calm the
fear-stricken Ahaz:

> Take care that you remain tranquil and have no fear; let not
> your courage fail before these two stumps of smoking firebrands,

---

[2] Their candidate to succeed the legitimate king, Ahaz, is called "the son
of Tab'el." He was very probably a son of either Uzziah or Jotham by a princess
of Tab'el, a district in northeastern Palestine whose full name, "Bet-Tab'el," has
turned up recently in the published Assyrian archives of Calah.

the blazing anger of Rezin and the Arameans, and of the son of Romelia, because of the evil that Aram (Ephraim and the son of Romelia) plots against you, saying, "Let us go up and tear Judah asunder, let us force our way in and set the son of Tab'el on the throne" (Isa. 7:4-6).

But it was too late. Not even the sign of Emmanuel, solemnly offered as a guarantee that the conniving of men cannot thwart the will of Yahweh, could dissuade the weakling from his appeal to Assyria. He rejected Isaiah's challenge to have confidence in God, a challenge which was coupled with a warning to the king and his followers:

> Unless your faith is firm
> you shall not be firm!
> (Isa. 7:9)

The failure of Isaiah's intervention during this first great crisis marked the end of a period in his public activity. He prepared to put down in writing a record of his early oracles and entrusted the document to a group of faithful disciples who were to keep them sealed until events had verified his teaching.

> The record is to be folded and sealed and kept among my disciples. For I will trust in Yahweh Who is hiding His face from the house of Jacob; yes, I will wait for Him. Look at me and the children whom Yahweh has given to me: we are signs and portents in Israel from Yahweh of hosts Who dwells on Mount Sion (Isa. 8:16-18).

Over thirty years later Isaiah again appeared, this time as the counselor of Hezekiah, who had foolishly allowed himself to join a revolt against the Assyrian overlord which had been fomented by Egypt, that "broken reed which pierces the hand of anyone who leans upon it." The Assyrian Sennacherib led his armies into Palestine to punish this latest act of rebellion. The revolt was crushed and the Egyptian forces, sent to aid the rebels, were swept away before the onrushing tide. Sennacherib boasted that he had shut up Hezekiah in Jerusalem "like a bird in a cage." Hezekiah submitted to the imposition of tribute but, when Sennacherib demanded total surrender of Jerusalem, he refused to give up and set about preparing for the siege. Isaiah, now an old man, intervened once again, not to taunt the king for the folly of his policy, but to strengthen his resolve to resist the dreaded Assyrian. The oracles of this time are full of hope, and the unalterable conviction that Yahweh would never allow Sennacherib to take the Holy City. Again he summoned the people to have faith, to trust in Yahweh's protection of the city in which He had placed His name. And Jerusalem was saved as Isaiah had foretold, when a pestilence broke out in the Assyrian ranks and forced them to withdraw before the walls of Jerusalem:

> Therefore, thus says Yahweh concerning the king of Assyria: "He shall not reach this city, nor shoot an arrow into it, nor advance before it with a shield, nor cast up siegeworks against it. He shall return by the same way he came, without entering the city, says Yahweh. I will shield and save this city for My own sake, and for the sake of My servant David."
> The angel of Yahweh went forth and struck down one hundred and eighty-five thousand in the Assyrian camp. Early the next morning, there they were, the corpses of the dead. So Sennacherib, the king of Assyria, broke camp and returned to Nineveh (Isa. 37:33-37).

The deliverance of Jerusalem again vindicated the faith of Isaiah, whose words had often gone unheeded if not positively contemned. To understand the strength of this faith, which carried him through a long and testing ministry of forty years, we must give some attention to the call of Isaiah, his inaugural vision which left a permanent mark upon the character of the man.

MY EYES HAVE SEEN THE KING, YAHWEH OF HOSTS

Very few are wholly unfamiliar with the sixth chapter of Isaiah, two parts of which have been incorporated into the liturgy of the Holy Sacrifice of the Mass. It was during this vision that the prophet received that overpowering awareness of God's holiness and majesty. In the presence of that holiness which is the standard of all holiness Isaiah could not fail to be aware of his own sinfulness, to say nothing of the people among whom he lived. For the holiness of God makes demands upon the will of man, weak by nature but capable, with God's grace, of an astonishing response in purity and love to the demands of God. "The Holy One of Israel" now became the prophet's own phrase to describe the nature of God, and it was this deeply-felt conviction which explains Isaiah's powerful reaction to the sins, especially the social evils, of his own people. Injustice is an offense against the Holy One, and sacrifices of atonement are worthless unless they are offered by one who is trying to live a holy life.

The year was 742 B.C. and the brilliant but deceptively prosperous reign of Uzziah was about to end with his death. We do not know what brought Isaiah to the Temple on this occasion, but it was probably some important religious feast which drew great crowds for the solemn celebration of the liturgy. As the young Isaiah watched the colorful, ancient rites being enacted, he was suddenly overwhelmed by a mighty spiritual experience, involving hearing and seeing, which was to determine the course of his whole life. His future work, as we have remarked, can scarcely be understood apart from this soul-shaking religious ecstasy in which Isaiah confronted God in all His majesty and holiness:

> In the year king Uzziah died, I saw Yahweh seated on a high and lofty throne, His train filling the Temple. Seraphim flew above; each of them had six wings; with two they veiled their face, with two they veiled their feet, and with two they hovered aloft.
> They cried one to the other, "Holy, holy, holy is Yahweh of hosts! All the earth is filled with His glory!" At the sound of that cry the frame of the door shook and the whole house was filled with smoke (Isa. 6:1-4).

With an overpowering realization that he was in the presence of the divine majesty, Isaiah saw the Holy of Holies transformed into a throne room with the seraphim as attendants upon the King, but forced to cover their faces before the splendor of God. The triple repetition of their cry was the Hebrew way of expressing the superlative degree of God's holiness. The dense cloud of smoke and the shaking of the thresholds to their foundations manifested the presence of God Whose glory fills the whole earth. Isaiah could think only of his own unworthiness as he beheld the divine majesty. Only the purging fire of divine forgiveness could remove his guilt:

> Then I said, "Woe is me, I am doomed! For I am a man of unclean lips, living among a people of unclean lips; for my eyes have seen the King, Yahweh of hosts!" Then one of the seraphim flew to me, holding a live coal which he had taken with tongs from the altar. He touched my mouth and said, "See, now that this has touched your lips, your wickedness is removed, your sin is purged" (Isa. 6:5–7).

The cleansing touch of the live coal prepared Isaiah for the voice of God Who now spoke for the first time. The purification of his heart had made the prophet capable of hearing the word of God and responding to His call with spontaneity and total self-dedication.

> Then I heard the voice of Yahweh saying, "Whom shall I send? Who will go for us?" I said, "Here I am, send me!" (Isa. 6:8.)

Without yet knowing what effect his work would have upon his people, Isaiah enthusiastically and without question accepted the divine invitation to proclaim God's word. The answer to his readiness was the dismaying assurance that his preaching of God's message would only increase their religious insensibility to the point of spiritual blindness.

> And He [God] replied: Go and say to this people,
> Listen carefully, but you shall not understand!
> Look intently, but you shall know nothing!
> Make the heart of this people sluggish,

> Dull their ears and close their eyes;
> Lest their eyes see, their ears hear,
> their heart understand, and they turn and be healed!
>
> (Isa. 6:9–10)

These words express the unhappy but fundamental truth that the proclamation of God's word may have an effect which is directly opposite to what the prophet intended. Instead of bringing men to the light and turning them away from evil, the message sometimes makes them more callous and insensitive to their own spiritual plight, leading to a blindness which makes them incapable of receiving the word of God. The harsh way in which this truth is expressed in the above passage is due, no doubt, to the Old Testament practice of referring all things to God and bypassing secondary causes. The willful hardening of the heart, in this manner of speaking, appears to be something intended by God whereas it is really the frustration of God's saving purpose by the sinful abuse of human freedom. The Hebrew manner of expressing a future certainty, in this case the stubborn resistance of the people, must not mislead us into assuming a causal relation between the divine will and the hardening of their hearts. It is impossible to think of God's purposes for man in any other terms than salvation, but the world He has created is a moral one in which the free decision of man is capable of defeating the saving purpose of God. What is more, repeated abuses of human freedom inevitably bring with them additional punishment in the hardening of the heart and blinding of spiritual vision which drive men further away from God. The same is true in the New Testament where we learn that God has sent His Son into the world, not to condemn, but to save. Because men willfully turned away from His Son and rejected Him, there is a sense in which the coming of the Savior has brought condemnation.

> Now this is the judgment: the light has come into the world, yet men have loved the darkness rather than the light, for their works are evil (Jn. 3:19).

The task of Isaiah would have frightened a lesser man. There was to be no easy repentance as the fruit of his preaching; the words of the prophet would only confirm them in their obduracy, their ears would become less and less attuned to the divine warnings. With perhaps a slight hint of protest in his voice, Isaiah then inquired of Yahweh about the finality of his people's impenitence, and he learned that judgment was at hand but that its inflexibility was tempered by the promise of a holy remnant which would be the foundation of a new and better Israel.

> "How long, O Yahweh?" I asked. And He replied:
> "Until the cities are desolate
>   without inhabitants,
> houses without a dweller,
>   and the earth a desolate waste.
> Until Yahweh removes men far away,
>   and the land is abandoned more and more.
> Should there still be a tenth part in it,
>   then this in turn shall be laid waste;
> as with a terebinth or an oak,
> of which, when their leaves have fallen, the trunk remains.
> The holy seed is its stump."
>
> (Isa. 6:11–13)

Even when the oak tree was cut down in judgment, the stump retained the principle of vitality out of which a new tree would spring up; even an Israel laid waste contained the seed of the future Kingdom of God. Notwithstanding the difficulties of the text, it would be very strange if one of the consistent themes of Isaiah's message were absent from the vision which inaugurated his vocation as spokesman of God. The doctrine of the remnant, as we shall see, is characteristic of Isaiah, who gave unusual expression to this conviction by naming one of his sons *Shear-jashub*, "a remnant shall return." We should not expect, then, that his vision should end on the hopeless note of inevitable and total destruction of Israel. Isaiah never repudiated the unique relation which existed between Yahweh and His people; Israel was still the community in which God had revealed Himself in a special way. But this divine choice could not overlook the infidelities of the nation, nor could God be indifferent to sins which amounted to rebellion against His sovereign lordship. In the face of Israel's alienation from the source of all its blessings, Isaiah, like the other pre-exilic prophets, was constrained to announce that punishment was imminent if men did not repent and begin to practice that full-bodied justice which Yahweh demanded. But experience was to prove how difficult it is to turn an obdurate people away from its rebellion against the Holy One of Israel.

SONS HAVE I RAISED AND REARED

The book of Isaiah is a collection of oracles pronounced at different times and later set down in what we would call an anthology of the prophet's writings. The material is certainly not arranged according to chronological sequence, and consequently it is often very difficult to match oracles with situations or incidents in Isaiah's life. Sometimes two or more oracles are joined together without any logical connection between them; and the compiler of this anthology has added to our difficulties by omitting transitional sentences between distinct passages, and even by placing side by side authentic material of Isaiah with sections composed by other authors. In these circumstances it is best to take a sampling of the prophet's work, concentrating on those oracles which scholars generally credit to Isaiah. The series of short poems in the first chapter may or may not belong to the first public utterances of Isaiah, but there is not the slightest doubt that these poems bear the authentic stamp of his genius and embody many of his central ideas — the break between Yahweh and His people, national disaster as a punishment for evil, the assurance of a remnant, and the futility of sacrifice without obedience to God's moral law. The keynote of the oracles is struck in the opening lines of a poem which shows that the fatherhood of God is found in the Old Testament as well as the New:

> Hear, O heavens, and listen, O earth,
>   for Yahweh speaks:
> "Sons have I raised and reared,
>   but they have disowned Me!
> An ox knows its owner,
>   and an ass, its master's manger;
> but Israel has not known,
> My people have not understood."
>
> (Isa. 1:2–3)

Following this reproach, Isaiah describes the calamities which have overtaken the land. The most likely historical situation for this charge against the faithless nation is the year 701 B.C., when Sennacherib laid waste the land and all but annihilated Judah. Were it not for the gracious mercy of a God they had spurned, Judah would have disappeared like the cities of the Plain:

> Ah! sinful nation, people laden with wickedness,
>   evil race, corrupt children!
> They have forsaken Yahweh,
>   spurned the Holy One of Israel,
>   apostatized!
> Where would you yet be struck,
>   you that rebel again and again?
> The whole land is sick,
>   the whole heart is faint.
> From the sole of the foot to the head
>   there is no soundness:
> wound and welt and gaping gash,
>   neither drained nor bandaged,
> nor eased with salve.
> Your country is waste,
> your cities burnt with fire;
> your land before your eyes
>   strangers devour;
> a waste, like Sodom overthrown,
> and the daughter Sion is left
> like a hut in a vineyard,
> like a shed in a melon-patch,
> like a city blockaded.

Unless Yahweh of hosts
  had left us a remnant,
we had become as Sodom,
  we had resembled Gomorrha.

(Isa. 1:4–9)

Yahweh's arraignment of His people rises to a climax as He indignantly rejects the persistent fallacy that elaborate formal worship can substitute for purity of heart and integrity of life. Once again, God was obliged to remind them that Temple services, no matter how splendid and well-attended, are hollow and worthless unless they symbolize an amendment of life and a desire to imitate His holiness. The sacrificial cult is not repudiated, as we have already seen, but the hypocritical association of meticulous ritualism with immoral lives is.

Hear the word of Yahweh,
  princes of Sodom!
Listen to the instruction of our God,
  people of Gomorrha!
"What care I for the number of your sacrifices?"
  says Yahweh.
"I have had enough of whole-burnt rams
  and fat of fatlings;
in the blood of calves, lambs and goats
I take no pleasure.
When you come to visit Me,
  who asks these things of you?
Trample My courts no more!
Bring no more worthless offerings;
your incense is loathsome to Me. . . .
Put away your evil deed from before My eyes;
cease doing evil; learn to do good.
Make justice your aim; redress the wronged,
hear the orphan's plea, defend the widow."

(Isa. 1:10–17)

A final picture of conditions in Judah during the lifetime of Isaiah is strikingly drawn in the Song of the Vineyard. The occasion was one of the happy vintage festivals, in all likelihood the Feast of Tabernacles following the harvest, and the prophet

appeared among the joyous throngs on the Temple esplanade.
The simple ballad of the "friend" who planted a vineyard
would gain the attention of his hearers; and even before he
made the application to his own situation, the listener would
have endorsed his own condemnation. In the last verse of the
Song, Isaiah underlined his conclusion by a play on words which
appealed to the Hebraic sensitivity to the power of the word
and clinched the meaning of the oracle as could no other
device. Where God had looked for judgment (mishpaṭ) He
found only bloodshed (mispah); instead of justice (sedaqa)
there was the cry of anguish (se'aqa):

> Let me sing now of my friend,
>   my friend's song concerning his vineyard.
> My friend had a vineyard
>   on a fertile hillside;
> he spaced it, cleared it of stones,
>   and planted the choicest vines;
> on it he built a watchtower,
>   and dug out a winepress.
> Then he looked for the crop of grapes,
>   but it yielded only wild grapes.
> Now, you citizens of Jerusalem and men of Judah,
>   judge between Me and My vineyard:
> What more was there to do for My vineyard
>   that I had not done?
> Why, when I looked for the crop of grapes,
>   did it bring forth wild grapes?
> Now, I will tell you
>   what I mean to do to My vineyard:
> take away its hedge, give it to grazing,
>   break through its wall, let it be trampled!
> Yes, I will make it a ruin:
>   it shall not be pruned or hoed,
>   but overgrown with thorns and briers;
> I will command the clouds
>   not to send rain upon it.
> The vineyard of Yahweh of hosts is the house of Israel
>   and the men of Judah are His cherished plant;
> He looked for judgment, and behold, bloodshed!
>   for justice, and behold, a cry of anguish!   (Isa. 5:1–7)

A REMNANT WILL RETURN, THE REMNANT OF JACOB

No one was more forthright in condemning the evils of his day than Isaiah, and he unhesitatingly warned his people that Yahweh was about to strike them down in anger. But there is, at the same time, a counterbalance. The doctrine of the remnant is associated in a special way with Isaiah; a small portion of the people, cleansed in the fire of judgment, would emerge as the faithful heir to the promises. This faith in the future was no lightly won optimism, but an unshakable conviction rooted in the faith of Isaiah. He did not make the mistake of simply identifying the remnant with the Judah which he knew so well and whose infidelities made her more and more unworthy of her privileged position as an elected people. Even if he saw in the few survivors of contemporary disaster the nucleus of a remnant, the prophet broadened his horizon and pushed it to the distant Messianic Age, that ideal state portrayed now as a restored Kingdom of David, now as a Paradise recovered. Whatever the imagery used, the fact is that the words of Isaiah came from a powerful faith in the divine decree to spare a remnant for His own purposes, and his prophecies of hope profoundly influenced subsequent generations, including the prophets Jeremiah and Ezechiel. The hope of Judah did not lie in mutual-defense pacts with unstable allies, as the experience of history clearly demonstrated, nor could the tiny nation count much on its own military strength. Only by trust in God and in His sovereign control over human affairs could they hope to survive the coming judgment:

> On that day
> the remnant of Israel,
>> the survivors of the house of Jacob,
>> will no more lean upon him who struck them;
> but they will lean upon Yahweh,
>> the Holy One of Israel, in truth.

> A remnant will return, the remnant of Jacob,
>   to the mighty God.
> For though your people, O Israel,
>   were like the sand of the sea,
> only a remnant of them will return.
> their destruction is decreed,
>   as overwhelming justice demands.
>
> (Isa. 10:20-22)

Yahweh held tenaciously to the people He had created on Sinai. His own *hesed* or covenant-love constrained Him to spare a remnant, the faithful few who would, not because of their merits but because of God's election, constitute the true Israel. Hosea taught the same truth but in accents of pathos never again attained in the literature of the Old Testament. After describing Israel's stubborn infidelities, God is shown soliloquizing:

> How can I give you up, O Ephraim!
> How can I surrender you, O Israel!
> How can I make you like Admah!
> How can I treat you like Zeboim!
> My heart recoils within Me,
> My compassion grows warm and tender.
>
> (Hosea 11:8)

The remnant is the answer to God's reluctance to give up His people and abandon them to the total destruction their apostasy had merited.

The prophetic teaching of the remnant links the two Testaments in a relation of promise and fulfillment. The early Christians, and especially St. Paul, saw the Church as the remnant of Israel, the new community which had inherited the promises made to Israel of old. Incorporation in this remnant was no longer a matter of physical generation but of a spiritual rebirth through divine grace:

> Even so, then, at the present time there is a remnant left, selected out of grace. And if out of grace, then not in virtue of works; otherwise grace is no longer grace. What then? What

Israel was seeking after, that it has not obtained; but the chosen have obtained it, and the rest have been blinded . . . (Rom. 11:5–7).

In the ninth chapter of the same Epistle to the Romans, St. Paul explicitly identifies the New Israel with the remnant of Isaiah 10:22–23. The new people of God had come into their inheritance. The estate was in their possession, since God's own people, in refusing to receive Him, had preferred the darkness to the light. What God had once promised to the people of His choice was now realized, beyond all expectations, in the Church of Christ.

To Isaiah is due the credit for holding fast to this hope for the future even when the circumstances of history seemed to be entirely against it. Only a man of his great faith in God's fidelity could maintain this conviction during the long and disappointing years of his ministry. Isaiah went further, by individualizing this hope in his well-known description of the messianic figure who should rule from David's throne over a Kingdom of peace and justice. It was probably during the reign of weak and vacillating Ahaz, an unworthy Davidic ruler if there ever was one, that Isaiah left us that unforgettable portrait of the ideal Davidic king whose rule of peace and justice would extend over the whole world:

> But a shoot shall sprout from the stump of Jesse,
>   and from his roots a branch shall grow.
> The spirit of Yahweh shall rest upon him:
>   a spirit of wisdom and understanding,
> a spirit of counsel and strength,
>   a spirit of knowledge and fear of Yahweh,
> and his delight shall be the fear of Yahweh.
> Not by what he sees shall he judge,
>   nor by what he hears shall he decide,
> but he shall judge the poor with justice,
>   and decide aright for the meek of the land.
>   (Isa. 11:1–3)

JEREMIAH

I HAVE SET MY FACE AGAINST THIS CITY

IN THE early months of 721 B.C. Samaria, the capital of the
Northern Kingdom, fell before the might of Sargon II, king
of Assyria. The disappearance of Israel as an independent state
left only the small Southern Kingdom of Judah, which was
spared destruction only at the high price of burdensome tribute.
In the century and a half which followed, the tiny state, compris-
ing the tribes of Judah and Benjamin, managed to preserve its
autonomy without ever being free from the fear of domination
by superior powers which surrounded it. But the day of reckoning could not be postponed indefinitely, and in the first quarter
of the sixth century B.C., Jerusalem met the same fate as her
sister-city, Samaria. The voice of the prophet, proclaiming the
word of Yahweh, had not been heard in Judah since the days
of Isaiah. Now God raised up at least four men who served
as His spokesmen: Zephaniah, Nahum, Habakkuk, and Jeremiah. Of these, the last-mentioned is easily the outstanding
personality and the man most closely involved in the critical
events which led up to the downfall of his country.

Since much, though not all, of a prophet's message has
relevance in view of the background against which it was delivered, we must look at the times in which Jeremiah lived and
the events which he tried, unsuccessfully, to guide. This was
an age of crisis, brought on by factors outside of Judah's control
as well as by her own obtuseness to the lessons of the past. We
can begin our survey of this swiftly moving history with the
call of Jeremiah, in 626 B.C., just five years before the religious
reform of Josiah. By this time the Assyrian hold on the ancient
Near East was beginning to weaken. With the disappearance of

her great military leaders, the Empire which had been held together by brute military force showed signs of cracking up. Its fall was inevitable, but few could have guessed how quickly it would come, with the overthrow of Nineveh in 612 B.C. by a coalition of Babylonians and Medes. Read the short prophecy of Nahum if you would hear the shout of triumph which resounded among the nations when the word came that Nineveh had been destroyed. Josiah had taken advantage of Assyria's declining strength by extending his political control into what had been, for almost a century, the Assyrian provinces of Samaria and Megiddo, established after the fall of the Northern Kingdom. But the act by which Josiah was best remembered by the Hebrew historians was the thoroughgoing religious reform which he inaugurated in 621 B.C., the year in which the book of the law, commonly identified with at least a part of the book of Deuteronomy, was found in the Temple.[1] The attitude of Jeremiah to the reform of Josiah has been the subject of keen debate, with the weight of evidence favoring the opinion that the prophet supported the measures of Josiah at first, but later, seeing that external legislation had failed to effect a true interior renewal, scored its insufficiency.[2]

If the failure of Josiah's reform proved a bitter disappointment to Jeremiah, a still more crushing blow was yet to come. The Egyptian Pharaoh Necho led an army into Palestine to give support to the tottering Assyrian Empire which had already lost its capital. Whatever may have been the ulterior motives of the Egyptian, he seems to have determined that he would

---

[1] Is is probable that Chapters 5 to 26 of Deuteronomy made up the law book discovered in Jerusalem and brought to Josiah. From the standpoint of successive editions of Deuteronomy — by no means an unlikely hypothesis — these chapters would constitute the nucleus of the book and were probably composed between the fall of Samaria (721 B.C.) and the beginning of Josiah's reign (640 B.C.). Deuteronomy is a seventh-century version of the Mosaic Law, more homiletic than legal in its style, and the public reading ordered by Josiah was meant to be a liturgical act in which the worshiper relived and participated in the mighty deeds which Yahweh had performed for His people.

[2] See H. H. Rowley, "The Prophet Jeremiah and the Book of Deuteronomy," *Studies in Old Testament Prophecy*, H. H. Rowley, ed. (Edinburgh: T. & T. Clark, 1950), pp. 157–174.

strike a blow at the rising new power in the ancient East, Babylon, even if it meant giving help to an old enemy of Egypt. Josiah came with his forces to stop the northward march of Necho, and the two armies met at the great strategic pass of Megiddo. Details of the conflict are obscure, but we know that Josiah was mortally wounded and his body was brought back to Jerusalem. This was in the year 609 B.C. and it not only marked the end of any further reforms, pushed by one of Judah's best kings, but it ushered in a train of events which culminated in the overthrow of Jerusalem.

Upon his return from the north, the Egyptian Necho placed a son of Josiah on the throne, giving him the name of Jehoiakim. He was known to be pro-Egyptian in his sympathies, at least as long as Egypt was strong, and he was the first to clash head-on with the prophet Jeremiah who recognized in this empty shadow of a noble father a pompous and vain weakling. There is not a stronger condemnation of a Judean king than the one uttered by Jeremiah against Jehoiakim. The desperate plight of the land did not prevent this vain puppet from enlarging and ornamenting his own palace with unpaid labor:

> "Woe to him who builds his house by injustice,
>   and his upper rooms by false judgment;
>   who makes his neighbor work for nothing,
>   and refuses him his pay;
> who boasts, 'I will build for myself a great house
>   with vast upper rooms,
>   and I will cut out windows for it
>   and will panel it with cedar,
>   and paint it with vermillion.'
> Do you play the king
>   because you compete in cedar?
> Did not your father eat and drink
>   and execute judgment and do justly?
> Then it was well with him.
> He judged the case of the needy and poor;
>   then it was well.
> Is this not knowledge of Me," says Yahweh?

"But your eyes and heart
   are set only on your own profit,
   on shedding innocent blood,
   on extortion and violence."
   Therefore, thus says Yahweh of Jehoiakim, son of Josiah,
king of Judah:
"They shall not mourn for him, crying,
   'Alas, my brother!' or 'Alas, my sister!'
They shall not mourn for him, crying,
   'Alas, my lord!' or 'Alas, his majesty!'
He shall be buried with the burial of an ass,
   dragged and thrown outside the gates of Jerusalem."
                                        (Jer. 22:13–19)

We are left in the dark as to the precise fulfillment of this
terrifying prediction, but it is certain that Jehoiakim died shortly
before the Babylonians, now the dominant power in Western
Asia, laid siege to Jerusalem for the first time. The recently
published *Chronicles of Chaldean Kings*, by D. J. Wiseman of
the British Museum, now makes it certain that Nebuchadnezzar
captured Jerusalem on March 16, 597 B.C. We might add that
the same tablets provide a much clearer picture of the international struggle for power in which the little Kingdom of
Judah was caught and perished.

Jehoiachin, the son of Jehoiakim, ruled only long enough
to surrender Jerusalem to the Babylonians, and he was carried
off with the first deportation of exiles to Babylon. The concluding verses of the last book of Kings describe his captivity
and eventual liberation from prison. The Weidner Tablets,
published in 1940, provide an illuminating footnote to the
account in this book of Kings. The Tablets describe the food
ration given to Jehoiachin and prove, at the same time, that
the Jews still hoped for a restoration of the Davidic dynasty
under Jehoiachin. Apparently the people had not taken to heart
the prophecy of Jeremiah that no descendant of the young king
would ascend the throne of Judah:

       O land, land, land,
       hear the word of Yahweh!

Thus says Yahweh:

> "Write this man down as childless,
> a man who will not prosper in his days;
> for none of his offspring will prosper,
> sitting on the throne of David,
> and ruling again in Judah."
>
> (Jer. 22:29–30)

In 597 B.C. the Babylonians, now in control of Jerusalem, placed Zedekiah on the throne of Judah. He was a son of Josiah and an uncle of Jehoiachin who had already gone into exile. Zedekiah was a well-intentioned but weak man, trapped between the pro-Babylonian and pro-Egyptian factions in Jerusalem. To his credit it should be said that he took seriously the advice of Jeremiah during the major part of his ten-year reign. This is especially clear in the case of the abortive conspiracy of 594 B.C., when representatives from surrounding states gathered at Jerusalem to plan their revolt against Babylon. Jeremiah was prepared for the envoys and dramatized his message by the well-known symbol of going about Jerusalem with a yoke upon his neck:

> Thus Yahweh said to me: "Make for yourself thongs and yoke-bars, and put them on your neck. Send word to the king of Edom, the king of Moab, the king of the sons of Ammon, the king of Tyre, and the king of Sidon by the hand of the envoys who have come to Jerusalem to Zedekiah, king of Judah. Let them bring back their message to their masters: Thus says Yahweh of hosts, the God of Israel: This is what you shall report to your masters: It is I Who by My great power and My outstretched arm have made the earth, along with the men and animals who are on the earth, and I give it to whomsoever I please. Now I have given all these lands into the hand of Nebuchadnezzar, the king of Babylon, My servant, and I have given him also the beasts of the field to serve him. All nations shall serve him and his son and his grandson, until the time of his own land comes; then many nations and great kings shall make him their slave" (Jer. 27:2–7).

But Zedekiah could not hold out indefinitely against the strong anti-Babylonian party, and he signalized his revolt by refusing to pay tribute to his Babylonian overlords. Once again, the army of Babylon invaded Judah, captured the surrounding cities which served as military outposts for the defense of Jerusalem, and laid siege to the Holy City in January, ´588 B.C. Shortly before the siege began, Jeremiah warned Zedekiah that the city was doomed and that resistance was useless. At the time of this warning only the fortified cities of Lachish and´ Azekah remained. The discovery, in 1935, of the Lachish Letters, inscribed on ostraca (broken pieces of pottery), permits us to date this warning to the summer or early fall of 589 B.C. Letter IV, written to a certain Yaosh, commander of the garrison of Lachish, serves as a striking archaeological footnote to Jeremiah 34:7. The plight of these outlying towns is underscored by the last line of the letter:

> And let him [my lord Yaosh] know that we are waiting for the fire-signals of Lachish, according to all the indications which my lord has given, for we cannot see Azekah.

Only a few months after this letter, with its ominous reference to neighboring Azekah, the town of Lachish fell to Nebuchadnezzar, and the way was cleared for the final assault on Jerusalem. The siege lasted for more than a year, during which Jeremiah was imprisoned for "weakening the hands of the soldiers in the city" by his counsel to submit. In August, 587 B.C., Jerusalem fell to Nebuchadnezzar. Though it is difficult for us to determine the precise date of composition, the following lamentation of Jeremiah over the city affords a fitting conclusion to this national tragedy:

> "Who will take pity on you, O Jerusalem,
>   or who will bemoan you?
> who will turn aside
>   to inquire about your welfare?
> You have cast Me off," says Yahweh,
>   "you keep going backward;
> therefore I have stretched out My hand against you
>   and destroyed you: —
> I am weary of relenting.

With a winnowing fork have I winnowed them
   in the gates of the land;
I have bereaved them, I have destroyed My people;
   for they turned not from their ways. . . ."

(Jer. 15:5–7)

A MAN OF STRIFE AND CONTENTION

About two miles to the northeast of Jerusalem, in the territory of Benjamin, lay the small town of Anathoth, birthplace of Jeremiah. The introduction to the prophecy tells us that the prophet belonged to the priestly family of Hilkiah, who may possibly have been a descendant of Abiathar, a priest in the time of David. There is no evidence that Jeremiah ever officiated as a priest. It is more than likely, however, that this shy and sensitive young man soon became acquainted with the messages of the great prophets who had preceded him, and if we are to single out one, it is Hosea who appears to have exercised the greatest influence on him. Hosea, the prophet of God's love for Israel, was of a temperament very much like Jeremiah; both suffered intensely from the evil they saw all about them and both interpreted Israel's sin in terms of marital infidelity, the callous refusal to respond to Yahweh's covenant-love. The reproach of spurned affection found utterance in the prophecies of both.

While still a young man, probably during the year 626 B.C., Jeremiah was called by Yahweh to the prophetic office. The vocation is described by Jeremiah in the form of a dialogue between himself and God:

Now the word of Yahweh came to me saying,

"Before I formed you in the womb I knew you,
   and before you were born I sanctified you;
   I appointed you a prophet to the nations."

Then I said, "Ah, Lord God! Behold, I do not know how to speak, for I am but a child."

But Yahweh said to me,

"Do not say, 'I am but a child';
  for to whomever I send you, you shall go,
  and whatever I command you, you shall speak.
  Fear them not for I am with you to deliver you."
                                    The utterance of Yahweh.

Then Yahweh stretched forth His hand and touched my mouth;
and Yahweh said to me,
  "Behold, I have put My words in your mouth.
  See, I have set you this day over nations
  and over kingdoms,
  to root out and to break down,
  to destroy and to overthrow,
  to build and to plant."

                                    (Jer. 1:4–10)

One could make an interesting comparison between this
episode and the call of Isaiah. For Isaiah, the Lord was the
all-holy One, clothed in majesty and splendor, before Whom
the seraphim veiled their faces. In the presence of this transcendent being, Isaiah could only stammer out his unworthiness,
removed by the cleansing coal of the seraph; then he was ready
to pronounce his courageous: "Here am I; send me!" God's
approach to Jeremiah was quieter, on a more personal level.
There was no overwhelming sense of personal guilt, only the
awareness of his own inadequacy and a natural shrinking from
the onerous task of being God's spokesman. The temptation to
draw back from the divine summons was met by the assurance
that God had predestined him for this work, a special mission
not only to Israel but to the nations. As far as we can determine,
no prophet before Jeremiah had received a call which was
world-wide in scope, constituting him a watchman over the
destinies of great empires. Finally, the revelation that the message he would preach was not his own but the very word of
Yahweh prevailed over the natural timidity of the man.

The circumstantial description of Jeremiah's call points ahead
to the inner conflict which characterized the life of the prophet.

Fortunately, we possess a series of passages in the book which reveal the inner life of Jeremiah and which have come to be known as the "Confessions of Jeremiah." They may be found in the following chapters: 11:18–12:6; 15:10–21; 17:9–10, 14–18; 18:18–23; 20:7–18. No other prophet in the Old Testament has left us so much autobiographical material in which the soul of a man is laid bare. Therein we see Jeremiah's awareness of his own weakness and, at the same time, his turning to God as the only source of strength. We are reminded of St. Paul, who learned that the grace of God would more than make up for the weakness in which he could finally boast, since his whole sufficiency was from God. Jeremiah was destined to be a man of contention, and the first lyric of the "Confessions" reveals his own sense of helplessness before his enemies. In this passage he raises, for the first time, the problem which will be one of the central themes of the book of Job, the good fortune of the wicked. It had been revealed to Jeremiah that his own people, the citizens of Anathoth, were planning to kill him. Unaware of the enmity he had provoked, he compares himself to an innocent lamb led to the slaughter and then cries out for vengeance on these men, who are God's enemies as well as his own. After receiving an assurance that the plotters would be punished severely, the prophet expostulates with God:

> Right would You be, O Yahweh,
> were I to complain to You;
> yet would I plead my case before You.
> Why does the way of the wicked prosper?
> Why do all who are treacherous thrive?
> You plant them and they take root;
>   they grow and bring forth fruit;
> You are near in their mouth
> but far from their heart.
> But You, O Yahweh, know me;
> You see me, and try my mind toward You.
> Pull them out like sheep for the slaughter,
> and prepare them for the day of slaughter!

> (Jer. 12:1–3)

The reply of God to this challenge was not an answer but a reminder that greater evils lay ahead and that Jeremiah must bring greater faith and resoluteness to the conflicts which still faced him:

> If you have raced with men on foot,
>   and they have wearied you,
>   how can you compete with horses?
> And if in a peaceful land you fall down,
>   how will you do in the jungle of the Jordan?
>   (Jer. 12:5)

Few men have been as sensitive as Jeremiah to the failure of a mission. But the thought of his prophetic words being rejected forced from his soul cries of protest, even against God. Jeremiah had been a laughingstock, the butt of ridicule, the object of curses from his own people. The apparent futility of his work, the absence of any confirmation of his message led him finally to protest to God with an intensity which could come only from desperation. Jeremiah had once compared God to the running water of a spring, a perennial source of refreshment. Now he would cry out:

> Why is my pain unending,
>   my wound incurable,
>   refusing to be healed?
> Will You be to me like a deceitful brook,
>   like waters that fail?
>   (Jer. 15:18)

Jeremiah has been called a prophet with a divided heart, torn between loyalty to the task imposed upon him by God, and the natural aversion of a sensitive man to proclaim the imminent doom of his own nation. He was even forbidden the quiet joys of married life and was obliged to forego the ordinary pleasures and sorrows of his own people. In the sixth century B.C., the office of prophet to Judah demanded an austerity which came hard to a man of Jeremiah's warm and emotional temperament. What the prophet's obedience cost in terms of interior suffering is clear from a passage which illuminates the inner life of the prophet and, at the same time, gives us some idea of how he felt divinely compelled to preach the word of God:

> Yahweh, You have deceived me,
> and I was deceived;
> You have overcome me,
> Yes, You have prevailed!
> I have become a laughingstock all day long;
> everyone mocks me.
> For whenever I speak, I cry out,
> I cry, "Violence and destruction!"
> For the word of Yahweh has become for me
> a reproach and derision all day long.
> If I say, "I will not mention Him,
> nor speak any more in His name,"
> there is in my heart as it were a burning fire
> shut up in my bones,
> and I weary myself with holding it in,
> and I cannot. . . .
>
> (Jer. 20:7–9)

While candidly recognizing the faults and limitations of Jeremiah, his petulancy, outbursts of anger, doubts, and cries of vengeance, we cannot overlook the magnificent courage and faith of a man who believed himself naturally unsuited for his task, and yet overcame his misgivings and reluctance. In union with God, intense and personal, he surmounted the disappointments and loneliness which are often the lot of those chosen to be the instruments of God.

WICKED MEN ARE AMONG MY PEOPLE

Two visions are closely associated with the call of Jeremiah, and both contained a warning that judgment upon the nation was near at hand. In the first vision there is a play on words as Jeremiah related that he saw an almond tree (shaqed) and God answered that He was watching over (shoqed) His word, to see that it was carried out. In the second vision Jeremiah saw a large boiling pot upon a stove whose opening faced the north, whence came the wind to fan the fire which would make the pot seethe. From the north would come the dreaded foe, Babylon, to administer God's judgment. In each case the message was fundamentally the same: God is active in these days and He is about to punish. There was nothing particularly new in all this, for there had been earlier prophets who had threatened punishment for the sins of Israel. But Jeremiah gave a new depth to the perception of evil by emphasizing the interior deordination which is the essence of sin. In this realization he was the forerunner of Christ, Who taught that the malice of sin consists in the inward spirit of rebellion against God.

The background for Jeremiah's denunciation of Judah's sin was Yahweh's loving act of espousing the nation at the time of the Exodus. In the desert Yahweh had taken Israel as His bride, but she had proved faithless. At the very beginning of Jeremiah's career the Lord told him to proclaim in the streets of Jerusalem:

> I [Yahweh] remember the covenant-love of your youth,
>   your love as a bride,
> how you sought Me in the wilderness,
> in a land not sown.
> Israel was holy to Yahweh,
>   the first fruits of His harvest.
> All who devoured her became guilty;
>   evil came upon them.
>
> (Jer. 2:2–3)

More than one prophet had looked upon the sojourn in the desert as an ideal time of mutual love between Yahweh and His people. Once they had entered Canaan the process of degeneration had begun and seems to have gone on with accelerated speed. In a rapid succession of images, very common in the Oriental literary style, Jeremiah pictured the degradation of Israelite religion through its contact with the sensuous, often abhorrent, religious practices of Canaan:

"For long ago I broke your yoke
and burst your bonds;
but you said: 'I will not serve!'
Yes, upon every high hill
and under every green tree
you bowed down like a harlot.
Yet I had planted you a choice vine,
wholly of pure seed.
How then have you become degenerate
nothing but a wild vine?
Though you wash yourself with niter
and use much soap,
the stain of your sin is still before Me,"
    says the Lord God.
"How dare you say, 'I am not defiled,
nor have I gone after the Baals'?
Look to your way in the valley;
know what you have done —
a restive young camel interlacing her tracks,
a wild ass used to the wilderness,
in her heat sniffing the wind!
Who can restrain her lust?
No need for those who seek her to weary themselves;
in her month they will find her.
Keep your feet from going unshod
and your throat from thirst.
But you said, 'There is no hope,
    for I have loved strangers,
    and after them I will go.'
But where are your gods
    which you made for yourself?
Let them rise up, if they can save you,
in your time of trouble;
for as numerous as your towns
are your gods, O Judah!"

                    (Jer. 2:20–25, 28)

Underlying these images of infidelity to Yahweh is that
"spirit of harlotry" which Hosea, a century and a half before
Jeremiah, recognized as the inner cause of Israel's apostasy.
Jeremiah has much in common with his predecessor, above all

in his insistence on the inwardness of sin, the evil heart as the source of external acts contrary to God's will. When Jeremiah says that "the heart is deceitful above all things, and desperately corrupt," he is tracing the deordination of any human action to its source. Our Lord did the same when He combated the sterile legalism of His opponents. More than once Jeremiah uses the phrase "stubbornness of heart" to underscore that moral apathy or indifference to evil which is the most dreadful effect of persistently sinful actions. There are many punishments attached to sin, but few so dreadful as that inner deterioration which makes a man all but impervious to the initiatives of divine grace.

It did not take Jeremiah long to see that the only hope of his people lay in a radical change of heart. The famous Temple sermon, delivered shortly after the death of Josiah, insisted on the need of interior reform and on the futility of reliance upon merely external worship, coupled with a superstitious belief in the inviolability of the Temple. The incident revealed the courage of Jeremiah in openly assailing this perversion of divine worship at a time when, due to the reform of Josiah, the Temple had become the center of Judah's religious life. It was before a great mass of worshipers, milling about the courts of the Temple, and blissfully unaware that their religious life, divorced from God's moral demands, was little more than large-scale hypocrisy that Jeremiah stunned priests and people with the announcement that the Temple was doomed:

Thus says Yahweh of hosts, the God of Israel, "Amend your ways and your deeds, and I will let you dwell in this place. Trust not in these deceptive words: 'This is the Temple of Yahweh, the Temple of Yahweh, the Temple of Yahweh!'

"For if you truly mend your ways and your deeds, if you truly execute justice one with the other, if you do not oppress the alien, the fatherless or the widow, or shed innocent blood in this place, and if you do not seek out other gods to your own hurt, then I will let you dwell in this place which of old I gave to your fathers for ever and ever.

"Behold, you trust in deceptive words to no avail. Will you

steal, murder, commit adultery, swear falsely, burn incense to Baal, and go after other gods whom you have not known, and then come and stand before Me in this house, which is called by My name, and say, 'We are delivered!' — only to go on doing all these abominations? Has this house, which is called by My name, become a den of thieves in your eyes? Behold, I Myself have seen it," says Yahweh. "Go now to My place which was in Shilo, where I first made My name dwell, and see what I did to it because of the wickedness of My people Israel.

"And now, since you have done all these things," says Yahweh, "and when I spoke to you persistently you did not listen, and when I called you, you did not answer, therefore I will do to the house which is called by My name, and in which you trust, and to the place which I gave to you and your fathers, as I did to Shilo. And I will cast you out of My sight, as I cast out all your kinsmen, all the offspring of Ephraim" (Jer. 7:3-15).

This was too much for priest and people, naïvely confident that the Temple, despite the empty formalism of the worship which went on there, was as imperishable as God's own word. A later chapter informs us that the crowd seized Jeremiah and threatened him with death because he had dared to speak against the Temple. A court was summoned and Jeremiah was put on trial but acquitted by the bench when they remembered the traditional right of the prophet to speak the word of Yahweh. To this argument was added the precedent of Micah who had spoken against the city without being condemned to death by Hezekiah. Jeremiah was released but, from this time, he was a marked man, suspected of subverting the state religion and its elaborate ceremonial. But Jeremiah's last word to his people was not one of condemnation. He lived to see the Babylonians batter down the wall of Jerusalem and destroy the Temple, as he had prophesied. The judgment of God on Judah's sin had been worked out in the tragic history of those days. Now it was time for God to show His mercy.

I WILL MAKE A NEW COVENANT

It is often darkest before the dawn. Judah's humiliation was complete and the nation lay in ruins. Naturally speaking, there was no hope for the people upon whom the hand of judgment had descended so heavily. But Jeremiah was the last man in Judah to live according to merely natural principles; his whole strength and the source of his hope lay in his vital and sustained union with God. For over forty years of prophetic work, the word of Yahweh, "I am with you to deliver you," enabled this heroic man to turn back every attempt to silence him, dilute his message, and even to take away his life. The moment of catastrophe would not find the aging prophet without hope, for he had been granted a revelation of God's redemptive purpose for men. In the vision of the New Covenant, Jeremiah reached the climax of his teaching:

> "Behold, days are coming," says Yahweh, "when I will make a new covenant with the house of Israel and the house of Judah. Not like the covenant which I made with their fathers when I took them by the hand to lead them out of the land of Egypt, for they kept not My covenant, though I was their husband," says Yahweh.
>
> "But this is the covenant which I will make with the house of Israel after those days," says Yahweh. "I will put My law within them, and I will write it upon their hearts; and I will be their God, and they will be My people. And no longer shall each one teach his neighbor and each his brother, saying, 'Know Yahweh,' for they shall all know Me, from the least to the greatest," says Yahweh; "for I will forgive their iniquity, and their sin I will remember no more" (Jer. 31:31–34).

A bridge between the two covenants is constructed in this passage. It is not a prophecy that the Law of Sinai will be repudiated, but rather that new means will be given to fulfill the Law once given. The covenant relation is not ruptured, but brought to a higher level of perfection. For, under the New Covenant, the grace of God, as contrasted with external precepts carved on the tablets of the Law, will act directly on the mind and heart of man, bringing him into a more perfect and interior relation to the will of God. In both the Covenant of Sinai and the New Covenant God takes the initiative, but there is advance in several directions.

The inward character of the new relation is expressed by the phrase, "I will put My Law within them, and I will write it upon their hearts." Good and evil are rooted in the heart of man. Just as a man's sin involves more than an external act of disobedience, as Jeremiah recognized so well, so his union with God involves more than an external conformity to law in a spirit of pure legalism. Jeremiah knew well, from personal observation of Josiah's reform, how impossible it was to legislate men into a proper relation with God. The prophet envisaged an interior transformation of man, not unlike the regeneration which is so prominent in the doctrine of St. John. This transformation was not to be the work of man but a mystery of grace which enables a man, through self-renunciation, suffering, and obedience, to share in the very life of God. The optimism of Jeremiah was grounded on his faith in God and God's fidelity to the promises made long ago; he had no illusions about his country's natural capacity to bring about a spiritual reform. A corollary of this interior renovation would be the personal response of the individual who would do God's will by a spontaneous surrender of his heart to the promptings of God's grace. Here was a foreshadowing of that Christian liberty which has replaced the service of a slave with the freedom of God's children, living under the New Covenant of grace.

It would be a mistake to conclude, from Jeremiah's emphasis on a personal relation to God, that he was concerned exclusively with the individual or that he should be called "the father of individualism." Aside from the fact that the individual, as a responsible agent, appears in some of the earliest sections of the Old Testament, notably in the Ten Commandments with their categoric "thou shalt," we should not forget that Jeremiah set his vision of the future in the context of a community, the New Israel. Individualism and collectivism were nicely balanced in the thought of Jeremiah, and one should not be stressed to the exclusion of the other. The personal, individual elements were there, notably in the promised "knowledge of Yahweh."[3]

---

[3] This "knowledge," which appears frequently in the Old Testament, is a

They were present as well in the promised "forgiveness of sins," but in the age of the New Covenant men were still to remember that they were members of a community and that it was through life in a community that they were to be saved. Excessive individualism has no place in either the Old or the New Testaments. The failure of his own people to make return of Yahweh's love tore at the heart of Jeremiah. But if the original community had shut its eyes to its true vocation, Yahweh could still create a New Israel with which He would enter into a New Covenant. The Church has, from the beginning, seen the fulfillment of this vision in that solemn scene in the Upper Room when Christ told His Apostles that the New Covenant was being inaugurated in the blood He was about to shed for the redemption of all men. Through the blood of Christ would come forgiveness, extended to the whole race of men, a New Law inscribed in the heart of man, and an outpouring of grace through which men could know God in all the richness of that biblical word.

The faith of Jeremiah brought him, as it has others, beyond tragedy and despair. From every human viewpoint the man of Anathoth must be set down as a failure. He failed to lead his people to repentance; he could not prevent them from putting their trust in senseless alliances; his motives were questioned and even his patriotism was put in doubt. He was not spared the grim sight of prophecy fulfilled when Jerusalem fell before the vastly superior Babylonian army. It does not seem that he was even granted the satisfaction of public vindication. With his faithful secretary, Baruch, the prophet was led away an unwilling captive to Egypt, shortly after the fall of Jerusalem. Instead of a chastened people he found the Jews in Egypt returning to the idolatrous practices which had so often aroused the wrath of Yahweh. Jeremiah could well repeat the prophecy of an

---

dynamic thing which combines intellectual apprehension of the truth with the fulfillment of God's commands. It embraces much more than what we are accustomed to associate with the term. To know God is, above all, to do His will.

earlier time: "I looked on the earth, and lo, it was waste and void; and to the heavens, and they had no light." Literally, only God was left. Through intimate, personal union with Him Jeremiah did not find the tranquillity which has been granted to many of the saints. From the time of his call, when he was a young man, to the last days of his long prophetic ministry, the inner struggle and unresolved tensions remained. The "Confessions" have given us a glimpse into the heart of this man who was torn between love of his people and the stern duty of announcing the downfall of a faithless nation. Union with God gave him strength to surmount his timidities and the stamina to bear this burden for almost forty years. More important still, it gave Jeremiah an insight into the nature of Israel's God Who, though bound to destroy what He had fashioned as a potter molds his clay, would still, through His infinite wisdom and goodness, offer salvation to all in the New Covenant sanctified by the blood of His Son.

EZECHIEL

EZECHIEL is the third of the Major Prophets, roughly contemporaneous with Jeremiah, and the greatest spiritual figure
of Judaism during the Exile. He belonged to the priestly family
of the Zadokites, a fact which may explain why, in his plans
for the restored Temple, Ezechiel restricted the office of priesthood to the sons of Zadok, the man who had been appointed
chief priest at the time of Solomon. Allowing for some exaggeration in the description of Ezechiel as a "priest in the mantle of
a prophet," there is little doubt that his plan for a Temple-
centered theocratic community, envisioned in the last nine
chapters of his book, exercised a profound influence on the
Judaism which emerged after the Exile. Because of this influence
Ezechiel has often been called the "Father of Judaism."

Before examining the priestly aspect of his life, let us see
him as a prophet in the great tradition of men like Amos,
Isaiah, and Jeremiah. We have insisted that a prophet must be
understood in the light of the times in which he lived. This is
pre-eminently true in the case of Ezechiel who was called to the
task of prophesying at a turning point in the history of his
people. Jerusalem was besieged and captured for the first time
by the Babylonians in 597 B.C. This was the occasion of the
first deportation of Judeans to Babylon and many of the most
capable citizens joined their king, Jehoiachin, in the long march
from Jerusalem to Babylon. Ezechiel was in this band of exiles
and, according to a solidly founded opinion, he never returned
to Jerusalem. Instead, he carried on his prophetic activity
exclusively among the *Golah*, the community of Jews settled
in the land of their conqueror. Ezechiel is unique among the

prophets in having received his call outside of the land of Israel. From the time of the conquest of the land under Joshua, religious leaders had been chosen in the land of Yahweh's dwelling and they were commissioned to prophesy in the same place, sanctified by the presence of Yahweh. For the first time in Israel's history a prophet received the spirit of God outside of Palestine and, though not neglecting those left in Palestine, the unprecedented charge to exercise the prophetic office in the pagan land of Babylon.

The Babylonian invasion devastated the small territory of Judah and led to such a depopulation of the country that, for over fifty years, the center of Jewish life shifted from the Holy Land to Babylonia, which was destined to be for many centuries one of the great settlements of the Diaspora. This is the name given to locations where Jews took up residence outside of Palestine. The attempts of some modern scholars to revise this traditional view of the catastrophe suffered by the Jewish people and to picture it as a relatively minor dislocation of life have foundered on the mounting evidence of archaeology which thoroughly supports the traditional picture of Judah's devastation. Excavations of the past thirty years at such sites as Beth-zur and Tell Beit Mirsim, to mention only a few, put the validity of the traditional view beyond question. It is no exaggeration to affirm, in the light of what is now known, that not a single town of Judah remained untouched and undisturbed by the invasion of the Babylonians. The facts unearthed by archaeologists proclaim in no uncertain terms that in the sixth century B.C. there was a radical and drastic rupture of continuity in the territory of Judah and that it took a number of centuries before anything like normal life was resumed.

The spiritual effect on the people was more serious than the dislocation of the material side of their lives. The book of Jeremiah draws a clear picture of the uncertainty and confusion which characterized the decade between the first and the last deportations (597–587 B.C.). Some looked for deliverance in an alliance with the "Broken Reed," Egypt. Others held tenaciously to an almost superstitious belief in the absolute inviolability of city and Temple, as though God, in no case, could allow the place where His name dwelt to be destroyed. Among the exiles this same fanatical belief was nourished by false prophets who predicted that God would soon intervene dramatically and break the yoke of Babylon. There appears to have been constant and fairly rapid communication between the survivors in Judah and the Babylonian Diaspora, and every reported uprising enkindled the false hopes of the exiles. What Jeremiah was doing in Jerusalem to stamp out these empty dreams of victory over Babylon, Ezechiel was doing among his exiled countrymen in Babylon.

Once the final blow had fallen and Jerusalem lay in ruins, the spiritual crisis became more acute among the exiles who had refused to believe that the nation could perish. A general disillusionment set in among those who seem never to have taken seriously the constant teaching of the prophets that this calamity, of great proportions it is true, was a judgment of God upon a sinful nation. It was not a defeat for Yahweh, as many might have fancied, but another step in His mysterious plan of salvation through a new and chastened Israel. Added to this disillusionment was the peril faced by a people uprooted from their ancient traditions, deprived of their sacred center of worship and their priesthood, and swallowed up in an environment where strange gods were worshiped at ceremonies of fabulous splendor. If an exiled Jew brought with him a paganized attitude toward Yahweh, in the sense that a kind of commercial bargain was struck between God and worshiper, it is not surprising that he would renounce this God Who had suffered thorough defeat at the hands of Babylon. What could be more natural than to take up the worship of Babylon's gods now that they had proved themselves superior to the God of Israel? How many succumbed to this temptation we shall never know, but the oracles of both Jeremiah and Ezechiel against idolatry sharply remind us of the menace which faced Israelite monotheism.

Ezechiel had come to Babylon with the first deportees,

including King Jehoiachin, the last of the Davidic line. Many of them settled in a colony named Tel-Abib, derived from the cuneiform (Mesopotamian) word *til abub,* meaning "primordial mound." This latter name was given to those low lying mounds along the Euphrates which represented the ruins of towns destroyed centuries before. Alongside this settlement ran the Kabar canal, close to the holy city of Nippur, and it was here that Ezechiel received his great throne-chariot vision and the mission to the people of Israel. It was the fifth year of Jehoiachin's Babylonian captivity, 592 B.C. The vision took the form of a great storm coming from the north, the traditional abode of God. There emerged from the midst of the storm four fantastic creatures, cherubim, each with four faces and four wings. This feature reminds us of the seraphim in Isaiah's inaugural vision when Yahweh appeared to him in the Temple. Beside each of the four living creatures was a wheel made of precious stone. The wheels moved at the command of the spirit which was in the living creatures. Above the living creatures was the firmament and above that, the likeness of a throne upon which Yahweh, in the likeness of a man, was enthroned. The language of the prophet broke down before this overwhelming experience as it often has in the case of Christian mystics. But Ezechiel had come face to face with the glory of Yahweh, and he fell upon his face when the Lord addressed him in these words:

"Son of man, stand upon your feet, for I would speak with you." And when He spoke to me, the Spirit entered into me and set me upon my feet; and I heard Him Who spoke to me. And He said to me, "Son of man, I am sending you to the people of Israel, to a rebellious nation which has rebelled against Me; they and their fathers have transgressed against Me to this very day. The sons are also brazen-faced and stubborn; to them I send you and you shall say to them, 'Thus says the Lord God'" (Ezech. 2:1-4).

The narrative continues with a description of Ezechiel's eating of the scroll on which were written words of lamentation and mourning. At the command of Yahweh he took the scroll, ate it, and found that it was as sweet as honey. The bizarre imagery of this and subsequent visions shows that Ezechiel was a man of unusual temperament and vivid imagination. Yet, one cannot help noticing that his vocation, in its essential elements, was no different from the great prophets who had preceded him and who were conscious that they spoke a word given to them. Knowing that God had spoken to them and that He had sent them to their fellow men, they had no fear of man. The approval or contempt of men was of no account as long as they were faithful to the task which Yahweh had laid upon them.

THEREFORE I HAVE POURED OUT MY INDIGNATION

During the five years which followed the call of Ezechiel, he was obliged to prepare the exiles in Babylon for the destruction of Jerusalem which was to occur in 587 B.C. Ezechiel knew that the hopes of many of the people in a restored Davidic monarchy were illusory, for Yahweh was about to deliver His city to the Babylonians. Like Jeremiah in Jerusalem, Ezechiel not only predicted the inevitable calamity but explained it in terms of God's punishing a sinful people. A nation which had taken idols to its heart would have to be cleansed. Ezechiel taught this bitter truth by means of symbolic actions which graphically expressed the revelation he had received. Three of these actions are recorded in the book. In the first, he was ordered by God to cut a picture of Jerusalem on one of the sun-dried bricks which are so common in Babylonia. Then he was to carry out a mimic siege against the city:

"Now take an iron plate, and set it like an iron wall between you and the city; and set your face toward it, and let the city be in a state of siege, and press the siege against it. Let this be a sign for the house of Israel" (Ezech. 4:3).

On a second occasion, he was told to eat rationed food and to measure out his drinking water. This was also a sign of the approaching doom:

Then Yahweh said to me, "Son of man, behold, I will break the staff of bread in Jerusalem; they shall eat bread by weight and in anxiety; and they shall drink water by measure and in dismay. I will do this that they may lack bread and water, and look at one another in dismay, and waste away in their iniquity" (Ezech. 4:16–17).

Finally, God ordered Ezechiel to take a sharp sword and cut off his hair, as a sign of mourning familiar to the ancient East, and dispose of it as a further sign of the fate in store for the inhabitants of Jerusalem:

"And you, O son of man, take a sharp sword; use as a barber's razor and pass it over your head and beard; then you shall take balances for weighing, and divide the hair. A third of it you shall burn in the fire in the midst of the city, when the days of the siege are fulfilled; and a third of it you shall take and strike with the sword round about the city; and a third of it you shall scatter to the wind . . ." (Ezech. 5:1–2).

The above are some of the symbolic actions performed by Ezechiel during the difficult years preceding the destruction of the Holy City. On another occasion (Chapter 9) he had an apocalyptic vision of judgment in which he saw the slaughter in the streets as resistance in the city collapsed. The "executioners" in the vision are reminiscent of the angel of Yahweh which slew the great multitude in the camp of the Assyrians. In both cases it was a divine judgment at work, and consequently all human agents receded into the background of the vision.

Of all the means Ezechiel used to prepare the exiles for Jerusalem's fall, the most effective was undoubtedly the terrible indictment of the city whose crimes the prophet set out in the bright light of God's holiness:

Moreover the word of Yahweh came to me saying, "And you, son of man, will you judge, will you judge the bloody city? Then let her know all her abominations! You shall say: 'Thus says the Lord God; a city that sheds blood in her midst, that her time may come, and that makes idols to defile herself! You have become guilty by the blood you have shed, and defiled by the idols you have made; and you have brought your day near, the appointed time of your years has come. Therefore I have made you a reproach to the nations, and a mocking to all the countries. Those near and far from you will mock you, you infamous one, full of tumult!' " (Ezech. 22:1–5.)

The weight of Israel's past and present sins was a heavy burden, and it would have to be borne and expiated by the present generation. Corporate responsibility for both good and evil was deeply ingrained in Hebrew thought; for centuries the belief in collective guilt was widespread among the Israelites, and they accepted the view that the children would be punished for the sins of the fathers. As noted in the chapter on Jeremiah, there is no warrant for holding that the idea of individual responsibility was nonexistent in the early days of Israel. Still, there was a long-standing emphasis on collective guilt which now appeared to have a disheartening effect upon the exiles. Thinking that they were paying the price for the sins of their ancestors, they cynically repeated a popular proverb which expressed the idea of group solidarity in sin: "the fathers have eaten sour grapes and the children's teeth are set on edge." To this saying Ezechiel felt forced to respond with a long discourse on personal responsibility. He was not innovating in stressing the close relation between personal conduct and reward or punishment, but calling them back to a concept as old as the religion of Yahweh:

The word of Yahweh came to me again: "What do you mean by repeating this proverb concerning the land of Israel, 'The fathers have eaten sour grapes, and the children's teeth are set on edge'? As I live," says the Lord God, "you shall no longer use this proverb in Israel. Behold, all souls are Mine; as the soul of the father so also the soul of the son is Mine; the soul that sins shall die. If a man is just and does what is lawful and right — if he does not eat upon the mountains or lift up his eyes to the idols of the house of Israel, does not defile his neighbor's wife or approach a woman in the time of her impurity, does not oppress anyone, but pays his debt, commits no robbery, gives his bread to the hungry and covers the naked with a garment, does not lend at interest or take any profit, withholds his hand from iniquity, executes true justice between man and man, walks in My statutes, and is careful to observe My ordinances — he is just, he shall surely live," says the Lord God (Ezech. 18:1–9).

The weight of Israel's guilt was not to rest on some impersonal community, much less on the community of the past. It was for the individual to shoulder, and each one could ask his conscience the extent to which he shared this responsibility. Ezechiel was not trying to eradicate the idea of communal responsibility, as though a man enjoyed no solidarity with the rest of his people; he was correcting an abuse of this principle, but his doctrine of individual responsibility, as in the case of Jeremiah, is only one part of the picture. Both viewpoints should be kept in mind if we want a balanced view of the Old Testament teaching on the individual and the corporate group.

When the news came that Jerusalem had fallen and that the nation no longer existed as an independent unit, Ezechiel saw the great danger that many of his countrymen, buoyed up by false hopes which they refused to relinquish, would now fall into apathetic despair. There was every likelihood that many would now give up the faith, and having thrown aside the one thing which made them a distinctive people, they would simply disappear in the great mass of the Babylonian population. Whatever it may mean now, assimilation in those days and under those conditions could only mean giving up the religion of Yahweh and adopting the paganism of their environment. In the first few years of his ministry Ezechiel was compelled to fight against a fatuous optimism; the attack now shifted to another front, and he would now have to bring a word of consolation and encouragement to the exiles.

"SON OF MAN, CAN THESE BONES LIVE?"

The deeply human side of the prophet, otherwise so obscured in the prophecy, comes out in the personal tragedy which climaxed the dramatic actions symbolizing the fall of Jerusalem. Ezechiel was not even permitted the privilege of private sorrow; his deeply felt loss must be turned into a public oracle of doom. The tender love between Ezechiel and his wife is brought out in one brief phrase, "the delight of your eyes" (*mahmadh 'eneka*). Again it was Yahweh Who spoke to him:

> "Son of man, behold, I am taking away from you at a stroke the delight of your eyes; yet you shall neither mourn nor weep nor shall your tears run down. Sigh, but not aloud; cease mourning for the dead. Bind on your turban, and put your shoes upon your feet; do not cover your lips, nor eat the bread of mourners."
> So I spoke to the people in the morning, and in the evening my wife died. And on the next morning I did as I was commanded (Ezech. 24:16–18).

Shortly after this sorrowful episode in Ezechiel's life, a fugitive from Jerusalem brought the news that the city had fallen. It was January 5, 585 B.C., and it marked the end of the period in which Ezechiel, acting under the command of God, could speak of nothing but the impending doom of Jerusalem:

> In the twelfth year of our exile, in the tenth month, on the fifth of the month, the fugitive from Jerusalem came to me saying: "Jerusalem has fallen." Now the hand of Yahweh had been upon me in the evening before the fugitive came, and He had opened my mouth by the time he came to me in the morning, so that I was no longer dumb (Ezech. 33:21–22).

Now it was time to awaken hopes of restoration among the disheartened exiles whose numbers were increasing daily as Judean captives straggled into Babylon. Jeremiah had refused to despair of the future even though Jerusalem lay in ruins; similarly, Ezechiel, once the prophet of inevitable woe, was now to be the consoler of his people in captivity. To him, more than to any other man among the exiles, belongs the credit for preventing the wholesale defection of his countrymen to the alluring paganism which surrounded them. The tone of the prophetic oracles changed, and there followed a series of prophecies concerning the restoration of Israel.

Yahweh Himself would now lead His people since their appointed shepherds had sought their own interest at the expense of Israel. Yahweh would make these hirelings answer for the sheep entrusted to them and He would intervene to rescue His people. One of the strongest condemnations in the Old Testament is found in Ezechiel's pronouncement of judgment against the faithless leaders of the people:

"Son of man, prophesy against the shepherds of Israel, prophesy, and say to them, even to the shepherds. Thus says the Lord God: Woe to the shepherds of Israel who have fed yourselves! Should not shepherds feed the sheep? You eat the fat, you clothe yourselves with the wool, you slaughter the fatlings: but the sheep you do not feed. The weak you have not strengthened, nor have you healed the sick; the crippled you have not bound up, the strayed you have not brought back; you have not sought the lost, but with violence and harshness you have ruled them. So they were scattered, because there was no shepherd; and they became food for all the beasts of the field" (Ezech. 34:2–5).

The vision of the prophet was then projected into the future where he discerned a new David, a King who would be faithful to the royal ideal as Yahweh had conceived it. Historically speaking, the dynasty had come to an end with the last king of Judah, but there was still the ancient promise of Yahweh that David's dynasty would last forever. The vision, then, was of the Messianic Era and of that King who would perpetuate the dynasty of David and establish the peaceful reign of God over the whole world. In Christ, the Son of David, would this hope be realized:

"And I will set up one shepherd over them, My servant David, and he shall feed them; he shall feed them and be their shepherd. But I, Yahweh, will be their God, and My servant David shall be prince among them; I, Yahweh, have spoken" (Ezech. 34:23–24).

In 1933 the American Mission of Yale University discovered and then excavated the now famous third-century Synagogue of Dura-Europos on the Euphrates. The reconstructed Synagogue is now one of the chief attractions in the National Museum of Damascus, where it has been fully restored according to its primitive appearance. Walls and ceilings are covered with polychrome paintings which depict scenes from the Old Testament. Among the most impressive painted panels is a scene from the book of Ezechiel based on the dramatic vision of the Valley of Dry Bones. To a dispirited nation, uncertain of its future, this magnificent vision responded with a promise of national restoration. To be sure, it was not the Old Israel walking in the old ways of disobedience which would come to life through the work of the spirit, but a new creation, an Israel resurrected by the grace of God and vivified by His spirit. We can only guess as to the precise location of the valley, but one attractive suggestion places it at the spot where Ezechiel received his call to prophesy. In that vision Ezechiel had received a revelation of Jerusalem's fate at the hands of the Babylonians; now he would learn that God's last word was not destruction but resurrection from the death of exile:

The hand of Yahweh was upon me, and He brought me out by the Spirit of Yahweh, and set me down in the midst of the valley, and it was full of bones. And He led me round among them; and behold, there were very many upon the plain; and lo, they were very dry. And He said to me, "Son of man, can these bones live?" And I said, "O Lord God, You know."

Then He said to me, "Prophesy to these bones, and say to them, 'O dry bones, hear the word of Yahweh . . .'" So I prophesied as I was commanded; and as I prophesied, there was a noise, and behold, a rattling; and the bones came together, bone to its bone. And I looked and lo, there were sinews on them, and the flesh had come upon them, and skin had covered them; but there was no breath in them. Then He said to me, "Prophesy to the Spirit, prophesy, son of man, and say to the Spirit: 'Thus says the Lord God: come from the four winds, O Spirit, and breathe upon these slain, that they may live.'" So I prophesied as He commanded me, and the Spirit came upon them, and they lived, and stood upon their feet, an exceedingly great host (Ezech. 37:1–10).

AND THE EARTH SHONE WITH HIS GLORY

The last nine chapters of the book describe in minute detail the restored Temple, with its ritual, and the distribution of the land according to the twelve tribes. The minute architectural description of the Temple and the concern for even the smallest details of liturgical service have made this a difficult section for all but the most persevering reader. In addition, it is now generally agreed that these chapters have undergone editorial revision and that secondary material has been added, though it would be hypercritical to deny the substance of these chapters to Ezechiel. If we are unable to arouse much sympathy for this form of literature, with its meticulous attention to measurements, decorative features of the Temple, and liturgical rubrics, we can nevertheless attempt to grasp the chief ideas which underlie the great vision of the restored, theocratic community.

It was in the year 572 B.C. that Yahweh, for a second time, brought His prophet in vision to Jerusalem. On the first occasion, nineteen years earlier, Ezechiel had been given a terrifying vision of the abominations which went on in the Temple, the slaying of the wicked by divine executioners, and the departure of God's glory from the city:

> Then the cherubim lifted up their wings, and the wheels were beside them; and the glory of God was over them. And the glory of Yahweh went up from the midst of the city, and stood upon the mountain which is on the east side of the city (Ezech. 11:22–23).

But this was not the end. The Temple of Solomon no longer existed and the country was devastated. Yet in this national catastrophe Ezechiel was granted a larger vision, full of hope, of an Israel faithful to its vocation as a holy people serving the all-holy God. Having been transported in vision to Jerusalem, the prophet was taken on a tour of the New Temple, with every feature so carefully described that it is possible to sketch the plan of Ezechiel's Temple. The journey completed, the prophet was brought to the East Gate,[1] where he saw God

---

[1] Professor C. G. Howie contributed a very interesting study of this East Gate in the *Bulletin of the American Schools of Oriental Research*, No. 117 (Feb. 1950), pp. 13–19. On the basis of a conservatively reconstructed text

returning to the city in the same majestic splendor with which
He had left:

> Afterward He brought me to the gate, the gate which faced
> the east. And behold, the glory of the God of Israel came from
> the east; and His voice was like the sound of many waters; and the
> earth shone with His glory. And the vision I saw was like the
> vision which I had seen when He came to destroy the city, and
> like the vision which I had seen by the Kabar canal; and I fell
> upon my face.
> As the glory of Yahweh entered the Temple by the gate facing
> the east, the Spirit lifted me up, and brought me into the inner
> court; and behold, the glory of Yahweh filled the Temple (Ezech.
> 43:1-5).

Ezechiel is the prophet of God's glory. Not that he is alone in
this, for Isaiah, too, was overwhelmed by the majesty of the
divine presence. But Ezechiel has elaborated his theme in a
series of unforgettable images, such as we have seen. When the
prophet uses the phrase "the glory of God," he has in mind
the living and sustaining presence of God among His people.
Before this glory Ezechiel could only bow in reverence and
acknowledge his own human weakness, summed up in his
use of the expression "son of man." As we shall see, this
phrase "son of man" can, under certain circumstances, have
a transcendent meaning. In the book of Ezechiel, however, it
contrasts with the "glory of God," that majestic presence which
was Israel's pledge that God was with them even though all
the external signs of independence and national greatness had
passed away.

Did Ezechiel expect his plans for the restored community
to be carried out to the last detail by the returning exiles? It
is difficult to answer such a question because it is next to im-

---

along with comparative material from archaeology, he was able to draw a plan
of the East Gate as envisioned by Ezechiel. It bears a striking resemblance
to the type of gate constructed by Solomon, one which was no longer built
after the early eighth century B.C. Professor Howie concluded that Ezechiel
must have known quite thoroughly the Solomonic Gate of the First Temple and
that his vision of the East Gate reflects that knowledge. Such knowledge was
obviously gained by the prophet during his years in Jerusalem before he was
brought away in the first deportation, 597 B.C.

possible to separate the visionary from the realistic planner who sought to apply the Torah to new religious conditions. At least we can say that this part of Ezechiel's prophecy had a great influence in determining the direction of Jewish religious life after the return from Babylon. With good reason, then, he has been called the "Father of Judaism," not in the pejorative sense of being a narrow legalist in love with ritual for its own sake, but in laying down the general lines along which Ezra and others were to proceed in building up a holy community intent upon the observance of the Law. Compared with the spacious vision of Ezechiel, the actual fulfillment was indeed disappointing. But if his hopes were only partially realized in the postexilic community there is no doubt that many of his fundamental themes, the need of repentance, the faithful shepherd, the holiness of God, and the outpouring of His Spirit by a sheer act of grace which could revivify a nation, reached out to that new presence of God among His people when the Word became Flesh. His vision of the Holy City provided the background for that opening of the heavens in which St. John caught a glimpse of the heavenly Jerusalem, the holy community of God's elect:

> And I saw a new heaven and a new earth. For the first heaven and the first earth had passed away, and the sea was no more. And I saw the holy city, New Jerusalem, coming down out of heaven from God, made ready as a bride adorned for her husband (Apoc. 21:1–3).

SECOND ISAIAH

DURING the last decade of the Babylonian Exile, between 547 and 538 B.C., an anonymous prophet delivered his message to fellow exiles in the captivity. Little or nothing is known of the personal life of the author who has come to be known as Second or Deutero-Isaiah and whose oracles have been attached to the work of Isaiah of Jerusalem who lived two centuries before him. The majority of scholars attribute chapters 40–55 to Second Isaiah, assigning chapters 56–66 to another prophet who lived and worked in Palestine shortly after the return from Babylon. This is not the place to discuss at great length the problems of authorship in the latter part of Isaiah. To eliminate controversy we shall include only chapters 40–55 in our treatment of Second Isaiah. Critical scholars are practically unanimous in assigning this section to the nameless prophet who may be called the greatest of Isaiah's disciples and in whose work the principles and faith of the eighth-century prophet were applied, in poetry of unsurpassed beauty and theological depth, to a new and critical situation.

What are some of the reasons for assigning this section to a period between Ezechiel and the two prophets of the restoration, Haggai and Zechariah? They are derived almost entirely from the book itself. The evidence is thus internal, based on such factors as the historical situation which appears to be supposed in these chapters, the style of writing and theological ideas which set these chapters apart. There is unquestionably an affinity in thought between the earlier and later Isaiahs, but this should not close our eyes to the real differences between the two in the factors mentioned above. In Second Isaiah, for example, all historical allusions come from the time just before Cyrus issued his decree allowing the Jews to return to Palestine. There is not a single reference in these chapters to events of the eighth century B.C.; on the contrary, the references to the captivity, the coming of Cyrus, the expectations of the people in Babylon, the ruined city of Jerusalem unmistakably point to the sixth century as the time of composition. It would be strange, indeed, if an eighth-century prophet, whose task was to be God's spokesman to the men of his time, delivered a message which was relevant only to people who lived two hundred years after him.

Second Isaiah's theology of history, with its emphasis on the universal gathering-in of the nations, shows a development over the earlier Isaiah's doctrine of Yahweh as the Lord of history. It may be said that Second Isaiah's distinctive view of God is based on his grasp of God's universal dominion. He is the God of the whole world which He has created and which He governs from one end to the other. Everything was brought into existence at His word, and He is to intervene decisively at the end of days, the eschaton. God is the true Alpha and Omega and all creation manifests His glory. All of these theological ideas might be found, at least inchoatively, in the Isaiah of the eighth century; however, their stage of development in Chapters 40–55 provides evidence for a real distinction between the two prophets as well as for the continuity of thought and ideals which join the two over a span of two centuries. In short, the author of Chapters 40–55 should be clearly distinguished from Isaiah of Jerusalem, without losing sight of the fact that Second Isaiah is a worthy descendant of the pre-exilic prophet, and that he perpetuates the tradition associated with the name of Isaiah.

The historical background of Chapters 40–55 is the spectacular career of Cyrus the Great, once a vassal king of the Medes, but eventually the creator of an Empire extending from

Egypt to India. By 550 B.C. Cyrus had successfully challenged the rule of the Medes in Western Asia by overthrowing their king, Astyages. This was followed by a brilliant campaign against the fabulous king of Lydia, Croesus, ending with the destruction of his capital, Sardis, in 546 B.C. The climax of the Persian's career came in the overthrow of Babylon in 539 B.C., marking the end of the Semitic empires in the Near East. The oracles of Second Isaiah probably date from the rise of Persian hegemony, but before Babylon actually fell, without a fight, to the new master of the world, Cyrus. The impending overthrow of Babylonian rule stirred up hopes among people long subject to their regime, including the Jewish captives who had been transported to Babylon some fifty years before. Until the coming of Cyrus, with its promise of restoration, the Judeans had little to hope for, especially when they reflected on conditions back in Palestine and on their own situation in Babylon, where they were just another minority among a large pagan population. Babylonian rule was not as harsh and tyrannical as that of Assyria, but there are indications in the prophecies of Second Isaiah (47:6; 42:22 ff.) that the defenseless captives were often treated with contempt and hostility. The morale of the exiles was very low; the fear and insecurity of life in a strange and unfriendly land had caused some to question the providence of God Who might have done wonderful things for their ancestors but Who now seemed to forget His own people. "My way is hidden from the Lord, and my right is disregarded by my God" was a complaint often heard among the captives.

When the exiles looked westward to what was once the Kingdom of Judah, they found little which could lift them from their despondency. The territory lay in ruins, most of its towns destroyed by the armies of Nebuchadnezzar, and the Holy City, its Temple burned to the ground, had no protecting walls to keep out marauders. Second Isaiah compared Sion to a widow who has lost her children and to a mother cursed with sterility:

> She has no one to guide her
>   of all the sons she has borne.
> She has no one to grasp her by the hand
>   of all the sons she had raised!
> Your misfortunes are double;
>   who will sympathize with you?
> Desolation and destruction, famine and sword!
>   Who will comfort you?
> Your sons lie helpless
>   at every street corner
>   like antelopes in a net.
> They are filled with the wrath of Yahweh,
>   the rebuke of your God.
>
> (Isa. 51:18–20)

To a people so badly confused and despondent Second Isaiah brought his revealed message of hope, rich with insight into the nature of God and His relation to the world as well as to the city where He chose to place His name. The great poet-theologian does not speak as the quiet comforter; he is rather the herald who has been admitted to the divine council and is now announcing the event which is to mark a turning point in history. The herald's personality recedes into the background; only the good news of God's imminent intervention is important. The first strophe of his work announces the end of Judah's travail:

> "Comfort, give comfort to My people,"
>   says your God.
> "Speak tenderly to Jerusalem, and proclaim to her
>   that her time of service is at an end,
>   her guilt is expiated.
> Indeed, she has received from the hand of Yahweh
>   double for all her sins.
>
> "A voice cries aloud:
> In the wilderness prepare the way of Yahweh!
> Make straight in the desert a highway for our God!
> Every valley shall be filled,
>   every mountain and hill shall be made low;
> the rugged land shall be made a plain,
>   the rough country a broad valley.

Then the glory of Yahweh shall be revealed,
>   and all flesh shall see His face;
>   for the mouth of Yahweh has spoken."
>
> (Isa. 40:1-5)

This is the overture of the message, announcing in vigorous
and imaginative language the prophetic theme, and describing
the great royal highway prepared for the triumphant coming of
the King. There may be an allusion here to the famous Procession Street of Babylon, where the images of the gods were
paraded at great festivals; but the predominant image is the
route from Egypt to Palestine which the Israelites took at the
time of the Exodus. The return from captivity as a new Exodus
is a constantly recurring image in the writings of Second Isaiah,
for Yahweh's great redemptive act of deliverance from bondage
in Egypt was about to be repeated in the new Exodus from
Babylon. St. Paul further enriched this image when he compared our deliverance from sin to a new Exodus from slavery.
The opening lines of Second Isaiah sing out that Israel's time
of affliction is over and deliverance is at hand. The dejected
exiles should lift up their heads, for God was about to take
them by the hand and lead them back to the Holy Land which
He had once given them as an inheritance. Despair had driven
many of the exiles down the dead-end road of idolatry; the
prophet would announce that God had not abandoned them;
He was approaching them and again summoning them to their
great mission. They had sinned and their sin would not go
unrebuked by the prophet, but uppermost in his thought was
the revelation that Yahweh had forgiven their rebellion and
was now about to "speak to Jerusalem's heart," in the beautiful
Hebrew phrase which disclosed the tender love of God for
His people.

TO WHOM CAN YOU LIKEN GOD?

The theology of Second Isaiah is centered on God as Creator
and Redeemer. Redemption is the culminating act of God just
as creation is His initial work; the world which He has created

will eventually be transformed when the new age of salvation dawns. Speaking in the imagery of the ancient Orient, he pictures the moment when the heathen nations shall be converted and confess that there is only one God, and He is Israel's Savior:

> Thus says Yahweh:
> "The wealth of Egypt, the gain of Ethiopia,
> and the Sabeans, tall of stature,
> Shall come over to you and belong to you;
>   they shall follow you, coming in chains.
> They shall fall prostrate before you,
>   uttering their prayer:
> 'God is with you alone, and nowhere else;
>   the gods are nought.
> Truly You are a hidden God
> O God of Israel, the savior!'"
>
> (Isa. 45:14–15)

The oracles of Second Isaiah move between the two poles of the beginning and the end, the two extreme moments of time. In the beginning was creation, at the end would be redemption; both are the work of God, and consequently all history is permeated with the divine purpose. If the captive Jew in Babylon felt the oppressive weight of a hostile world all about him, here was a prophet to announce that the whole universe was created and governed by the God of Israel. Many might have been tempted to forsake Yahweh because they thought that He was powerless before the might of Babylon; but Second Isaiah laughed to scorn the dumb idols carried about in the religious processions.

The prophet was fond of contrasting the majesty and incomparableness of God with the helplessness of idols which cluttered the temples of Babylon. It is God, and no idol, Who has proved Himself to be the Lord of history, initiating and shaping future events, determining their outcome and revealing all to His servants, the prophets. What god could have predicted the events of these days, in which the People of God were to be liberated? It was not the prognosticators of Babylon who fore-saw the rise of Cyrus; but Yahweh knew because Cyrus was His anointed, an instrument of the divine purpose in directing history's course. Let the gods point out past predictions of theirs which were verified in the course of time! Second Isaiah's biting satire on the idols and their makers was in perfect keeping with his teaching on the transcendence of Yahweh. It was done, however, with a derision and scorn which suggest that the author was set on laughing his countrymen out of their senseless flirtation with idolatry. Detail after detail heightened the ridicule of a religion which compelled men to fall down before a block of wood:

> All idol makers amount to nothing and their precious works are of no avail. Their witnesses neither see nor know — to their shame — and they are more deaf than men are. . . . The black-smith fashions an image, works it over the coals, hammers it into shape, and forges it with his strong arm. But he becomes hungry and weak, drinks no water and becomes exhausted. The carpenter stretches a line and marks with a pencil the form of an idol. He shapes it with a plane and measures it off with a compass, making it into the figure of a man, to occupy a shrine. He cuts down cedars, takes a holm or an oak, and lays hold of other trees of the forest; he plants a cedar and the rain makes it grow. It becomes fuel for man, and with a part of the wood he warms himself, or makes a fire for baking bread; but with another part he makes a god which he adores, an idol which he worships. . . . Of what remains he makes a god, his idol, and prostrate before it in worship he begs, "Rescue me, for you are my god!"
>
> The idols have neither knowledge nor reason; he coated their eyes so that they cannot see, and their hearts so that they cannot understand. . . . He is chasing ashes; he will be consumed by the flames, yet he does not save himself, nor say, "Is not this thing in my right hand a fraud?" (Isa. 44: 9–20.)

Babylon had trusted in its gods to bring it to the summit of world power. Now that the Empire was about to collapse ignominiously before Cyrus, the gods, far from saving the city, were loaded onto the backs of straining beasts or carted off in headlong flight by their panic-stricken worshipers. This is one of Second Isaiah's last and most derisive satires on the impotence of Babylon's gods:

> Bel bows down, Nebo stoops,
>> their idols ride upon beasts and cattle;
> they must be borne up on shoulders,
>> carried as a burden by the weary.
> They stoop and bow down together;
>> unable to save those who bear them,
>> they too go into captivity!
>
>> (Isa. 46:1–2)

The polemic against idols is in the great tradition of the earlier prophets whose intransigence rests upon the revelation at Sinai. There Israel had learned of a God Who would not tolerate other gods. Epithets similar to those in Second Isaiah can be found in Amos, Isaiah, Jeremiah, and others who deride the gods as frauds, vanities, no-gods, and even as pellets of dung. Second Isaiah differs from his predecessors only in degree.

On the more positive side, we find in Second Isaiah some of the most memorable passages on God as Creator. In words reminiscent of Job, the prophet addresses to his hearers a series of questions which bring out the incomparable greatness of Israel's God as Creator of the world:

> Who has measured in his hand the waters of the sea,
>> and marked off the heavens with a span?
> Who has measured out the dust of the earth,
>> weighed the mountains in scales
>> and the hills in a balance?
> Who has directed the spirit of Yahweh,
>> or has instructed Him as a counsellor?
> Whom did He consult to gain knowledge,
>> who taught Him the path of judgment,
>> or showed Him the way of understanding?
> Behold, the nations are like a drop in the bucket,
>> as dust on the scales are they reckoned;
>> the isles weigh no more than powder.
> Lebanon would not suffice for fuel,
>> nor its animals for a holocaust.

Before Him all the nations are as nothing,
    as emptiness and void He accounts them.
To Whom can you liken God?
    With what likeness can you compare Him?
An idol, cast by the craftsman,
    which the smith plates with gold,
    and forges silver chains for it?

                     (Isa. 40:12–19)

The word of God, abiding and steadfast, is contrasted with the frailty and impermanence of man whose works are as perishable as the grass of a summer season. No human power can stand in the way of God's word; those who oppose Him will be blasted by the searing wind of divine judgment:

A voice says, "Cry out!"
    I answered, "What shall I cry out?"
"All flesh is grass,
    and all its glory like the flower of the field.
The grass withers, the flower wilts,
    when the breath of Yahweh blows upon it. . . .
The grass withers and the flower wilts,
    but the word of our God stands forever."

                     (Isa. 40:6–8)

This was the God to Whom they were called to bear witness; this was Israel's mission, the corollary of her election. Israel's history was the visible manifestation of Yahweh's activity and no human force, much less idols of stone and wood, could defeat His purpose. The challenge of Sinai, to serve God alone, is recalled by Second Isaiah:

"You are My witnesses," says Yahweh,
    "My servants whom I have chosen
to know and believe in Me
    and understand that I am He.
Before Me no god was formed,
    and after Me there shall be none.
It is I, I Yahweh;
    there is no savior but Me.
It is I who foretold, I who saved;

I made it known, not any strange god among you;
you are My witnesses," says Yahweh.
"I am God, yes, from eternity I am He;
there is none who can deliver from My hand;
I work and who can undo it?"

(Isa. 53:10–43)

RETURN TO ME, FOR I HAVE REDEEMED YOU

We have noted that the imagery of the Exodus pervades the poetry of Second Isaiah. It was in the period of the Exodus that Israel had become the peculiar possession of God, His chosen people. This election of Yahweh, wholly unmerited, gave eloquence to the poet's conviction that the same God Who had sent them into Exile was now about to liberate them from their captivity. Israel was to be restored to her inheritance now that her guilt had been expiated during the years of Exile. Now was the time to speak to the heart of the people, to show them God as the Redeemer of His people. Israel should put aside her fears, for Yahweh was to make her a mighty instrument of judgment:

"Fear not, O worm Jacob,
    O maggot Israel;
I will help you," says Yahweh;
    "your redeemer is the Holy One of Israel.
I will make you a threshing sledge,
    sharp, new, and double-edged,
to thresh the mountains and crush them,
    to make hills like chaff.
When you winnow them, the wind shall carry them off
    and the storm shall scatter them.
But you shall rejoice in Yahweh,
    and glory in the Holy One of Israel."

(Isa. 41:14–16)

Yahweh's choice of Israel was irrevocable; though scattered to the ends of the earth they were the offspring of Abraham, meant to be a light to the nations instead of a scandal to them. Since they had been created and fashioned by God, their history was in His hands and determined by His gracious purposes:

"But now," thus says Yahweh
> Who created you, O Jacob, and formed you, O Israel:
"Fear not, for I have redeemed you;
I have called you by name: you are Mine.
When you pass through the water, I will be with you;
> in the rivers you shall not drown.
When you walk through fire, you shall not be burned;
> the flames shall not consume you.
For I am Yahweh, your God,
> the Holy One of Israel, your savior."

> > > > > > > (Isa. 43:1–3)

The most tangible proof of the national restoration, viewed here as a covenant-renewal, was the imminent victory of Cyrus and the return to Palestine. Wrath once directed against Israel because of her infidelities was now turned against her enemies. The jarring imagery of the passage, immediately following a gentle reference to the children of Sion, recalls the passionate outbursts of imprecation in some of the psalms:

> Thus says Yahweh:
> "Can booty be taken from a warrior?
> > or captives be rescued from a tyrant?
> Yes, captives can be taken from a warrior,
> > and booty be rescued from a tyrant.
> Those who oppose you I will oppose,
> > and your sons I will save.
> I will make your oppressors eat their own flesh
> > and they shall be drunk with their own blood
> > as with the juice of the grape.
> All men shall know
> > that I, Yahweh, am your savior,
> > your redeemer, the Mighty One of Jacob."

> > > > > > (Isa. 49:24–26)

In the same chapter the prospect of return from Exile suggested the figure of Sion, the bereaved mother mourning her lost children, about to be adorned with her returning children as a bride is adorned with her jewels. Sion's complaint was answered by the oath of Yahweh that the bridal gown would replace the widow's garments of mourning. The affectionate love of God for

His people found here an expression which is one of the high points of the Old Testament. Hosea had compared the love of Yahweh to that of bride and groom; here it was shown to be deeper and more lasting than the most tender of human loves, that of a mother for the infant at her breast:

> "But Sion said, 'Yahweh has forsaken me;
> my Lord has forgotten me.'
> Can a mother forget her infant,
> show no tenderness to the child of her womb?
> Even should she forget,
> yet I will never forget you.
> Behold, I have drawn you upon the palms of My hands,
>   your walls are ever before Me.
> Your rebuilders make haste,
>   as those who tore you down and laid you waste
>   go forth from you.
> Lift up your eyes and see,
>   they are all gathering and coming to you.
> As I live," says Yahweh,
>   "you shall be arrayed with them all as with adornments,
>   like a bride you shall fasten them on you."
>
> (Isa. 49:14–18)

Return of the exiles was near at hand, a thought which sets the tone of exuberant joy in succeeding oracles. Sion had stumbled and reeled after drinking the cup of wrath which Yahweh had held to her lips. The humiliating experience of exile had left her prostrate, like a woman neglected by the wayside with no sons to help her. Now the cup of reeling was to be given to her enemies: Yahweh, Who made Israel taste the bitter cup of affliction, would now visit retribution on her tormentors. The sudden reversal of Sion's fortune is dramatized in a hymn of redemption announcing that the days of enslavement and abjection are finished. The repetition of imperatives adds to the elation of the song which contrasts sharply with the "taunt-song" against Babylon in Chapter 47:

> Awake, awake!
> Put on your strength, O Sion!

Put on your glorious garments,
  O Jerusalem, holy city!
For no longer shall the uncircumcised
  or the unclean enter you.
Shake off the dust!
Ascend the throne, O Jerusalem!
Loose the bonds from your neck,
  O captive daughter Sion!
For thus says Yahweh:
"You were sold for nothing,
  and without money you shall be redeemed."
(Isa. 52:1–3)

From Second Isaiah's magnificent descriptions of Yahweh as Creator and Redeemer, we turn to that contribution for which he is best remembered and which has had such a profound influence on the theology of the New Testament. This is the theme which gave to the earliest Christian preachers the key to understanding the redemptive death and resurrection of Christ. The Saviour Himself saw and interpreted His own mission in terms of the Suffering Servant.

SEE, MY SERVANT SHALL PROSPER

The first mention of Israel as the Servant of God occurs in the dramatic trial scene built around the stirring events of those days. To the court of law over which God presides the nations are summoned; the crises of contemporary history are reviewed and the impotence of the gods exposed. The feverish activity of craftsman and goldsmith, turning out idols in their shops, is useless in the face of the Persian advance. The end of the Semitic Empires and their idols is at hand. At this cross-road of history the Lord turns to Israel, His Servant, and announces her inevitable victory over her enemies of long standing. The image of the Servant comes up again in a series of four poems embedded in the oracles of Second Isaiah and most probably composed by him.[1]

---

[1] The Servant Songs may be found in the following passages: 42:1–7; 49:1–6; 50:4–9; 52:13–53:12. The fourth Song is by far the most important since it speaks of the expiatory death of the Servant and His glory.

An enormous amount of scholarship has been expended on the task of identifying the enigmatic figure of the Servant of Yahweh. Is he the nation of Israel? And if this is true, is the Servant the historical Israel or some idealized Israel of the future? Or is he some individual roughly contemporaneous with the prophet? Perhaps the Servant is an individual person of the future who shall fulfill the destiny of Israel. Finally, is it possible to combine the collective and individual interpretations of the Servant figure? It would be out of place to review all the solutions offered during the past few hundred years.[2] Instead, let us see how the author develops the portrait of the Servant, at one moment highlighting the collective traits, at another the individual. There is an unmistakable fluidity in the prophet's description of the Servant, a shifting from the individual to the community or, it might be more accurate to say, combining the collective and individual traits in one and the same figure. Thus the Servant of Yahweh stands for both the nation Israel and for Him Who would later fulfill, in the most perfect way, her mission to the world. The Servant would do this by dying for the world and His death would be expiatory as was no animal sacrifice offered on Israel's altars; the fourth Servant Song reached across the centuries and found its fulfillment on Calvary.

The first Song, in part, describes the mission of the Servant, and in terms which strongly suggest that the nation, Israel, is in the forefront of the author's mind. In the preceding chapter, Israel had already been addressed as "My Servant" so that we are prepared for the designation of Israel, either the entire nation or only a remnant, under that figure of speech. The missionary task of God's chosen people is proclaimed:

> Behold, My Servant, whom I uphold,
>   My chosen one in whom I delight,
>   upon whom I have put My spirit;

---

[2] The best summary of these questions will be found in the historical and critical study of C. R. North, *The Suffering Servant in Deutero-Isaiah* (London: Oxford University Press, 1948). A second edition appeared in 1956.

> he shall bring forth justice to the nations,
> he will not cry out nor shout,
> nor make his voice heard in the street.
> A bruised reed he shall not break,
> and a flickering wick he shall not quench,
> until he establishes justice on the earth;
> and the coastlands wait for his teaching.
>
> (Isa. 42:1–4)

In other parts of Second Isaiah the community of Israel is described as Yahweh's Servant, chosen and sustained by God. Thus there is good precedent for holding that the first Servant Song has Israel in view. On the other hand, it is evident that the description of the Servant would be very suitable to an individual. The same can be said of the second and third Songs, in which collective and individual elements can be discerned. In the climactic fourth Song it is difficult to see how anything but a definite individual, to appear in the future, can be in the mind of the prophet.

To return for a moment to the first three Songs, how is it possible for a writer to oscillate between community and individual as the subject of a given piece of literature? To understand this fluidity we should keep in mind a characteristic of Semitic writing which goes by the name of "corporate personality." Over twenty years ago the late Professor H. Wheeler Robinson described in considerable detail this trait of Semitic writing, and then used it as a key to understanding many passages in the Old Testament, including the Servant Songs. He observed that the entire group or nation, including past, present, and future members of the group, might be pictured as an individual by means of one of those members taken as representative of the group. It is a mistake, then, to place too sharp an antithesis between the collective and individualistic elements of a passage, as though it had to be one or the other. In this Semitic way of thinking both could coexist in the same piece of writing, so that the figure of the Servant in the Songs could be both individual and the community at one and the same time.

With the fourth Song we reach one of the summits of Old Testament thought, the portrayal of suffering which expiates sin, along with the triumph of victory achieved through suffering. Christian tradition has seen in this Song a picture of the passion, death, and resurrection of Jesus, unfolded in prophetic vision centuries before they were to be accomplished:

> Behold, My Servant shall prosper,
> he shall be greatly exalted, lifted up
>   and set on high.
> As many were appalled at (him) . . .
> I have so altered his aspect from the rest of men,
> his form from that of the sons of men.
> So shall he startle many nations,
> kings shall stand aghast at him.
> For things untold shall they have seen,
> and things unheard shall they have understood.
> Who has believed our report?
> To whom has the arm of Yahweh been revealed?
> As a young plant he grew up before Him,
> like a root out of thirsty soil.
> He had neither form nor comeliness
> that we should look upon him,
> nor beauty that we should delight in him.
> He was despised and forsaken of men,
> a man of pains and acquainted with wounds,
> as one from whom men hide their faces,
> he was despised and we esteemed him not.
> Truly he bore our wounds,
> our pains he made his burden,
> and we esteemed him as one smitten,
> struck down by God and afflicted.
> Yet he was wounded for our sins,
> crushed by our iniquities.
> The chastisement of our peace was upon him,
> and by his stripes we were healed.
> All of us had gone astray like sheep,
> each had followed his own way,
> but Yahweh fastened upon him the iniquity of us all.
> Though oppressed he submitted
> and opened not his mouth,
> like a lamb led to the slaughter,

> like a sheep dumb before his shearers,
> for he opened not his mouth.
> By a coerced sentence he was taken away,
> and who concerned himself with his lot?
> For he was cut off from the land of the living,
> smitten (to death) by the sin of My people.
> With the wicked they buried him,
> his tomb was with the corrupt,
> though violence he had not committed,
> nor was deceit on his lips.
> But Yahweh was pleased to crush him with suffering;
> truly he offered his life as a guilt-offering.
> He shall see a posterity, he shall enjoy length of days,
> the good pleasure of Yahweh shall prosper at his hand.
> After life's sorrow he shall see light and be satisfied.
> By his knowledge shall My servant justify many,
> and their sins he shall bear.
> Therefore I shall apportion him many,
> the multitudes shall he receive as booty.
> Because he poured out his soul in death
> and with sinners was he numbered;
> since he bore the sin of many, and for sinners
> he made entreaty.

                                    (Isa. 52:13–53:12)

We may say at once that neither the historical community of
Israel nor any individual before or after Christ answers to this
description of the humble Servant offering his life for the
redemption of mankind. On this point the majority of commentators will agree. Can we see at work here the same concept of corporate personality as we noted in the first three
Songs? With Professor Rowley and others we may hold as more
probable that this picture of sacrifice willingly accepted as atonement for sin contains a certain oscillation between the community, Israel, and Him Who is the perfect representative of
that community and Who is destined to fulfill the mission of
Israel.[3] The development in the fourth Song is not a linear one,

---

[3] The problems of interpretation connected with the Servant Songs have
been treated with great thoroughness and objectivity in the first two chapters of
H. H. Rowley, *The Servant of the Lord* (London: Lutterworth Press, 1952).

from community to individual, but rather there is a compenetration of the two in the picture of the Servant. He is, in a sense, both Israel and Christ. The strong sense of solidarity, with its emphasis on man as a member of a community, permits the Hebrew prophet to expand and contract the idea of the Servant. At one moment it may stand for the covenanted nation of Israel; again, it may stand for the faithful remnant, a purified Israel which inherits the mission of the nation; finally, and most clearly in the fourth Song, the Servant stands for the Redeemer of the future Who accomplishes the mission of Israel through His own innocent and vicarious suffering.

This fluid concept of the Servant of Yahweh prepares the way for the Pauline idea of the Church as the Body of Christ. The New Israel is a community with a mission, the salvation of the world, but this can be accomplished only by union with Him Whose relation to that community is so vital and intimate that Paul can describe it only in terms of the relation which exists between the head and the body. The Church is the Body of which Christ is the Head, and when the New Testament tells us that we must make up what is lacking in the sufferings of Christ it reminds us that the New Israel has been called to share in the world-mission of the Suffering Servant, our representative Who has died on a Cross for the sins of the world. We are members of Christ, on Whom was laid the sins of us all, but we will be worthy of this awesome dignity only when we can say with Paul: "With Christ I am nailed to the cross. It is now no longer I that live, but Christ lives in me. And the life that I now live in the flesh, I live in the faith of the Son of God, Who loved me and gave Himself up for me" (Gal. 2:20).

NEHEMIAH

IN THE autumn of 539 B.C. Babylon fell without even a battle, marking the end of the Neo-Babylonian Kingdom. Not for a thousand years would Semites again hold sway over the Near East. Persians, Greeks, and Romans, in that order, would rule from the Nile to the Euphrates, while the great Semitic Empires became memories of a dimly remembered past. The last ruler of Babylon was Nabonidus (555–539 B.C.) who appears to have taken a much greater interest in cultic and archaeological matters than in administering the Empire. In his ambition to reinstate ancient religious practices he incurred the enmity of the powerful priesthood of Marduk, and it was with little or no regret that the Babylonian priests saw his kingdom collapse before the assault of the Persian. In addition to his antiquarian interest, Nabonidus spent a good part of his reign at Tema, an oasis in the desert of Arabia, leaving royal affairs in the hands of his crown prince, Bel-shar-uṣur, whom we meet in the book of Daniel as Belshazzar, presiding over the fatal banquet at which the doom of Babylon was pronounced.

As the Assyrians and Babylonians departed from the stage of history there came to the fore one of the most extraordinary leaders of the ancient world. Cyrus the Great, once a vassal of the king of the Medes, managed to unite his own people and, in 550 B.C., subdued the last of the Median kings and established a kind of dual monarchy of Media and Persia over which he was sole ruler. We have already mentioned his capture of Croesus, the king of Lydia, whose formidable capital city, Sardis, is now being excavated under the auspices of the American Schools of Oriental Research and sponsored by the Bollingen Foundation, Harvard and Cornell Universities. With Media and Lydia conquered Cyrus felt that the time had come to put an end, once and for all, to Babylonian power. Having defeated the Babylonian army in the field, a detachment of the Persian forces was able to enter the city of Babylon without a struggle, and a few days later Cyrus took formal possession of the capital which had once ruled the ancient Near East.

With the entrance of Cyrus into Babylon the hopes of the Judean captives welled up once again, and Second Isaiah did not hesitate to interpret the victory of Cyrus in terms of the divine plan. It would have surprised the Persian leader to hear that his great feats were performed for the sake of some despised Jewish exiles who were dreaming of return to Palestine. But the sacred writer knew that Cyrus was Yahweh's instrument and that, all unknowingly, he was fulfilling the divine purpose.

> Thus says Yahweh to His anointed, Cyrus,
>   whose right hand I grasp,
> subduing nations before him,
> and disarming kings,
> opening doors before him
> and leaving the gates unbarred.
> "I will go before you
> and level the mountains.
> Bronze doors I will shatter,
> and iron bars I will snap.
> I will give you treasure out of the darkness,
> and riches that have been hidden away,
> that you may know that I am Yahweh,
> the God of Israel, who calls you by name.
> For the sake of Jacob, My servant,
> of Israel, My chosen one,
> I have called you by name.
> I have given you a title, though you knew Me not.
> I am Yahweh and there is no other,
> there is no God besides Me.
> It is I Who arm you, though you know Me not,
>   so that toward the rising of the sun,
> and toward its setting
> men may know that there is none besides Me."

(Isa. 45:1–6)

The book of Ezra opens with the proclamation of Cyrus, issued during his first year as the king of Babylon, 538 B.C. In keeping with the Persian policy of religious toleration, the Decree of Cyrus, which Ezra has preserved for us in both Hebrew and Aramaic versions, gave the Jewish captives permission to return to Palestine and promised assistance in rebuilding Jerusalem and its Temple:

> Thus says Cyrus king of Persia: "Yahweh, the God of heaven, has given to me all the kingdoms of the earth, and He has commanded me to build Him a house in Jerusalem, which is in Judah. Whoever is among you of all His people — his God be with him — let him go up to Jerusalem, which is in Judah, and rebuild the house of Yahweh, the God of Israel; He is the God Who is in Jerusalem" (Ezra 1:2–3).

Before the period of archaeological discovery a number of scholars placed little confidence in the historicity of this Edict, preferring to treat it as a forgery of the sacred writer who imitated Persian models in order to give the decree the appearance of authenticity. Granting that the decree does not reproduce the words of Cyrus *verbatim*, there is no reason to question the substantial authenticity of an edict which fits in perfectly with the known religious policy of the Persian king.

It would be a mistake to think that there was an overwhelming response of the exiles in Babylon to the Decree of Cyrus, permitting them to return to the homeland. For one thing, many of the exiles had already adjusted themselves to life in Mesopotamia and had arisen to places of prominence and wealth, as we know from the Murashu family archives and other business documents of the period. The ancient city of Nippur, where a rather large colony of Jews settled, has yielded many documents which show how well the exiles had been integrated into the social and economic life of Babylonia. Such a situation, for which there are modern parallels, helps us to understand why there was no such thing as a mass return of all the exiles to Sion. It took great courage and unusual religious zeal to pull up roots and start the long and arduous journey to

Palestine, now a tiny province in the fifth satrapy of the Persian Empire. The land had not recovered from the devastation wrought by Nebuchadnezzar fifty years before, especially since the best of the citizenry had been forced into exile and hostile neighbors had secured a foothold in territory once controlled by the Davidic monarchy. Edomites, for example, had occupied that part of the southern hill country around Hebron. The leaders of the Persian province of Samaria proved most troublesome, since they laid claim to Jerusalem and its environs and strongly resented the resettling of the land by the exiles returning from Babylon. We shall see in a moment how much Nehemiah suffered from this hostile attitude when he undertook to rebuild the walls of Jerusalem, as late as the second half of the fifth century B.C.

One of the first objectives of the returning Jews, who might be called proto-Zionists, was to rebuild the Temple, completely destroyed by the Babylonian armies in 587 B.C. The vicissitudes of this project may well serve as a gauge of national morale during this difficult period of the Restoration. Although the foundations were laid just a year after the arrival of the exiles, as we learn from the third chapter of Ezra, it was not until 515 B.C. that the work was finished and the Temple dedicated. The work lagged for over a decade, largely because of the poverty and insecurity of the people, but by 520 B.C. the fiery prophet Haggai and his contemporary, Zechariah, probably spurred on by rebellions breaking out in the Persian Empire, moved the people to resume the work. An excerpt from the prophecy of Haggai shows the kind of exhortation which was necessary to raise the morale of the people:

> Thus says Yahweh of hosts: "Take to heart your ways. Go up to the hills and bring wood and build the Temple, that I may take pleasure in it and that I may be glorified," says Yahweh. "You looked for much and, behold, it came to little; and when you brought it home I blew it away. For what reason?" says Yahweh of hosts. "Because of My house which lies in ruins, while each one is busy about his own house. Therefore the heavens above you have withheld their dew and the earth its produce. And

I have called for a drought upon the land and the hills, upon the corn, the new wine, the oil, upon everything the soil brings forth, upon men and cattle, and upon all at which they labor" (Hag. 1:7–11).

Little wonder that there was considerable disillusionment among the Jews when they saw the contrast between their great expectations of a restored Jewish state under a successor of David, and the harsh realities of life in an impoverished land open on all sides to incursions from its foes. It took scarcely a generation, from the Edict of Cyrus, for the repatriated to realize that Judah was not destined to play any great role as a military or political power among the nations. It required one of Israel's great historians, whom we call the Chronicler, to remind the descendants of the returned exiles wherein their true greatness lay.[1] We have very little evidence for the period between the completion of the Second Temple and the coming of Nehemiah in the middle of the fifth century B.C. For this reason the era of the Restoration is tantalizingly obscure in Hebrew history; but no one can for a minute doubt that it was also a very important one.

THE SOURCES

Aside from what the excavation of Palestinian sites discloses about the cultural and religious life of the time, and this is relatively meager, our essential source of information is that

---

[1] The Judeans of the late fifth century might have been expected to exercise great influence on Jewish communities outside of Palestine and to have drawn, in steadily increasing numbers, Jews of the Diaspora anxious to return to Sion. But interest among these Jews in exile tended to wane once it was seen that the hopes of an earlier generation stood little chance of being realized. Why return to a land where one thought more of survival than of setting up an ideal Jewish community? As a consequence, the Jewish people began to set up communities in other parts of the world, thus extending the Diaspora instead of accelerating the ingathering. Verse 20 of the prophecy of Obadiah contains an interesting reference to Sepharad, which is Sardis, the capital of Lydia in Asia Minor. An Aramaic inscription from the ancient city informs us that the Jews had settled there as early as the tenth year of Artaxerxes, generally believed to be Artaxerxes Longimanus (465–424 B.C.). Later translators of the Hebrew Old Testament mistakenly connected Sepharad with Spain and thus Spanish and Portugese Jews became known as Sephardim.

great historical work produced by an unknown author who did for his people what Herodotus did for the Greeks. The Chronicler, like the Greek historian, interpreted for his contemporaries the meaning and direction of their history, and the Chronicler found in the principle of divine retribution the key to understanding Israel's past and present.[2] This great historical work repeats many things found in the earlier historical books, since he intends to give not a simply factual account, but a theological interpretation of events in Israel's history from Adam to the time of Nehemiah. The foundation stone of his sacred history is the choice of Israel by Yahweh. Israel is a holy community, bound to Yahweh in an everlasting covenant, especially through David, the model of an Israelite king. In fact, David is consistently idealized by the Chronicler. Judah also shares this idealization since she remained loyal to David; it is in Judah, and not in North Israel, that the theocracy is formed. To restore this manner of life under God was to be the glorious task of the post-exilic community. But where was the Davidic king? Granted that the royal line had ceased to exist, the holy community was a present reality, and in obedience to the Law and cult of the Temple, this community could enjoy the blessings promised to the theocracy formed by David but over which God ruled as the true King.

The two books of Ezra and Nehemiah, originally one composition, belong to this large historical work which interprets the history of Israel from Adam to Nehemiah. Though they precede the two books of Chronicles in the Hebrew Bible because of their prior acceptance in the Canon, the Ezra-Nehemiah work belongs after the two books of Chronicles. Let the reader, for example, compare the last two verses of 2 Chron-

---

[2] There are two other large historical collections in the Old Testament. The first is confined to the first four books of the Pentateuch and includes the history of Israel from creation to the eve of the Conquest. The second collection is known as the Deuteronomic History and includes the books of Deuteronomy, where the dominant themes are stated, Joshua, Judges, the two books of Samuel and the two books of Kings. This history covers the period from the time of Moses to the end of the Judean kingdom. The third historical collection is that of the Chronicler.

icles with the first two verses of Ezra; the repetition strongly supports the sequence already mentioned as well as the unity of all four books in one historical collection. In addition, there are literary characteristics and theological viewpoints common to both parts, inclining scholars to conclude that the four books are the product of one school of thought and probably of one man who has received the name of the Chronicler. A date around 400 B.C. is likely for the composition of his work.

For the time in which Nehemiah lived and worked for his countrymen we have one of the most remarkable and authentic sources in ancient historical writing. The memoirs of Nehemiah, set down in writing not long after 432 B.C., are incorporated with very few changes into the Chronicler's history. Other figures in the Old Testament, such as Hosea, Jeremiah, and Ezechiel, have left autobiographical data, but no one has given us so complete and personal a picture of his work, from beginning to end. Without the recollections of Nehemiah the period would be far more obscure than it is now. What kind of man emerges from this record, left by his own hand and possibly deposited in the Temple as a memorial of his work?

REMEMBER ME, O MY GOD, FOR GOOD

Nehemiah, whose name means "The Lord has comforted," was the cupbearer of Artaxerxes I Longimanus, and a man of considerable wealth and influence in the Persian community of the Diaspora. The memoirs open with a fixed date, sometime in December of 445 B.C., when the royal court had moved to the winter residence of Susa. Hanani, one of the brethren of Nehemiah, came to the palace with disturbing news:

> Hanani, one of my brethren, came with certain men from Judah; and I asked them about the surviving Jews, who had escaped exile, and about the city of Jerusalem. And they said to me: "The survivors in the province [of Judah] who escaped exile are in great distress and shame; also the wall of Jerusalem is broken down, and its gates have been destroyed by fire" (Neh. 1:2–3).

The report was a great blow to the man who, despite his high position in the Persian court, never cut himself off from the interests of his own people. After a period of fasting and prayer, offered as a national confession of guilt for past sins, Nehemiah determined to seek a royal interview and request permission to visit the province of Judah and rebuild the walls of Jerusalem. Artaxerxes was sympathetic toward the plan and provided him with letters which identified Nehemiah as a servant of the king and gave him the proper authorization for his task. The opposition which lay ahead appears in a brief notice which says, "But when Sanballat the Horonite and Tobiah the servant, the Ammonite, heard this, they were very angry that a man had come to seek the welfare of the children of Israel." The former proved to be a relentless adversary of Nehemiah during all his efforts to rebuild Jerusalem. Sanballat, as governor of Samaria, pressed claims on the province of Judah which went back to the days of Babylonian rule. Jealous of these prerogatives, Sanballat did everything possible to interfere with the rebuilding of Jerusalem's walls. But Nehemiah had come armed with royal authority and he moved so fast that appeal to the Persian king would be of no avail; so Sanballat and his colleagues were forced to resort to other tactics in the hope of halting the work. Tobiah, the governor of Ammon in Transjordan, was another inveterate foe of Nehemiah. Like Sanballat he probably saw in the arrival of Nehemiah a curtailment of his own powers, which appear to have included some kind of supervision over the province of Judah.

Three days after he arrived in Jerusalem, Nehemiah, with a few loyal friends, set out to inspect the ruined walls by moonlight and made this report to the leaders of the city:

> Then I said to them, "You see the distress we are in, how Jerusalem is ruined and its gates burned. Come, now, let us build the wall of Jerusalem, that we may no longer suffer disgrace." And I told them of the hand of my God which had been upon me for good, and also of the words which the king had spoken to me. And they replied, "Let us rise up and build!" So they strengthened their hands for the good work (Neh. 2:17–18).

The personal courage and determination of Nehemiah were already beginning to raise up the morale of the people who now volunteered to work upon the walls. Chapter three interrupts the narrative with a list of the workers and the sections of the wall built by each group. It is a record of co-operative enterprise and a valuable source for the topography of the city at this time.

The work on the wall provoked resistance from the enemies of the Jews, and their first step was to ridicule the work. The following account is found in the memoirs:

> Now when Sanballat heard that we were building the wall, he was very angry and greatly enraged, and he mocked the Jews. And he said in the presence of his own people and of the army of Samaria, "What are these feeble Jews doing? Will they restore things? Will they offer sacrifice? Will they finish the job in a day? Can they bring to life the stones from the rubbish heaps, even those that are burned?" Tobiah the Ammonite was at his side and taunted, "Yes, as for what they are building — should a fox go up on it he would break down their stone wall!" (Neh. 3:33–35.)

The work was not to be stopped by ridicule, and Nehemiah turned on his adversaries with an imprecation whose violence may startle us but should also serve to recall the desperate circumstances in which the leader found himself, fighting the discouragement of his own people and the threats of outsiders:

> Hear, O our God, for we are despised; turn back their taunt upon their own heads, and give them up to be plundered in a land of captivity. Cover not their guilt and their sins blot not from Your sight; for they have provoked You to anger in the presence of the builders (Neh. 3:36–37).

After ridicule had failed, the enemies tried another line of attack, the threat of an armed assault on Jerusalem. This was an ancient "war of nerves," made more serious by the growing discouragement among the workers. But Nehemiah was again equal to a very difficult situation and devised a defense system which enabled the work to go on:

When I saw their fear I arose and said to the nobles, the officials and the rest of the people, "Fear them not! Remember Yahweh, Who is great and terrible, and fight for your brethren, your sons, daughters, wives and homes."

When our enemies heard that it was known to us and that God had frustrated their plan, we all returned to the wall, everyone to his work. From that day forth, half of my servants worked on construction and half held the spears, shields, bows, and coats of mail; and the leaders were behind the entire house of Judah (Neh. 4:8–10).

Sanballat and another ally, Geshem, attempted a final stratagem as they saw with dismay that the wall was finished except for the final task of setting the doors of the city gates in their sockets. They attempted to draw Nehemiah out to a "summit conference" at Ono, in the Sharon Plain; there they hoped to eliminate this stubborn adversary, lured beyond the protecting walls of Jerusalem. Nehemiah did not reveal his suspicions to them when they summoned him four times to the conference. By messenger he sent the forthright answer, "I am doing a great work and I cannot come down. Why should the work stop while I leave it and come down to you?" Four attempts having failed they sent a fifth letter, this time accusing Nehemiah of sedition. The repair of the walls, they claimed, was only the prelude to rebellion against their Persian rulers. Nehemiah's answer was a blunt refutation of their lie together with another appeal for God's help:

Then I sent to him [Sanballat] a message saying, "No such things as you say have been done, for you are inventing them out of your own heart." For all of them sought to frighten us, thinking, "Their hands shall be weakened so that they will cease working, and it will not be done." But now, strengthen my hands (Neh. 6:8–9).

The last and most subtle of the enemies' stratagems consisted in hiring false prophets, particularly the prominent Shemaiah, who appears to have been a friend of Nehemiah. He proposed that both of them should take refuge in the *hekhal* or principal room of the Temple, from which one entered the Holy of Holies. This was abhorrent to Nehemiah for several reasons; his own quick flight would seriously weaken the morale of his people, and his use of the Temple for this purpose would be a violation of the sacred edifice. Nehemiah flatly refused and then realized that the prophet Shemaiah was speaking as a hireling and not as a messenger from God. The incident ended with an imprecation against Sanballat, Tobiah, and any others implicated in the plot.

We are told that the walls were completed in the amazingly short time of fifty-two days, but it is not until the twelfth chapter that the dedication of the walls of Jerusalem is described. The liturgical ceremony began with an act of purification, followed by a procession about the walls in which two great companies took part, and the rite of dedication was climaxed by sacrifices and rejoicing:

> And they offered great sacrifices that day and rejoiced, for God had made them rejoice with a great joy; the women also and the children rejoiced. And the joy of Jerusalem was heard afar off (Neh. 12:4).

But if the chief goal of Nehemiah's visit to Jerusalem was to repair the ruined walls it was not his only one. He sought to repopulate Jerusalem, now that it was properly fortified, and this was accomplished by a casting of lots to determine who should live in the Holy City. Before the determination by lot was completed, however, some had volunteered to live in Jerusalem. The prestige of the city was thus increased and it was ready to become the great center of the holy community, as it had been in the time of David. Nehemiah also took measures to remedy the deplorable economic condition of the poor who were forced to give up the small property which they inherited and, in some cases, to sell their own children into slavery in order to pay their taxes. His moral sense aroused, Nehemiah frankly spoke of his anger:

> I was very angry when I heard their outcry and these words. I consulted with myself and brought charges against the nobles and rulers, saying, "You are exacting interest from your own

brothers." And I called a great assembly and said to them, "We, as far as in us lay, have redeemed our Jewish brethren who have been sold to the Gentiles; but you even sell your brethren that they may be sold to us!" They were silent and found not a word to say (Neh. 5:6–8).

Nehemiah's care for the poor, often at his own expense, is one of the endearing traits of the man. The heavy bondage of his people moved him to pity and, like the prophets of an earlier age, he fearlessly took their part against those who would exploit them. The Law of Moses, which defended the poor, deeply influenced his life; it was therefore not as an innovator that he undertook his reforms.

Nehemiah remained for twelve years in Jerusalem, carrying out his program of reform as governor of the province. Then he returned to Persia as he had promised, but shortly thereafter, again asked and received permission to go back to Jerusalem. During his absence all had not gone well; the pledge to support the Levites had not been honored, the Sabbath was being profaned, and in the Temple itself Nehemiah found his old enemy Tobiah installed in rooms once reserved for sacrificial offerings. Nehemiah wasted no time in taking care of this situation:

> And being very angry I threw all the household furniture of Tobiah out of the chamber. Then I ordered them to cleanse the chamber; and I brought back the vessels of the house of God, with the meal offering and the frankincense (Neh. 13:8–9).

After restoring the Levitical support which the laymen had neglected, Nehemiah forbade the Levites to engage in secular work and brought them back to the Temple and re-established them in their stations. Using his full authority as governor, Nehemiah stopped the abuses which had turned the Sabbath into another business day. Finally, he turned to the delicate problem of mixed marriages, to "the Jews who had married women of Ashdod, Ammon, and Moab." Ezra had to face the same situation in the post-exilic community but, whereas Ezra largely turned his anger on himself, Nehemiah vented his fury on the offenders and even beat them physically:

And I contended with them and cursed them and struck some of them and pulled out their hair; and I forced them to take an oath in the name of God, saying, "You shall not give your daughters to their sons nor take their daughters for your sons or for yourselves. Did not Solomon, king of Israel, sin because of such women? There was no king like him among the nations, and he was loved by his God, and God made him king over all Israel; yet foreign women made even him to sin. Shall we then listen to you and do all this great evil and act treacherously against our God by marrying foreign women?" (Neh. 13:25–27.)

These bursts of anger were characteristic of the man who, for all his faults, must go down as one of Judaism's religious leaders. As a layman he had no special consecration, nor could he appeal to any prophetic call; what authority he possessed upon his arrival in Jerusalem came from the Persian king. But he proved to be a dedicated servant of God, working without thought of personal gain, and turning even his shortcomings into means of furthering the necessary reforms. His bluntness and quick temper brought results, especially since the people realized that he sought no personal gain in his correction of abuses. The memoirs of Nehemiah reveal, with great frankness and sincerity, a human man of action, but with great faith in God, wholly concerned with the welfare of his own people in the province of Judah. Luckily, in his memoirs he left us an authentic historical document which sheds welcome light on the history of Judah between the time of Haggai and the Hellenistic age. The memoirs close with a brief and incomplete summary of what had been accomplished during his second mission along with the customary plea that God would remember his deeds.

So I cleansed them from everything foreign, and I settled the duties of priests and Levites, every one in his own task; and I made provision for the wood offering, at appointed times, and for the first fruits. Remember me, O my God, for good (Neh. 13:30–31).

JOB

WHEN the Hebrew writer described Solomon's wisdom as surpassing the wisdom of all the children of the East and all the wisdom of Egypt, he was acknowledging the international character of this quest for the meaning and values of human life. Modern discoveries of Egyptian, Canaanite, Babylonian, and Sumerian wisdom literature have brilliantly confirmed this observation and made it possible for us to set the wisdom of Israel in the framework of the ancient Near East. From the Valley of the Nile to the Land of the Two Rivers men from the earliest times wrestled with the great problems of man's existence and his destiny. Why does the good man suffer while the wicked prospers? What can a man do in the face of adversity for which he can find no adequate cause? How can the inequities of life be reconciled with divine justice? What is the use of trying to live a perfect and upright life? These are the perennial questions which have troubled the human spirit whenever man reflects on the realities of our human condition. In new and reliable translations we can read some of the answers which the wise men of the past gave to these questions. The Egyptian who has suffered all manner of ill treatment pessimistically looks to death as a release from his sorrows and contemplates the taking of his own life:

> Death is in my sight today
>   Like the *passing away* of rain,
> Like the return of men to their houses
>   from an expedition.
> Death is in my sight today
>   Like the clearing of the sky,
>   like a man *fowling thereby* for
>   what he knew not.

> Death is in my sight today
>> Like the longing of a man to see his house [again],
>> After he has spent many years held in captivity.[1]

In a composition entitled "I will praise the lord of wisdom," a Babylonian sage voices the complaint of the just man in his misery. Fortunately, the story had a happy ending; for Marduk, the great god, released him from his woes and restored him to health and happiness. Here is a description of the "Babylonian Job":

> .... I have become like a deaf man.
> .... Once I behaved like a lord, now I
>> have become a slave ...
> The fury of my companions destroys me.
> ....
> The day is sighing, the night is weeping;
> The month is silence, mourning is the year.
> ....
> I have arrived, I have passed beyond life's span.
> I look about me: evil upon evil!
> My affliction increases, right I cannot find.
> I implored the god, but he did not turn his countenance;
> I prayed to my goddess, but she did not raise her head.[2]

In the book of Job, the supreme achievement of Hebrew poetry, the Old Testament comes to grips with those profound problems which are the stuff of great literature. We do not know the name of the author nor can we determine with precision the literary sources on which he drew. Nor are these questions of any great importance. As in other works of Wisdom literature, notably the book of Proverbs, one should always distinguish between the ancient, traditional material in the work and the much later, finished form of the actual biblical composition. The hero of the story is a traditional figure going back as far as the first half of the second millennium B.C. The name of Job appears under the archaic form of Ayyabum in the Egyptian Execration texts of the twentieth century B.C. and

---

[1] See *ANET*, p. 407.
[2] See *ANET*, p. 434.

also in the Mari texts of the eighteenth century B.C. Twice the prophet Ezechiel brackets Job with Noah and Daniel, the latter being an ancient Canaanite hero, well known in their literature as early as the fifteenth century B.C. From this and other indications it would appear that the poet-author, who lived and wrote around the fifth century B.C., made use of a traditional figure whose piety was already legendary among his readers. But to draw hard and fast lines between what is traditional and what is due to the creative genius of the writer is no longer possible. Suffice it to say that there once lived a character named Job who suffered great misfortunes, argued his case before friends who represented the traditional views on suffering and sin, and was finally vindicated by God Whom he never abandoned in his misery. Above all, we must remember that the question of an historical nucleus for the work is of secondary importance, since the writer's purpose is not to give us the detailed history of a certain individual but to discuss a mystery which will always be relevant as long as man's life deserves the name human.

As a rule of thumb we might say that the traditional portions of Job are in prose while the truly creative parts, where the author deals with his great theme of innocent suffering, are written in poetry. It is interesting to note that, in a thoroughly Jewish work, Job is not represented as an Israelite but as one belonging to a people, the Edomites, who were considered enemies of the Jews at least since the fall of Jerusalem in 587 B.C. The book falls easily into five parts: (1) The Prologue, introducing Job and the misfortunes which overtook him. (2) The discourses, in three cycles, between the innocent sufferer and the three friends, Eliphaz, Bildad, and Zophar. (3) The discourses of Elihu, a young bystander who suddenly enters the debate. Some commentators believe that these passages were added by another writer but it is equally probable that the author himself added this section at a later date. (4) The discourses of Yahweh, addressed to Job. (5) The Epilogue, in which the fortunes of Job are restored. The reader might as well know that many of the discourses are so similar in mood and content that they can become a trifle tiresome when taken in one large dose. Selected sections should be read slowly and meditatively.

MY SERVANT JOB

The prose prologue introduces the hero and the chief protagonists of the drama:

> There was a man in the land of Uz, whose name was Job; and that man was blameless and upright, one who feared God, and turned away from evil.

His large family and great wealth were proof enough that he was God's friend, for Job did not for a moment question that there was an equation between material prosperity and obedience to the law of God. Could harm ever come to one who feared God? In a later chapter, after the blow had fallen, Job looked back and enlarged the picture of his own virtuous life:

> For I delivered the poor who cried out,
> the orphan who had none to help him;
> the blessing of one about to perish came upon me,
> and I made the widow's heart sing for joy.
> Justice I put on and it clothed me,
> judgment was like a robe and a turban.
> I was eyes to the blind,
> and feet to the lame;
> a father was I to the poor,
> and I searched out the cause of the stranger,
> the fangs of the wicked I smashed,
> and I snatched the prey from his teeth.
> (Job 29:12–17)

In the great soliloquy of Chapter 31, one of the ethical peaks of the Old Testament, Job solemnly swore under oath that he had led a life of innocence and inward purity. Nothing in his conduct could bear any relation to his tragic suffering; having made his "oath of clearance," Job challenged the Almighty to answer him.

I made a covenant with my eyes;
    how then could I look upon a virgin?
What would my portion be from God above,
    or my inheritance from the Almighty on high?
Does not calamity befall the wicked,
    and misery those who work iniquity?
Does He not see my ways,
    and number all my steps?
If I have walked in falsehood,
    and my foot has hastened to deceit,
let me be weighed in a just balance,
    let God know my integrity!
If my step has wandered from the way
    and my heart has followed my eyes
    or a blemish has clung to my hands;
then let me sow but another eat;
    and let my planting be rooted up!
If my heart has been ensnared by a woman
    and at my neighbor's door I have lain in wait;
then let my wife grind for another,
    let others violate her!
For that would be a wicked crime,
    to be condemned by the judges;
it would be a fire burning down to Abaddon
    until it burned to the roots my possessions.
If I have refused justice to servant or maid,
    when their case came before me,
what then could I do when God rises up?
What answer could I make when He calls me to account?
Did not He who made me in the womb make him,
did not the same One fashion us in the womb?

                        (Job 31:1–15)

Toward all, God and men, Job had lived up to the highest standard of conduct, and his material wealth was but a sign of his spiritual well-being. So Job reasoned, and all the sages of that day. But then the scene shifts to the heavenly court where, in the dialogue between God and Satan, the drama is set in motion. These are the lines which reach to the heart of the drama by raising the question of whether or not a man can ever serve God out of disinterested love:

Then Satan answered Yahweh, "Is it for nought that Job fears God? Have You not put a hedge about him and his house and all that he has, on every side? You have blessed the work of his hands, and his holdings have increased in the land. But put forth Your hand now and touch all that he has and he will curse You to Your face." And Yahweh said to Satan, "Behold, all that he has is in your hands, only lay not your hand upon his person." Then Satan went forth from the presence of Yahweh (Job 1:9–12).

The series of misfortunes, culminating in a loathsome disease, are familiar to all. The next cry is heard from his frantic and desperate wife, tempting Job to abandon God. Death by cursing God was far better than the agonizing suffering of this outcast from civilized men:

> Then his wife said to him, "Do you still cling to your integrity? Curse God and die!"
> But he said to her, "You speak as one of the foolish women. We accept good things from God and, verily, evil as well." In all this Job sinned not with his lips (Job 2:9–10).

Job overmastered the first temptation, coming from the wife who loved him so sincerely. Where his reason could give him no light, faith led Job to formulate an answer in which he became the spokesman of all who suffer. His own suffering did not make him forget the goodness of God, and his humble and silent submission must be accounted his first victory over Satan. But other and greater trials lay ahead.

SORRY COMFORTERS ARE YOU ALL

Three friends, with the best of pastoral intentions, appeared before Job to offer consolation. At first their sympathy could find no voice as they looked with horror on the wreck of a man who once moved among them in patriarchal dignity. For seven days and seven nights they sat in silent vigil beside the sufferer. Then followed Job's first outburst of pent-up grief in which he called down a curse upon the day of his birth. He had not yet come face to face with the problem of the drama, the mys-

tery behind this suffering. His first soliloquy was the release
sought by a man overwhelmed with grief:

> Perish the day in which I was born,
>   and the night which said,
> "A man-child is conceived."
> May that day be darkness,
>   let not God above seek it,
>   nor light shine upon it.
> May the day's darkness terrify it. . . .
> Why was I not hidden away like an untimely birth,
> like infants who have not seen the light?
> There the wicked cease from troubling,
>   and there the weary find rest.
> There the prisoners are at ease together,
> and hear not the voice of the taskmaster.
> Small and great are there the same,
>   and the slave is free from his master.

(Job 3:3–5, 16–19)

Job's repudiation of the gift of life and his melancholy longing,
against all Semitic tradition, for Sheol's "surcease of sorrow,"
must have unsettled his friends; it was time for the oldest and
most honored of them, Eliphaz, to offer his friendly sympathy
and advice. With tact and deference he proposed the orthodox
view of reward and punishment, reminding Job that he had
often counseled others and strengthened them with this traditional doctrine:

> Behold, you have instructed many,
>   and the hands of the weak you have strengthened.
> You raised up a stumbler with your words,
>   and the knees of the weak you have made firm.
> But now your time has come, and you are vexed,
>   it touches you and you are terrified.
> Is not your fear of God your support,
>   and the integrity of your ways your hope?
> Remember, I beg of you, what innocent man ever perished,
>   or when were good men ever blotted out?
> As I have seen, those who plough iniquity and
>   plant trouble harvest the same.

(Job 4:3–8)

The three friends, each in his own way, adopted this doctrine of retribution as an unquestionable principle of divine government in the world. Since they knew that God was both all-powerful and concerned with the moral conduct of men, it stood to reason that He must punish evil and reward goodness. It was but another step to draw the conclusion that wherever there is suffering and material privation there you must find sin. Baldly stated, if a man suffered it was only because he was a sinner.

Job himself seems to have held this conventional theory at least until, to his shock, the theory applied to his own case. Never for a moment had it occurred to him that his suffering could be the punishment for his sins, and his share in the debate consists largely in denying that the orthodox doctrine has any applicability to his case. The theory simply did not square with his situation no matter how valid it might have been in the past: His own personal experience was the refutation of conventional wisdom, but Job had no theory to put in its place. All he had was the consciousness that he was suffering without apparent cause. Job's first reply to Eliphaz brings out the failure of friendship, as he compares the three to dried up brooks which give no refreshment to the thirsty and weary traveler:

> Whoever withholds kindness from a friend
>> forsakes the fear of the Almighty.
> My brethren are treacherous as a torrent-bed,
>> as streams that pass away,
>> which are dark with ice
>> and where the snow hides itself.
> In the hot summer they disappear,
>> when the heat comes they vanish from their place.
>
> (Job 6:14–17)

The other two friends add little to what Eliphaz had said about the problem. Bildad, impatient at what he thinks is the irreverence of Job, begins by disposing of the mystery with a rhetorical question:

> Does God pervert judgment?
> Or does the Almighty pervert justice?
>
> (Job 8:3)

The experience of the past is Bildad's argument that God cannot be unjust. Since God has never rejected the blameless man, all Job has to do, if he is innocent, is to wait for God to restore his fortune. Bildad represents the wisdom which has centuries of experience to support it; he cannot see that his pat formulas no longer meet the situation of Job. Zophar appeals neither to his own long reflections on the problem, as Eliphaz had, nor to the teaching of experience, as Bildad had argued. With scarcely a trace of sympathy and with no consideration for the feelings of Job, he accuses the sufferer of mocking God and follows this up with a direct charge of guilt. The others had insinuated and hinted; Zophar comes out with, "Know then that God exacts of you less than your guilt deserves" (Job 11:6).

In the succeeding cycles of speeches the three friends return again and again to these considerations, tenaciously upholding the prevailing orthodoxy in its explanation of human misery. With increasing anguish Job clings to his innocence and insists that their arguments utterly fail to solve his problem. Job even goes so far as to say that the three men, and not he himself, are the offenders against God because they have spoken falsely in their efforts to defend God. The justice of God is not served by those who wrongly accuse Job of sin in their futile attempts to save the traditional teaching:

> Will you speak falsehood for God,
> and deception for His sake?
> Will you show Him favor
> and plead His case?
> Will you fare well when He searches you out
> or can you deceive Him as
> you would any man?
> He will certainly rebuke you
> if in secret you show favor.
> Will not His majesty dismay you
> and dread of Him fall upon you?

Your maxims are proverbs of ashes,
  your lofty words are mounds of clay.
              (Job 13:7–12)

Finding no understanding among his friends, Job turned to God as his vindicator.

I WOULD SPEAK TO THE ALMIGHTY

No character in the Old Testament has spoken to God with the unrestrained aggressiveness and defiance of Job. Not that he, for a moment, questioned the existence of God. It was the nature of God which was in question, not His existence. If we weigh the physical suffering and mental agony of the man, his felt estrangement from God, we will judge him no more severely than Yahweh did. Job knew full well that God was responsible for his suffering; to Him he turned to seek the reason, sometimes in plaintive lament but just as often in outright defiance. Some of the most powerful and frightening passages in the drama come from Job's confrontation with God, Who had placed this heavy and mysterious burden upon him. With a bitterness which can be explained only as the language of one who is spiritually sick, Job compared the relentless hostility of God to the fury of a wild beast, and then to an implacable enemy:

His wrath has torn me, and
He has hated me;
He has gnashed His teeth at me.
My enemy sharpens His eyes against me.
They have gaped at me with their mouth,
  they have smitten me scornfully on the cheek,
they unite against me.
God delivers me to the evil man,
  into the hands of the wicked He casts me.
I was at ease and He broke me asunder;
He has taken me by the neck
  and dashed me to pieces.
He set me up as His target,
  His archers hem me in on all sides.

> He cut open my kidneys and spares not,
>   my gall He pours forth on the ground.
>   (Job 16:9–13)

The nineteenth chapter is a mirror of Job's rapidly changing states of soul, from near-despair and bitter complaint to the soaring act of faith which is one of the climactic passages of the book. In replying to the traditional wisdom of Bildad's second discourse, Job cries out in anger against their constant accusations and their failure to comprehend. Again he blames God for his misfortune; the creature denounces and rebukes the Creator:

> Behold, I cry "Violence!" but I am not answered;
> I cry aloud but there is no justice.
> He has walled up my path so that I cannot pass,
>   in my way He has set darkness.
> He has stripped me of my glory
>   and removed the crown from my head.
> On every side He breaks me down
>   and He has uprooted my hope like a tree.
>   (Job 19:7–10)

In the extremity of his wretchedness, abandoned by God and men, Job makes his sublime act of faith in God Who has seemed so insensible to Job's mystery. It is the appeal to God as his *go'el*, the "blood avenger" of ancient Semitic law:

> As for me I know that my redeemer lives
>   and that at last He will stand up on the dust;
> and even after this skin of mine has been stripped off,
>   in my own flesh I shall see God,
>   Whom I myself shall see.
> And my own eyes shall behold, and not some stranger.
> My emotions are spent within me.
>   (Job 19:25–27)

Whether this vindication will take place before Job dies or after his death will probably never be settled by scholarly research. In either alternative, the important thing is that Job has turned to God for vindication; He will furnish the ultimate guarantee of Job's innocence. Job has claimed a kinship with God and let his accusers beware of a kinsman's vengeance!

OUT OF THE WHIRLWIND

We might expect the drama to end with Job's vision of God, momentary though it is. But the debate is resumed; Job returns to earth and continues the dispute with his friends, who continue to hammer home their traditional views on divine retribution, while Job stubbornly reaffirms his innocence. Another character joins the discussion, the young and self-confident Elihu. He is as critical of the friends as he is of Job; with the friends because they were unable to answer the sufferer; with Job because he has not seen the disciplinary value of suffering, and has justified himself rather than God. Elihu's positive contribution to the debate consists in setting before Job a picture of God as just, wise, and merciful. When God inflicts punishment He intends to purify the heart of man and to turn him away from sin. Following a hymn-like discourse on the unsearchable wonders of God in nature, Elihu finally calls upon Job to put aside his questioning and humble himself before God:

> The Almighty, we cannot find Him;
>   mighty is His power.
> Judgment and abundant justice He does not violate.
> Therefore men fear Him;
> He does not regard those who are wise in their own heart.
> (Job 37:23–24)

Job had often challenged God to appear and tell him why he suffered. But God often refuses to give us reasons. Where Job was looking for answers God counters by asking more questions. The speeches of Yahweh contain no simple solution to the mystery of innocent suffering; certainly the incomparable poetry of these lines could not be called a direct answer to the struggle going on in the soul of Job:

Then Yahweh answered Job out of the whirlwind and said:
"Who is this who darkens counsel
  by words without knowledge?
Now gird up your loins like a man,
  for I will question you, and you answer Me.
Where were you when I laid
  the foundations of the earth?
Tell Me if you understand!
Who determined its measurements —
  surely you know!
Or who stretched the line upon it?
How were its foundations fastened,
  or who laid its cornerstone,
when the morning stars sang together,
  and all the sons of God shouted for joy?"

(Job 38:1–7)

Job has been brought face to face with the wisdom and power of God, manifested in the unfathomable mysteries of nature. Before the whole magnificent panorama of the created world, all ordered and directed by God, Job could only answer in words of humble surrender:

Then Job answered Yahweh and said:
"I know that You can do all things,
  and that no purpose of Yours can be thwarted.
Who is this who hides counsel without knowledge?
Therefore I have spoken what I understood not,
  things too wonderful for me, and I knew them not."

(Job 42:1–3)

Job has learned the great lesson that childlike humility is the only state of soul in which we can meet the mystery of suffering. There is, ultimately, no spurious seeking after "answers"; in the end of the book of Job, as in the beginning, the mystery of innocent suffering remains inviolate. All we can say is that Job has come to know that it is not for man to question the hidden purposes of God. Job had suffered to the limits of human endurance, and he was tempted more than once to cry out that it was all meaningless. Now he realizes that, even though he might never come to know the meaning of that suffering, the evils which befell him were not to be charged to any callousness or moral imperfection on the part of God. They were a part of some divine purpose which he would never understand but which he could now accept. The traditions of the ancients had taught him something about God and His ways. That knowledge had come from "the hearing of the ear," the inherited wisdom of his own people. Their view of God had stood up well when Job was rich and honored, but it had broken down under the blows of physical and spiritual suffering. Now Job has "seen with his eyes" and learned that the wisdom and plans of God are above those of men. Just as man cannot pierce the mystery of the created world, though he can see its harmony and beauty, so he cannot expect to comprehend the moral order where God deals with man. What he cannot grasp with his reason he must accept in faith and love. In his humble acceptance of this mystery, and his own limitations, Job was released from the prison of his own doubts and self-pity, and in that final vision of God's glory Job learned that God had never forsaken him.

OOHELETH (ECCLESIASTES)

> Vanity of vanities, says the Preacher,
> vanity of vanities! All is vanity.
> What does man gain by all the toil
> at which he toils under the sun?
> (Qoh. 1 : 2–3)

THIS is a statement of the theme around which one of the most enigmatic and appealing books of the Old Testament has been written. So puzzling is Qoheleth's thought and so unpredictable are his changing moods that one is hardly surprised to learn that his book has been labeled "the quintessence of skepticism" by one and "the quintessence of piety" by another. That Qoheleth is skeptical goes without saying, and it is because of this quality that he has also been called the most modern of writers, and his book has turned out to be one of the most quotable of ancient literature. It is undoubtedly a disturbing book. Nobody would be ruffled if the sacred writer confined his amused doubts to the petty strivings of men or to the hollow platitudes which collapse before the experience of everyday life. But he becomes particularly disconcerting when his skepticism touches, not the beliefs of the arrogant and the wicked, but the code of the simple and pious. The men of this age were instructed, by the traditional wisdom of the sages, to seek after justice and wisdom; but here was a man, whose work was accepted in the sacred Canon, telling them that these aspirations were futile, and recommending a rule of life which some modern commentators have not hesitated to call "hedonistic." Before passing judgment on the man, however, it is worth the trouble to set his literary work in its context of time and place.

There were wise men in Israel long before the Babylonian Exile, but it was not until after the return from captivity that

the wisdom movement came into its own. While we must
never forget that wisdom has its roots in the distant past, it
is nevertheless a safe generalization that every wisdom composition we possess in the Old Testament was set down in its
present form in the post-exilic period. This is true of Proverbs,
Job, and Qoheleth, to mention three typical examples of wisdom literature. When we match the subject matter of the
wisdom writers with the spirit of the times, it will not appear
accidental that such literature flourished at this particular period
of Jewish history. The days of great national prosperity, conquest, and independence were a thing of the past. The reigns
of David and Solomon were little more than memories of a
Golden Age, unlikely to return even though some of the
prophets portrayed Israel's hope for the future in terms borrowed from the splendors of that age. The harsh reality of
history found Judaism under the dominion of great world
powers, and this subjection was to last for many centuries before
anything like a shred of national independence would be
achieved.

Little wonder, then, that in the generations after the return
from Babylon, less and less emphasis was placed on national
glory. What chance had the helpless little province of Judah
of throwing off Persian, Greek, or any kind of foreign rule?
With this decline of interest in the nation as a collectivity, the
individual came into his own and much of the wisdom literature was pointed toward his needs. Into the background had
receded the great prophetic theme that the nation stood in
unique covenant relation with Yahweh, with all the corporate
responsibilities and hopes which went with the idea of a chosen
people. Gone were the majestic interventions of Yahweh in history, His mighty acts of deliverance or His terrifying outbursts
of wrath. In wisdom literature God deals with man as an individual; on that basis would a man be judged.

The wise men were not philosophers in the Greek sense, and
systematic treatises were foreign to their genius; but they managed to raise very important questions, such as we have seen in

the book of Job, and they formulated many a shrewd observation on life and its tangled problems.

The Hebrew word for wisdom is ḥokmah and, at the time of which we are speaking, it was a practical virtue according to which a man might live successfully in the sight of God and men. The wise men of Israel are sometimes called "humanists," but this should not be understood as if their wisdom were purely secular. The true wisdom of man consisted in knowing the divine Wisdom, and it began by recognizing and serving the source of all wisdom, God:

> Trust in Yahweh with all your heart and lean not upon your own understanding (Prov. 3:5).

Nor is this wisdom of the sages completely unrelated to the prophetic and legal traditions of Israel. We should realize that the wise men, in giving their advice on what constituted the good life, took for granted without bringing to the fore the great truths of Israel's spiritual heritage. There is no justification, therefore, for holding a radical discontinuity between prophet and wise man.

Like everything else, wisdom was a gift of God, but it was accessible to all and only the fool would not strive to acquire it. The most typical and conventional expression of Hebrew wisdom can be found in the book of Proverbs, where virtues such as hard work, reverence for authority, moderation, and high ethical conduct are constantly inculcated. But the conventional teachers of wisdom, with all their practical counsel on how to get along in a world which they had rather neatly schematized, were not destined to have the last word. In the book of Job we saw how one wisdom writer, refusing to accept the traditional views on reward and punishment, grappled with the mystery of innocent suffering for which no maxim of the traditionalists could supply a solution. Among the dissidents must also be ranked the author who is called Qoheleth. He is unlike Job in many ways, but like him inasmuch as he fearlessly faced up to the facts of experience, the limitations of human nature and the complexity of the world which God had created.

Apart from general agreement that the book of Qoheleth was written after the Exile, there is no unanimity as to the precise date of the work, its original language, or the place where it was written. Without going into any of these critical questions, it may be proposed as probable that the writer came from the coastal plain of northern Palestine or southern Phoenicia, and that he wrote in Hebrew around the year 300 B.C. The name Qoheleth is a substantive derived from the Hebrew verb *qahal*, meaning "to assemble or convoke"; the noun form probably means "preacher" or "leader of an assembly." The Greek translators of the Old Testament called the book Ecclesiastes, the name which has also been adopted by the Vulgate of St. Jerome. As to the question of outside influences on Qoheleth, attempts to show that the writer depended directly on Greek philosophical works have not been successful, since practically all of the alleged borrowings from Greek are now seen to have perfectly good Hebrew and ancient Semitic parallels. It would be going too far, however, to assert categorically that Qoheleth was in no way influenced by ideas and attitudes current in the Hellenistic world of which he was a part.

In the matter of structure, it is quite impossible to discern in Qoheleth any logical development of thought, and there are even times when the writer puts forth views which can hardly be reconciled. For example, the pessimistic view that the dead are more fortunate than the living (4:2) contrasts with the author's conviction that a living dog has it better than a dead lion (9:4). In one place Qoheleth tells us that sorrow is better than laughter (7:3) and a little later he will say that he praised joy (8:15). What are we to make of these discrepancies and sudden shiftings of viewpoint? One German scholar believed that he could detect the work of six authors, others were more moderate in postulating several interpolators who touched up the book in order to make it more palatable for Jewish readers. Today the tendency is to recognize that there is a basic unity in the book and that it reflects the varying moods of the writer and the complexity of the world on which he was reporting.

Qoheleth will use formulas but he seems to be dissatisfied with them; he makes use of mood but mood is very imprecise. In addition, a single point of view would never do justice to the breadth of his own experience. So the author walks around his subject, writes about it from different angles, probes it with different instruments, and even judges it from different standards. He might even be said to give the impression that he is dissatisfied with the resources of his own thought and language. Father Roland Murphy, O.Carm., has made the excellent suggestion that Qoheleth should be classed in the same category with Pascal's *Pensées*, where we find random reflections on life and its values.[1] Once this is recognized we can more easily reconcile ourselves to the lack of order and the changing viewpoint of a thinker who was profound but very unsystematic. As a writer whose opinions are based on experience, it might also be said that many of his views are tentative and that he is often groping for a solution without insisting on the absolute validity of his own views. As we have seen, summarizing such a book is next to impossible — Qoheleth surely would have called it "vanity" — but it may be of some help to join Qoheleth as he puts to the test our human endeavors.

"THE TEARS OF THINGS"

To pursue wisdom was a cherished ideal of the post-exilic era, but Qoheleth, speaking as a royal personage, sadly recounts his disappointment in this quest:

> I Qoheleth was king over Jerusalem. And I applied my heart to seek out by wisdom all that is done under heaven; it is an unhappy task that God has given to the sons of men to be concerned with. I have seen all the works that are done under the sun; and behold, all is vanity and a striving after wind.

---

[1] R. E. Murphy, "The *Pensées* of Coheleth," *Catholic Biblical Quarterly*, XVII, April (1955), pp. 184–194. On page 186 of his article Father Murphy notes: "No one will ever succeed in giving a satisfactory outline of the contents of the book. Any schematic outline superimposes upon the meditations of Coheleth a framework that he certainly never had in mind."

> What is crooked cannot be set straight,
> what is wanting cannot be numbered.

I said in my heart: "Behold, I have acquired great wisdom, surpassing all my predecessors in Jerusalem; and my heart has acquired much wisdom and knowledge." And I applied my heart to know wisdom, and madness, and folly. This also I perceived is but a striving after wind.

> For in much wisdom is much grief, and increase of knowledge brings increase of sorrow.
>
> (Qoh. 1:12–18)

Why is this search for wisdom so unhappy a business, bringing only fresh problems and failing to solve anything satisfactorily? After all his efforts to acquire wisdom he could say with Job:

> Whence, then, comes wisdom?
> And where is the place of understanding?
>
> (Job 28:20)

But Job found in this very mystery his answer to the question which tormented him. There was a divine order in the world, established by a just and loving God, but this order was incomprehensible to man. In that faith Job found peace. Qoheleth reacts to this inscrutability with the frustration of one who can see no purpose at work in the events of daily life. For all its vaunted blessings wisdom could give its possessor no ultimate and permanent good, since death is the lot of both wise man and fool:

I knew that one lot befalls both of them. So I said in my heart: "If the fool's lot is to befall me also, why then should I be wise? Where is the profit for me?" And I concluded in my heart that this too is vanity. Neither of the wise man nor of the fool will there be an abiding remembrance, for in days to come both will have been forgotten. How the wise man dies just like the fool! (Qoh. 2:15–16.)

Time and again Qoheleth returns to the inevitability of death, that dark portal through which must pass both wise man and fool. And with death comes the end of all those activities in which man has found joy, for "there is no work or thought or knowledge or wisdom in Sheol, to which you are going." In one melancholy and often misunderstood passage, Qoheleth goes so far as to say that man and beast are equal in their final destiny, for both return to dust:

> For the lot of the sons of men and of beast is one lot; the one dies as well as the other. Both have the same life breath, and man has no advantage over the beast; but all is vanity. Both go to the one place: all were made from the dust, and to the dust they all return. Who knows if the life breath of the sons of men goes upward and the life breath of beasts goes earthward? (Qoh. 3:19–21.)

In the Garden of Eden the shadow of mortality descended upon all of us. Qoheleth has seen by experience the carrying out of this sentence and, in this, we have no advantage over the beast. Another Old Testament poet has written: "When you take away their breath, they die and return to the dust" (Ps. 104:29). One would have no right, however, to conclude that Qoheleth is a materialist who denies that there is any difference in the natures of man and beast. The life breath is not the equivalent of the soul, but stands for the physical "breath of life" which God has bestowed on all living beings. When this is taken away, the creature, whether man or beast, ceases to live. While Qoheleth knew very well that man was essentially superior to the beast insofar as man, made in the image of God, was a responsible moral person, he did not raise the question of the spirituality of man's soul since such a question was foreign to the Hebrew approach to the study of man.

What hope did Qoheleth hold out for man in the afterlife? Would the injustices he saw all about him be righted in another world where the wicked would receive their just deserts and the virtuous would live in eternal union with God? The answer to all these questions could be bluntly given by saying that Qoheleth simply did not know. Like the author of Job, he had no clear revelation on the fact of eternal life; nor did he know that God would make right in a future life the injustices and crimes which are committed in this life. If either he or Job had been given this revelation it would be hard to explain their anguish over the fact that the good often suffer in this life while the wicked prosper. Neither one is a Christian and both testify to the imperfect character of revelation in the Old Testament.

The recurring theme of man's mortality gives a haunting sadness to the work of Qoheleth. But it would not be too wide of the mark to claim that all great literature is sad. Remember the place of tragedy in ancient drama or the pathos of an Aeneas plodding along the weary path charted for him by Destiny. Horace's *Eheu fugaces* and the *Mors perpetua dormienda* of Catullus have the authentic note of all great literature. It is not easy to penetrate the ethos of the ancient classical world, with its different customs, traditions, ways of thinking, and ideals. But there is one chord from the treasury of ancient song to which all of us are attuned, and that is their ineluctable sadness, their melancholy stance before the oppressive majesty of death, their deeply felt sorrow bordering on despair at the thought of man's mortality. Man has his great moments and he is capable of mighty achievements, but the great writers knew in their hearts that none of these were lasting. Man and everything about him were doomed to perish. It is this affirmation of man's contingency which accounts for the lasting appeal of this literature. Qoheleth is the teacher of our contingency, set against the backdrop of the absolute transcendence of God, Who is never absent from his thought. Man can attain some joy and contentment but they will not last; he acquires possessions but his dominion over them is transitory. In one place Qoheleth says that God has put the "timeless" into the heart of man, only to add "without man's ever discovering from beginning to end the work which God has done" (Qoh. 3:10–11). Man forever presses against the limits of the finite, but God remains veiled in mystery.

WHERE IS WISDOM?

In probing the meaning of our lives, Qoheleth has looked at wisdom, pleasure, power, and toil. All of them leave man with that sense of futility and weariness which allows the author to sum it all up in the one word, "vanity." Everything moves in a cycle of endlessly repeated activities within which man is trapped by the limitations of his being. There is order in the world; but it is beyond his control, and he must try to adapt his own futile efforts to this vast cycle of recurrences which he can neither control nor comprehend. The author is probably best known for his melancholy, chant-like description of the activities which sum up the existence of man:

> Everything has its appointed season
> and there is a time for every affair under heaven;
> A time to be born, and a time to die;
> A time to plant, and a time to uproot what is planted;
> A time to kill, and a time to heal;
> A time to tear down, and a time to build up;
> A time to weep, and a time to laugh;
> A time to mourn, and a time to dance;
> A time to cast stones, and a time to gather them;
> A time to embrace, and a time to refrain from embracing;
> A time to seek, and a time to lose;
> A time to keep, and a time to cast away;
> A time to rend, and a time to sew;
> A time to be silent, and a time to speak;
> A time to love, and a time to hate;
> A time for war, and a time for peace.
>
> (Qoh. 3:1–8)

This is not equivalent to a denial of man's free will about which Qoheleth never seems to have had any doubts. But it certainly proclaims that the order in the world is due to God and that man cannot interfere with the design nor remake the world. Nor can he comprehend the overarching purpose of God's design. Although the author had tried earnestly to search out the meaning of all that is done under heaven, he could only confess with weary resignation:

Who knows what is good for man while he lives the few days of his vain life, which passes like a shadow? For who can tell man what will be after him under the sun? (Qoh. 6:12.)

What can a man do in the light of these disillusionments? Is Qoheleth inculcating a thoroughgoing pessimism from which there is no escape? Such an attitude, leading to despair, is unthinkable in a man who never lost faith in God, Who had made everything beautiful in its time and had put it in the heart of man to reach out to this fleeting beauty. The joys of life are a gift of God, and Qoheleth enjoins a moderate use of them while there is still time. For the days are coming when they too will vanish. His practical, measured rule of life comes through like a refrain in his reflections:

> Here is what I recognize as good: it is well for a man to eat and drink and enjoy all the fruits of his toil under the sun for the few days of life God gives him; for this is his lot. Every man also to whom God gives riches and property, and grants power to enjoy them, so that he receives his lot and finds joy in the fruits of his toil, has a gift from God. For he will hardly dwell on the shortness of his life, because God keeps him busy with the joy under the sun (Qoh. 9:5–6).

Many other passages could be cited to show how Qoheleth counterpoints his pessimism with the advice to enjoy in moderation the pleasures which God has put in his power to attain. Face the unpleasant facts of life, the folly of excessive striving, our helplessness before the injustices of man to man, the hiatus between desire and attainment. Enjoy the few pleasures offered us while life permits, for death, the lot of all, will mean the end of enjoyment:

> For the living know that they will die, but the dead know nothing, nor do they have any more reward, for memory of them is forgotten. Their love, their hate, and their envy as well have long perished nor do they have any more share in all that is done under the sun (Qoh. 9:5–6).

from the purpose he set himself. He writes as a critic of con-
Qoheleth must be studied in the context of his time and

ventional views and his indictment rests upon years of observation and reflection. Here we search in vain for the fiery religious enthusiasm of the prophets who looked beyond the calamities of the present and discerned a Golden Age in which the promises made to Israel would be richly fulfilled. Qoheleth, like other wisdom writers, prescinds from past and future, except in the ever present thought of death, and concentrates on the values of the present, the here and now. He wrote in a language which does not easily lend itself to well-differentiated statement. The literary genre is suited to the ambiguities of life as Qoheleth saw it, but notably deficient for the expression of well rounded, categoric propositions intended as absolute norms of belief and conduct. The confident assurance of Proverbs is missing in this book, whose author is far from sure that wisdom inevitably brings happiness or that the cruel injustice about which he spoke so feelingly could be swiftly remedied. Experience had taught him that the ways of God are indeed mysterious and that the joys of man are not beyond the reach of chance and change. His candid treatment of human limitations puts him a step ahead of earlier sages who were too sure of the just man's reward and the evil man's punishment.

Where others had followed the path blazed by their predecessors, Qoheleth felt obliged to strike out on his own and, through long and varied experience, to question the established wisdom of his contemporaries on the values of human life. It is difficult to imagine what the reaction of his readers was to the melancholy advice offered by Qoheleth. But many a man must have felt that this teacher of human limitations, this prober of our contingency, was expressing what he had come to know in the innermost recesses of his heart. Qoheleth has raised some of the most fundamental questions about life, and his honest, if not very optimistic, answers probably account for his great appeal today. His elemental sadness is not only the trademark of great literature; it is, I believe, thoroughly Hebraic. In an unusual but real sense, the book which Qoheleth wrote helped to prepare the human spirit for the "fullness of time."

DANIEL

IN THE Hebrew Bible the book of Daniel, which is the first great apocalyptic work of Judaism, is not found among the prophetic writings but in that category of miscellaneous works known as the "Writings." It is sandwiched in between the books of Esther and Ezra-Nehemiah, a position which serves to remind us that those who were responsible for fixing the Hebrew (Palestinian) Canon did not consider the book to be the work of a prophet. In the ancient Greek and Latin versions we find several additions which are missing in the Massoretic (Hebrew) text. The additions fall into two groups: in chapter 3 of Daniel, the prayer of Azariah and the Canticle of the Three Young Men in the fiery furnace have been inserted between verses 23 and 24; in the Latin Vulgate and modern Catholic translations, the stories of Susanna, and Bel and the Dragon make up Chapters 13 and 14, supplementing the twelve chapters of the book as it is found in the Hebrew Bible.

It will not be out of place to look for a moment at the well-known Susanna incident. The observations we make on the literary form used in this story have some applicability to the stories about Daniel and his friends found in the first six chapters of the book. During the last few centuries before Christ there arose a popular form of writing which might be called the "martyr-legend," an edifying, didactic literary piece designed to inculcate some virtue or to point up some lesson. The stories of Esther, Tobiah, and Judith belong to this class. To call these "legends" does not mean that they were made out of whole cloth with absolutely no foundation in fact. Events in history most likely furnished the starting point of these stories but, stated very bluntly, the historical nucleus in this kind of writing is of little or no importance. The sacred writer, in making use of this literary form, was trying to exhort, or encourage, or bring out some religious truth; he was not giving a sober historical account in the manner of an eyewitness, and we only deceive ourselves and miss the point of his writing if we interpret it from a viewpoint which was foreign to his intention and literary genre. To put it another way, the stories have theological, not reportorial, value.

The "historicity" of the Susanna story is purely secondary to the lesson taught. That lesson was precious to the author's contemporaries and it has enduring value for us. What was the writer trying to accomplish by his charming narrative of the faithful Susanna? This was written in a time of persecution, under Antiochus IV as we shall see, when many pious Jews were faced with martyrdom. Often they were left only the choice between capitulation to paganism and death. The early chapters of Daniel recount several of these tests; but, happily, Daniel and his friends always emerge successfully from them, thanks to divine intervention. In the Susanna incident the innocent woman is also saved by the intervention of God, Who gives to Daniel the wisdom whereby Susanna's innocence is proved and she is spared the death of an adulteress. But more often than not the loyal Jew gave up his life during these dreadful times; he died a martyr without even being absolutely sure of an eternal reward in the next life. In the Susanna story, as in those of Daniel, it has very plausibly been suggested that the divine intervention might be interpreted as a guarantee of the eternal happiness promised to those who actually undergo martyrdom. In other words, the miraculous deliverance of the heroes and heroines of these stories was intended as a symbol of the reward in store for the martyrs who actually chose to die rather than to offend God. If there was ever a time when such a teaching, and the use of such a symbol, was appropriate, it was during the second century B.C. when heroic men and women died rather than give up their faith in the God of Israel.[1]

The supplements or additions to the Hebrew-Aramaic text of Daniel belong to what Catholics call "Deuterocanonical Writings," so called because they were accepted as sacred and canonical only after some doubts about their canonicity had delayed their full acceptance into the Canon. These Deuterocanonical Writings are commonly referred to as "Apocrypha" by non-Catholics, and they are not accepted in the Jewish and Protestant Canons of the Old Testament. While recognizing the religious value and great influence of the Apocrypha, Jewish and Protestant authorities restrict the Old Testament Canon of sacred books to those books which are found in the Hebrew Bible.

The distinction between protocanonical and deuterocanonical sections is, unfortunately, but one of several problems connected with the book of Daniel, one of the most misunderstood and misused writings of the Old Testament. We shall restrict our remaining remarks to the book of Daniel as it is found in the Massoretic text of the Old Testament, i.e., to the protocanonical part of Daniel. This is written in two languages, Hebrew and Aramaic. Apart from the first chapter and a few verses of the second, everything up to chapter 8 is written in Aramaic, the rest in Hebrew. What is the reason for this abrupt change of language, especially when there is no corresponding change of subject matter? As we shall soon see, there is indeed a clear difference in subject matter and literary form in the book, but it does not dovetail with the use of Hebrew and Aramaic. There have been countless theories to explain the shift from one to the other language, but not one theory on which all have agreed. From a negative viewpoint, let it suffice to note that the diversity of language is not an adequate argument against the unity of the book. In other words, it still remains probable, and it

---

[1] R. A. F. MacKenzie, "Susanna the Martyr," *Scripture*, January, 1957, pp. 15–20.

will be the opinion followed in this treatment, that the book as we now have it comes from one and the same author, who lived and wrote in the second century B.C. during the persecution of Antiochus IV Epiphanes (175–163 B.C.).

HOW GREAT ARE HIS SIGNS!

The book of Daniel, at first glance, appears to be the work of a Jewish exile in Babylon during the sixth century B.C. In the first half, Chapters 1–6, there is a collection of stories centering around Daniel and his friends who heroically stood by their Jewish faith during the reigns of Nebuchadnezzar, Belshazzar, and Darius the Mede, the last of whom is a complete mystery to historians of the period. The second half recounts a series of visions, chapters 7–12, in which Daniel learns of the ultimate triumph of the Kingdom of God. Daniel is told to seal up the visions until the time of the end. Chapter 7 serves as a transition and a unifying link between both parts, which are further bound together by the purpose of the writer — to sustain and encourage his fellow Jews in the great trial of faith through which they were going. The book is the answer of a fervent Jew to an all-out attack against his religion by a powerful adversary who was bent on replacing the religion of Judaism by a Hellenized oriental cult based on a fusion between Hellenism and Judaism. To a loyal Jew, participation in such a cult would be nothing less than apostasy. Although the book was composed during the persecution of Antiochus Epiphanes, it does not mean that the author made no use of already existing traditions, whether written or oral, upon which he could draw to put across his message.

That there was a literary and oral prehistory to this composition appears practically certain, and a recent discovery among the Dead Sea scrolls at Qumran not only confirms this position but throws some very interesting light on the obscure question of the origins of the book. Father J. T. Milik, a member of the team of scroll experts in Jerusalem, published in 1956 some fragments of a document discovered in Cave IV of Qumran. He has entitled this composition the "Prayer of Nabonidus."

On the basis of this text it now appears certain that chapter 4 of Daniel is based on a story of Nabonidus and not the better-known Nebuchadnezzar. The new find describes, for example, how Nabonidus was stricken with a dreadful disease "by the decree of the Most High God," and how he was set apart for seven years from the company of men and dwelt in the North Arabian oasis of Tema. The sojourn of Nabonidus has been independently confirmed by cuneiform evidence from Babylon. It would seem that, on the basis of this discovery, there was an earlier story, originating in Babylon, about the affliction and banishment of Nabonidus and that, in the course of time, Nebuchadnezzar was substituted for the comparatively obscure Nabonidus. This does not necessarily mean that the Palestinian author of our Daniel made the shift; it may have long antedated him and he then simply incorporated in his book the tradition as it had come down to him. In Chapter 5 which follows, it now seems that the original story of the feast of Belshazzar gave the correct name of his father, Nabonidus. Once again, in the course of oral or written transmission, Nebuchadnezzar has been substituted for Nabonidus, who dropped out of sight until he was rediscovered and reinstated through the Qumran discovery. If the author of Daniel gave himself out as a strict historian, intent on an accurate reconstruction of the Babylonian period, we would find these substitutions embarrassing, to say the least. But once we reckon with the intention of the author and the literary form he chose to implement his intention, the difficulty ceases to be real.

As far as we are able to determine, our author, for his first 6 chapters, drew upon a fund of well-known stories about a wise man, Daniel, who was one of the Jewish captives in Babylon and who courageously resisted all temptations to give up the practice of his faith. Besides successfully resisting religious assimilation, Daniel and his companions attained to positions of prominence in Babylonian affairs, all the while undergoing severe trials to preserve their faith. The point of all this is that the stories of the first 6 chapters of Daniel undoubtedly have a traditional basis, though it is now impossible to determine where fact ends and legend begins. But this should cause us no difficulty, since the author is not attempting to provide us with a history of precisely what happened in Babylon many centuries ago; he is reworking his traditional material to suit his immediate and compelling purpose which is to show that God does not desert those who serve Him faithfully but will certainly deliver them, eventually, from even the most powerful foes.

It is not difficult to believe that the Jewish reader, undergoing his trial of faith under Antiochus, would see that the author of Daniel had done a "rewrite job" on his traditional material and that, in each of the stories, there was something pertinent to his own predicament. Recognizing the relevance of the stories and visions to his own time he would, it was hoped, take courage and resist the aggressive Hellenizing policy of the enemy. After briefly surveying the historical situation which underlies this book, and which must be known if we are to read Daniel intelligently and according to the mind of the original author, we may point out instances of how the stories about Daniel had a very special meaning for readers in the second century B.C. But who was the foe whose persecution called forth this unique book, the second part of which (Chapters 7–12) is thoroughly apocalyptic and the forerunner of many other apocalyptic works, culminating in the mighty Apocalypse of St. John?

THERE SHALL BE A TIME OF TROUBLE

The ancient Near East had, in its long history, known many conquerors, but none so brilliant and resourceful as the young Macedonian who, before his death at the age of thirty-two, had established the greatest Empire the world had ever known. This man was Alexander the Great (336–323 B.C.) whose military genius crushed the power of Persia and brought his armies as far as India before he turned back westward to consolidate the vast territory which had fallen to him. At Babylon, while making plans for further conquests, he died without leaving an heir. Alexander was more than a military hero; he considered himself an apostle of Hellenic culture and he had every intention of Hellenizing the Orient and bringing to it the blessings of Greek culture whose elements he had learned from no less a tutor than Aristotle.

After Alexander's untimely death the Empire broke up into factions headed by his bickering generals who assumed the title of king. Four dynasties were established but of these only two concern us here, the Ptolemies who secured control of Egypt, and, most important of all, the Seleucids who fell heir to Mesooptamia and Syria. The Seleucids ruled as a dynasty from 312 to 65 B.C., and their Empire extended from the Mediterranean to India. They also gave their name to a system of chronology, the Era of Seleucus. Among their number was the infamous Antiochus IV Epiphanes, whose ruthless assault on Judaism precipitated the Maccabean War of Independence. With good reason was Antiochus Epiphanes mockingly called Epimanes (madman). The Ptolemies, however, were the first to gain control over Palestine, then as ever a small country caught between warring powers. But in 198 B.C. the Seleucid armies thoroughly defeated the Ptolemies at Panium, close by the sources of the Jordan. From this time Palestine became a part of the vast Seleucid Empire and the new rulers, Hellenized orientals, were not slow in pushing ahead Alexander's vast program of imposing Greek culture on lands under their control. It is unfortunate that their efforts were seconded enthusiastically by some of the Jews who were all too ready to compromise their ancestral religion by coming to terms with Hellenism. Even some of the priests went over to the Hellenizers, among them Jason and Menelaus, who bought the office of high priest from Antiochus IV.

Matters reached a head when Antiochus made up his mind to put an end to Judaism and, in 168 B.C., desecrated the holy Temple in Jerusalem. The author of the first book of Maccabees recounts with horror the story of the measures taken by this unscrupulous despot to exterminate Judaism:

And the king wrote to his entire kingdom, ordering all to be one people and that every one should give up his religious practices. All the Gentiles acquiesced in the command of the king. Even many in Israel were glad to adopt his form of worship; they offered sacrifice to idols and profaned the sabbath. In addition, the king sent messengers with letters to Jerusalem and to the towns of Judah, directing them to follow customs foreign to the land; and to stop offering burnt offerings and sacrifices and drink offerings in the sanctuary, and to profane the sabbaths and feasts, to defile the sanctuary and its ministers, to build high places, and sacred groves, and shrines for the idols, to sacrifice swine and other unclean animals, and to leave their sons uncircumcised. They were to make themselves abominable by means of everything which was unclean and profane, in order to forget the Law and change all the traditional ordinances. "And whoever disobeys the command of the king shall die" (1 Macc. 1:41–50).

A careful reading of this passage will turn up interesting parallels between the anti-Jewish tactics of Antiochus and those of Nebuchadnezzar in the Daniel narratives; it is not difficult to imagine harassed Jews of the Maccabean period taking courage from the heroic example of Daniel and his companions. This was an age in which many Jews were compelled to choose between apostasy and martyrdom. Those who had already cast in their lot with the Hellenizers had no trouble in obeying the edict of Antiochus. But this was not the whole picture:

But many in Israel were fully resolved and determined in their hearts not to eat unclean things. And they chose to die, that they might not be defiled with the meats, and that they might not profane the holy covenant; and they died. And very great wrath came upon Israel (1 Macc. 1:62–64).

Many determined to fight for their faith no matter what the odds against them. They rallied around a venerable priest named Mattathias who had refused to offer sacrifice and had even slain a Jew who capitulated, along with the king's officer who was presiding over the idolatrous sacrifices. Mattathias had struck his blow for the faith, but he was too old to carry on a military campaign in which Jewish irregulars were pitted against a strong and disciplined army. On his deathbed Mattathias turned over the leadership to one of his five sons, known to history as Judas Maccabeus.

It is during this critical period, when victory was far from achieved, that the book of Daniel was written down in its present form. The author would attain his goal in two ways, by recalling the fortitude of a great hero of the past, and by interpreting the meaning of this persecution in the light of apocalyptic visions which proclaimed the invincibility of God's Kingdom against the evil powers of the world. The apocalyptic writers are the successors of the prophets and share with them the conviction that history is under the control of God, Who is directing events according to His own mysterious purposes. The distinctive note of apocalyptic writing is its emphasis on the great divine initiative at the end of history, when God would intervene decisively in human affairs and establish the Kingdom. We find, it is true, apocalyptic passages in the prophets, but their chief aim was to correct the evils of their day, lead men to repent of their sins, and to threaten them with judgment if they refused. The prophets were very forthright in their language, whereas the apocalyptists express their theology in strange, cryptic language, bizarre visions of great beasts, and symbolic numbers whose meaning is often disclosed to the visionary by an angel. Through all the bewildering details of these visions runs a theology of history, the assurance of an imminent divine breakthrough in history, the triumphant vindication of the suffering faithful and the definitive establishment of the Kingdom of God.

As already noted, the first half of the book consists of six edifying stories about Daniel and his companions who were living in the Babylonian Exile. The setting is the royal court at Babylon; four of the stories take place in the reign of Nebuchadnezzar and one each during the reigns of Belshazzar and the enigmatic Darius the Mede. In common, all of them sound the call to absolute loyalty in time of trial, coupled with the assurance that their enemies will be thwarted. Antiochus

Epiphanes had tried to force the Jews to eat the flesh of swine which had been sacrificed on pagan altars. Let those who were tempted to violate this law of God read the first chapter, in which Daniel and his friends refused to take any of the defiling food even though it came from the king's table. What were the consequences of an act which a despotic monarch might take as a personal affront?

> Then Daniel said to the steward whom the chief of the eunuchs had put in charge of Daniel, Hananiah, Mishael, and Azariah: "Test your servants for a period of ten days; let them give us vegetables for food and water for drink. Then let them see in your presence our appearance and the appearance of the lads who eat the king's choice food; and according to what you see deal with your servants." So he listened to them in this matter, and he tested them for ten days. After ten days it was seen that their appearance was better and their bodies fatter than all the lads who ate the king's choice food. So the steward took away the choice food and the wine they were to drink, and gave them vegetables (Dan. 1:11-16).

Antiochus had outraged the religious sensibilities of the Jews by setting up an idol, probably an image of himself as Zeus incarnate, in the Temple. But this was a relatively insignificant gesture by a petty tyrant compared to the colossal image of gold set up by Nebuchadnezzar in the Plain of Dura. All were commanded to fall down and worship the hideous statue under pain of being cast into a fiery furnace. The three friends of Daniel had their answer when they were brought before the king and accused of refusing to worship; a reader living at the time of Antiochus could not miss the point:

> Shadrach, Meshach, and Abednego made answer to the king: "O Nebuchadnezzar, we do not need to answer you in this matter. If the God Whom we serve is willing, He can deliver us from the fiery furnace and from your hand, O king, He will deliver us. But if not, let it be known unto you, O king, that we will not serve your gods nor worship the golden image which you have set up" (Dan. 3:16-18).

In this same chapter are inserted two deuterocanonical additions, the Prayer of Azariah (the Hebrew name of Abednego) and the triumphal Song of the Three Young Men, the former a confession of national guilt and a plea for deliverance, the latter a majestic hymn of exultation which has become one of the favorite prayers of the Christian liturgy.

GOD-HEWN STONE AND SON OF MAN

To set the persecution let loose by Antiochus Epiphanes in a broad, worldwide perspective, the author recounted two parallel dreams, one by Nebuchadnezzar in Chapter 2 and the other by Daniel in Chapter 7. In both cases the mighty kingdoms of the world, symbolized by parts of a colossal image or by hideous beasts, were swept away by the power of God in preparation for the establishment of His everlasting Kingdom. The same four great Empires of the ancient world, the Babylonian, Median, Persian, and Greek were represented in the vision of the statue as well as in the vision of the four fantastic beasts; both visions were climaxed by a revelation which fits in with the author's immediate purpose of encouraging his contemporaries. Each vision contributes an important element to the messianic doctrine of the Old Testament. The images of the stone not made with hands and the Son of Man do not stop with the book of Daniel but are caught up in that Messianic process which culminates in Christ. Both of these images, closely associated with the divine triumph over the powers of the world, find their fulfillment in Him Who came to establish the Kingdom of God.

Chapter 2 reports a dream of Nebuchadnezzar which troubled his spirit. All the wise men of the court were summoned to explain the dream but none of them could give the interpretation. Only Daniel, to whom God had revealed the mystery, could explain the dream which foretold the victory of God over the kingdoms of the world, symbolized by the great statue. While Nebuchadnezzar looked at the great statue, a stone hewn from a mountain, without a hand being put to it, struck the feet of the statue and it crumbled to the ground. But the

stone which struck the statue became a great mountain and
filled the whole earth. What was the meaning of this?

> In the lifetime of those kings, the God of heaven will set up a
> kingdom that shall never be destroyed or delivered up to another
> people; rather, it shall break in pieces all these kingdoms and put
> an end to them, and it shall stand forever. This is the meaning
> of the stone hewn from the mountain without a hand being put
> to it, which broke in pieces the tile, iron, bronze, silver, and gold
> (Dan. 2:44–45).

This Kingdom will be the work of God and not man, and it
shall be a universal Kingdom, for the stone, symbol of the
Kingdom, shall become "a great mountain and fill the whole
earth." It would be hazardous to assert that the author, in his
image of the stone, intended to portray solely a personal Messiah; but it is quite in keeping with the Hebrew way of thinking
to say that he saw in this mighty stone both the everlasting
Kingdom and its ruler, the Messiah.

As we have seen in the passages describing the Suffering
Servant, the Hebrew easily oscillated between the group and
the individual, especially when the latter was uniquely representative of the group. This theory of corporate personality,
characterized by a fluidity of transition between group and
individual, applies equally to another and better known messianic figure, the Son of Man, appearing in Chapter 7. This
vision, like the previous one of Chapter 2, was built around
the four-Empire concept with the same climactic intervention of
God to overthrow the last great power and establish His everlasting Kingdom. In the earlier vision, the Empires were pictured
under the imagery of metals; here they were symbolized by
monstrous beasts. The fourth beast was the Empire of the
Greeks and the "little horn with eyes like a man and speaking
great things" was Antiochus Epiphanes who epitomized the evil
power of the world. There follows immediately the majestic
vision of heavenly judgment upon the world Empires, the slaying of the last beast and the presentation of an everlasting
Kingdom to "one like a son of man":

As I looked, thrones were placed and one
who was the ancient of days took his seat;
his raiment was white as snow,
and the hair of his head like pure wool;
his throne was fiery flames,
its wheels were a burning fire.
A fiery stream issued
and came forth from before him;
a thousand thousands ministered unto him
and ten thousand times ten thousand
rose up before him;
the court sat in judgment,
and the books were opened.
Then I looked up because of the
noise of the great words which
the horn spoke. While I
looked the beast was slain, its
body destroyed and handed over
to be burned with fire. And as for the
rest of the beasts, their dominion was taken
away, yet their lives were prolonged for
a season and a time.
I saw visions in the night,
and behold, there came with the
clouds of heaven one like unto
a son of man,
and he came to the ancient of days
and he was presented before him.
And to him there was given dominion
and glory and a kingdom,
that all peoples, nations and languages
should serve him.
His dominion will be an everlasting dominion
which shall never pass away,
and his kingdom is one which
shall never be destroyed.

(Dan. 7:9–14)

In the New Testament our Lord's favorite designation for Himself was "Son of Man." He alone used it sixty-nine times in the Gospels. What significance did the term have on the lips of Jesus and what was its origin? The first part of this question is easier to answer than the second, because the problem of origin and sources of the Son of Man idea is a very complicated one. As for the meaning of the term, the texts in which it appears fall into two categories. One stresses the humanity of Christ, His identification with mankind. The second evokes the picture of a glorious and transcendent figure who is to come in glory on the clouds of heaven and to pass definitive judgment on the world. From the two uses of the phrase we see that it can express both the humility and majesty of our Lord, that the phrase has all the tension of a paradox; yet this paradox is but the reflection of the great mystery of the Incarnation in which He Who was on high in glory emptied Himself and was born in the likeness of man. There is one solemn incident during the passion, when Christ stands before His judges and announces the eventual coming of the Son of Man in glory, where the reference to Daniel 7 is unmistakable. It is true that, in its context, the Son of Man in Daniel 7 appears to be a collective figure inasmuch as he stands for the "saints of the Most High," just as the beasts represented the four Kingdoms. But the concept of corporate personality which we have seen in the figures of the Suffering Servant and the Stone appears to be operative here. The Son of Man in this chapter could thus stand for the holy community and, at the same time, be individualized as the representative of that community. He would thus sum up in His own person the mission and destiny of the holy community over which He is to enjoy sovereign rule. In His clear reference to the Daniel passage, Jesus again showed how He has taken to Himself the traditions of His own people, developed them and combined them,[2] all the while bringing a rich fulfillment to themes which were only imperfectly stated and partially

---

[2] It seems quite likely, for example, that the figures of Messiah, Suffering Servant, and Son of Man, originally very distinct and separate concepts, have, in the New Testament, been united in a unique synthesis by Jesus Himself. He saw His mission as the fulfillment not only of the royal son of David theme but of the Suffering Servant and Son of Man themes as well. In other words, various and sometimes disparate strands of Old Testament Messianism have been united for the first time in the Person of Christ, and in that union each theme has been enriched.

comprehended in the Old Testament. Among these themes the Son of Man, with its more immediate origins in the Old Testament and the apocryphal books of the intertestamental period, served to express not only the humanity of Christ but, more importantly, the supernatural and transcendent lordship of Jesus over the messianic community which another New Testament writer would call the Body of Christ.

THE TIME OF THE END

Divine judgment had already been passed on Antiochus, who had set his heart against the holy covenant. It does not seem as though the book was finished after the death of the great adversary, but the author is sure that "he shall come to his end, with none to help him." With Antiochus out of the way, we are prepared for the final consummation, described in the last chapter of the book. It shall be a time of great tribulation, a constant theme of apocalyptic writing, but deliverance will not be far away. In that hour the faithful who have suffered death for their faith will rise from the dead to share in the joy of the everlasting Kingdom:

> And at that time shall Michael arise, the great prince who stands over the children of your people. And there shall be a time of tribulation, such as there never has been since there was a nation up to now.
> But at that time your people shall be delivered, every one whose name is found written in the book. And many of those who sleep in the dust of the earth shall awake, some to eternal life, others to shame and everlasting abhorrence. And they who are wise shall shine as the brightness of the firmament; and they who turn many to justice as the stars for ever and ever (Dan. 12:1–3).

For the first time in the Old Testament a resurrection of the just and the wicked is expressly taught, as well as the everlasting destiny reserved for both. There is no need to look for outside influence in the progressive unfolding of this doctrine of blessed immortality for the just and eternal punishment for the wicked.

The revelation was prepared in earlier works of the Old Testament, and its development in the book of Daniel may be said to grow out of the historical circumstances in which the book was written. More often than not God's revelation is attuned to the rhythm of history. The author did not for a moment doubt that God would deliver those who remained loyal to Him. But what about the faithful Jews who had already undergone martyrdom during the persecution of Antiochus? Would they share in the Kingdom which was to be established on the ruins of the world Empires? It is in this context that the doctrine of the resurrection and eternal reward, only hinted at in earlier books of the Old Testament, should be regarded not only as providential but also as a normal development of the author's burning faith in Him Who would vindicate those who had died in His cause. From Daniel to the Apocalypse of St. John there is a straight line; the men who wrote in this literary genre have left us a stirring message, to hold fast in the time of tribulation. They put little trust in man, for their concern was with the divine control of events and the power of God to trumph over the the iniquity of man. Many other things they left unsaid, and they would be supplied by further revelation in both the Old and New Testaments. But it is for their unflinching confidence in the victory of God, together with those who are loyal to Him, that we owe them, especially in our days of trial, so immense a debt.

BIBLIOGRAPHY

Introduction

Bouyer, L., *The Meaning of Sacred Scripture* (South Bend, Ind.: Univ. of Notre Dame Press, 1958). A series of 22 short essays, introducing the reader to such themes as the Covenant, the qualities of God as revealed in the prophets, the presence of God, Jewish mysticism, the Christian mystery, etc. The *Leitmotiv* of the volume is the progressive development of divine revelation.

Charlier, C., *The Christian Approach to the Bible* (Westminster, Md.: Newman Press, 1958). A leader of the European Catholic biblical movement provides, with selectivity and economy, the introductory knowledge necessary for an intelligent and Christian reading of the Bible.

Dougherty, J. J., *Searching the Scriptures* (New York: Hanover House, 1959). A sanely critical and lucid survey of the Old and New Testaments, written from the Catholic viewpoint. Highly recommended for study clubs.

Jones, A., Rochford, V., and Hastings, C., *Pattern of Scripture* (New York: Sheed & Ward, 1959). A Canterbury Book.

Moriarty, F., *Foreword to the Old Testament Books* (Weston, Mass.: Weston College Press, 1954). A brief, up-to-date introduction to each book of the Old Testament.

Vawter, B., *The Bible in the Church* (New York: Sheed & Ward, 1959). This is a Canterbury Book which helps the reader to understand the place of the Bible in the Catholic Church.

Biblical History

Albright, W. F., *The Biblical Period* (The Biblical Colloquium: 731 Ridge Ave., Pittsburgh 12, Pa.). A 65-page essay which surveys the history of Israel from the Patriarchal Age to the coming of Alexander the Great.

—— *From the Stone Age to Christianity* (New York: Doubleday Anchor Book, 1957). A brilliant personal synthesis of monotheism and the historical process by one of the world's foremost Orientalists.

Bright, J., *A History of Israel* (Philadelphia: Westminster Press, 1959). The best and most comprehensive history we now possess. The text is interestingly written and thoroughly reliable in its handling of Israel's many-faceted history.

Heinisch, P., *History of the Old Testament*, trans. W. Heidt (Collegeville, Minn.: Liturgical Press, 1952). A companion piece to the author's *Theology of the Old Testament*; the translator has furnished supplementary notes for the English edition.

Ricciotti, G., *The History of Israel*, trans. C. della Penta and R. T. Murphy, 2 vols. (Milwaukee, Wis.: Bruce, 1955). A major work, intended for more advanced students, by one of the best known Italian biblical scholars. The most important of the many books he has written.

Biblical Archaeology and Geography

Albright, W. F., *The Archaeology of Palestine* (Baltimore, Md.: Penguin Books, 1956). An authoritative survey of the ancient peoples and cultures of the Holy Land.

Baly, D., *The Geography of the Bible* (New York: Harper & Bros., 1957). Fills the gap which has existed since George Adam Smith wrote his classic, *The Historical Geography of the Holy Land*, over sixty years ago. Contains 97 photographs and 47 maps and diagrams.

Grollenberg, L., *Atlas of the Bible*, trans. J. Reid and H. Rowley (New York: Thos. Nelson & Sons, 1956). A magnificently illustrated volume with an accurate and well-written text covering the historical background of both the Old and New Testaments. The maps alone are a mine of valuable information.

Pritchard, J., *Archaeology and the Old Testament* (Princeton, N. J.: Princeton Univ. Press, 1958). An appraisal of the impact of recent discoveries, showing how our knowledge of the history written in the Old Testament has been modified and enlarged by a century of archaeological work.

Wright, G., *Biblical Archaeology* (Philadelphia: Westminster Press, 1957). A thoroughly reliable summary of archaeological discoveries which directly illumine biblical history. Especially valuable for teachers.

Wright, G. and Filson, F., *Westminster Historical Atlas to the Bible* (Philadelphia: Westminster Press, 2nd edition revised and improved, 1956). The authors have condensed a vast amount of geographical, historical, and cultural knowledge within a reason-

able space. Written in clear and nontechnical language, it is
accompanied by many full-page plates carrying a map or series of
maps. There is an excellent survey of the Qumran discoveries.

Biblical Theology

Gelin, A., *The Key Concepts of the Old Testament*, trans. G. Lamb
(New York: Sheed & Ward, 1955). Those who have been baffled
by the complexity of the Old Testament will find here a brief
and well-organized survey of the essentials in Old Testament
thought.

McKenzie, J., *The Two-Edged Sword* (Milwaukee: Bruce, 1956). A
provocative and challenging treatment of the most important
themes in Old Testament theology. Pioneer work.

Rowley, H., *The Faith of Israel* (Philadelphia: Westminster Press,
1957). An extremely readable exposition of the distinctive and
enduring elements in Israel's faith by an outstanding non-Catholic
scholar.

Sullivan, K., *God's Word and Work* (Collegeville, Minn.: Liturgical
Press, 1958). A welcome and pleasantly written guide for those
who seek to enrich their liturgical life through a better acquaintance with the Old Testament.

INDEX

Abner, 71 f

Abraham, 1–18; association with Hebron, 71; call of, 103; election of, 17; faith of, 1, 14 ff; at Haran, 9; offspring of, 180; Yahweh's promise to, 79

Absalom, defection of, 76

Adam, 194

Aeneas, 223

Agag, king of Amalekites, 66

Agape, New Testament equivalent of hesed, 35

Ahab, 100; and worship of Baal, 94 f

Ahaz, 124 ff, 137

Ai, 52

Albright, W. F., composition of the Pentateuch, 4 f; excavations at Gibeah, 67; relation between older and later prophets, 90

Alexander the Great, 232 f

Amalekites, attacked Israelites at Rephidim, 44; Saul's victory over, 66

Amarna Letters, as source for knowledge of Canaan, 48 f

Amaziah, priest of Bethel, 117

Ammonites, attacked Jabesh-gilead, 65

Amorites, invasion of, 8 f

Amos, 103–119; call of, 106, 112 f, 117; as "Prophet of Social Justice," 108 f; visions of, 104 f

Anathoth, birthplace of Jeremiah, 144; citizens of, 146

Antiochus IV, 228; edict of, 234

Apocalyptic, 227, 235

Apocrypha, 229, 241

Aristotle, tutor of Alexander, 233

Ark of Covenant, 78; brought to Jerusalem, 73; captured by Philistines, 63; symbol of religious unity, 59

Artaxerxes Longimanus, 193 n, 195–196

Ashirat, in Canaanite pantheon, 93

Assimilation, danger to exiles, 164

Assyria, 107; decline of, 138 f; rise of, 122 ff

Augustine, St., City of God and sacerdotal tradition, 8

"Author," meaning for Hebrew, 82 ff

Azariah, prayer of, 227, 237

Baal, 59; Canaanite hymns to, 87; prophets of, 89, 95 ff; storm-god, 91; storm-god of Canaanites, 93

Babylon, fall of, 189; gods of, 177 f; instrument of divine judgment, 149; overthrown by Cyrus, 173; Procession Street, 175; wisdom of, 202 f

Babylonians, invasion of, 158

Bathsheba, and David, 77

Beasts, imagery of, 238 f

Bel, story of, 227

Belshazzar, 230; crown prince of Babylon, 189; feast of, 231

Benjamin, tribe of, 11

Berit, see Covenant

Bethel, 52, 106 ff; destruction in thirteenth century B.C., 21; shrine at, 90 f

Bethlehem, 103; David of, 67

Bethshan, 69

Bildad, 209 ff

Blindness, spiritual, 128 f

Bride, symbol of, 182

Bronze Age, Late, 52; Middle, 12 f, 38

Canaan, archaeological findings in, 48; during Patriarchal Age, 11; land of, during Patriarchal Age, 13 f; religion of, 92–94, 149 f; in time of Joshua, 46 f; wisdom of, 202

Canon, Palestinian, 227

Carmel, 89, 95 f

Catullus, 223

Charismatic leaders, 63, 76

Christ, Body of, 188, 241; Church of, 137; Person of, 240 n

---

* Where index items refer to books of Bible, they are set in **bold** type to distinguish them from individuals of the same name.

Psalms, 81 ff; authorship of, 81 ff; classification of, 84 f
Psalter, text of, 87
Ptolemies, 233

Qahal, 219
Qoheleth, date of, 219; discrepancies of, 219 f; language of, 219; pessimism of, 225; sadness of, 223, 226; unity of, 219
Qoheleth, **216–226;** enigma of, 216; skepticism of, 216 ff
Qumran, *see* Dead Sea scrolls

Rameses II, most likely candidate as Pharaoh of the Exodus, 21; non-aggression part with Hittites, 22
Ras Shamrah, *see* Ugarit
Redemption, hymn of, 182 f; theme of Second Isaiah, 175 f
Red Sea, *see* Sea of Reeds, 29
Remnant, 81, 99, 130, **135–137**
Restoration of the Kingdom, 192 ff
Resurrection, doctrine of, 241–242
Retribution, doctrine of, 209, 226
Richards, H. J., on Old Testament morality, 55
Robinson, H. Wheeler, "corporate personality," 185
Romans, 43
Rowley, H. H., on Jeremiah and Josiah's Reform, 139 *n*; on Servant Songs of Second Isaiah, 187

Sacerdotal tradition, 6 f
Sacrifice, attitude of prophets, 110, . 133; definition of, 110
Salvation, history of, 14, 17, 55, 103; mystery of, 43
Salvation history, and Exodus, 28; in Joshua, 45; and Yahwist tradition, 5
Samaria, 97; destruction of, 120; excavations at, 107; fall of, 138; new capital of Northern Kingdom, 91 f; Persian province of, 192; women of, 108
Samuel, 63 ff, 89; appears to Saul, 69
Sanballat, opposition to Nehemiah, 196 ff
Sarah, 9
Sargon II, captured Samaria, 138

Satan, in Job, 206 f; victory of, 14
Saul, **58–70;** anointing of, 64; appearance of, 64; jealousy of David, 68; moods of, 67
Sea of Reeds, 29 ff
Sea people, *see* Philistines
Second Isaiah, authorship of, 171 f; date of, 173
Second Isaiah, **171–188;** creation in, 176 f; imagery of return, 41; oracles of, 171
Seleucids, 233 ff
Seleucus, Era of, 233
Sennacherib, 132; attack on Jerusalem, 125 f
Servant, Jesus as, 186, 187 f; mission of, 188; Suffering, in Second Isaiah, 183
Servant Songs, list of, 183 *n*
Shechem, battle at, 48; ceremony at, 57; Joshua at, 1; sanctuary of, 46
Shemaiah, false prophet, 198 f
Sheol, 222; longing for, 208
Shephelah, 61
Shilo, 152; destruction of sanctuary at, 63; sanctuary at, 59
Sin, essence of, 149, 151, 154
Sinai, challenge of, 179; Covenant of, 15, 34 f, 115, 153; Law of, 153; names of, 24; revelation of, 178; site of, 24, 32
Sinuhe, Egyptian contemporary of Abraham, 13
Sion, complaint of, 181; Songs of, 74 f
Solomon, 217; and cult centers for alien gods, 90; sin of, 201; Temple of, 78; wives of, 90; wisdom of, 202
Song of Deborah, 62 f
Son of Man, **237–241**
Soul, spirituality of, 222
Southern Kingdom, comprised tribes of Benjamin and Judah, 138
Stone, symbol of, 238
Suffering, mystery of, **213–215,** 218
Suffering Servant, *see* Servant, Suffering
Sumer, wisdom of, 202
Susa, winter residence of Artaxerxes Longimanus, 195
Susanna, literary form of, 228; story of, 227 f

Tabernacles, Feast of, **133**